Sally's Diary:
Leaving home in the 1970s
Peterborough - Cardiff - Birmingham

Acknowledgements: Peter Arthur for enhancing the photographs and Susan Neave for reading the draft. Quotes and spellings are as written in the original Diary.

© by Sally George the author and publisher of this book 2014. The book author retains sole copyright to his or her contributions to this book.

The Blurb-provided layout designs and graphic elements are copyright Blurb Inc. This book was created using the Blurb creative publishing service. The book author retains sole copyright to his or her contributions to this book.

Sally's Diary: Leaving home in the 1970s
Peterborough - Cardiff - Birmingham

My best friend Brenda gave me a Diary as a present for my 14th birthday. Since then I have kept my Diary written up and have never missed a day. What we are given in this world is time, and no-one knows how much that is. Therefore I have recorded what I did with that time. So what do I do with 46 years' worth of Diaries? Well, I started reading them and was fascinated and couldn't put them down. They have become historical documents reminding me of items and words no longer used. The words 'crummy', 'grotty', 'groovy', 'jarsville' to name a few. How technology has moved on......I recorded songs from Radio Luxembourg on to my tape recorder, used a twin tub washing machine, golf ball typewriter, Tipp-Ex, button A and button B in the telephone box! Our first convenience food was a packet of Vesta Curry and we thought nothing of giving a lift home to six people in the car! The first computers I ever saw were the size of wardrobes with reel to reel tapes on the top half....in a locked, dust free room! The television (telly) gave us most of our entertainment with Morecambe and Wise, The Partridge Family, Top of the Pops featuring Pans People and Monty Python's Flying Circus. I have concentrated my Diary entries on the early 70s when I was leaving college and starting my first job at the age of 17. Before that I had a sheltered but happy home life so most days "nothing special happened"! My first ever entry on my 14th birthday reads "January 12th 1967: Brenda bought me this Diary. Didn't get 'bumps' until afternoon break. Had needlework exam. Got more 'bumps' in the gym when the whole class joined in. Saw film of the Monkees to the tune of 'I'm a Believer' - it was fab, great, lovely! Saw it on Top of the Pops!" Oh how I dreaded the birthday bumps, when everyone took an arm and a leg and bumped you to the ground for how many years old you were! Does any one else remember this and does it still happen? Sadly, my Diary for the year 1971 is missing, the year I was 16 and my first year at Peterborough Technical College of a two year 'Commercial Course'.

Photographs: Front cover - on holiday with my best friend Brenda (left) in Great Yarmouth 1970.
            Back cover - my A35 car 'Buttercup' dog Gem inside and a neigbour's daughter.

12th January, 1967 started something I have never finished!

My best friend Brenda gave me this Diary on my 14th birthday.

26th May 1970: Radio Luxembourg (1933-1992)
"In Games we just sunbathed - rushed dinner down to go to the Park to see the boys from Kings and Deacons Schools. Met up with Burgess, Terse, Whisky and Shady. Saw "light blue jumper" - groovy. Brenda went off with Prunes. At night took dog for a walk hoping to see David Gibson on his paper round but didn't - jarsville. Taped records off Radio Luxembourg".
Reader: This was Peterborough and there were 2 grammar schools for boys, and only 1 county high school for girls. I ended up going out with Kings Schoolboy "light blue jumper" for 2 years which rather cramped my style!

Saturday 30th October 1970: In the doghouse again!
"Came home at 2 a.m. and accidentally woke everyone when I lost my shoe in the garden after the heel got stuck in the mud! I am now grounded so will have to stay in and watch Morecombe & Wise on the telly - or maybe Monty Python's Flying Circus."

16th November 1970: I'll be grounded for life at this rate!
"More power cuts, and at work 2 secretaries went to have their hair done in the lunch hour and had to come back to work with hair in rollers! In trouble at home again after waking everyone up as I'd forgotten my key. My angry Mum opened the front door to find me kneeling over the contents of my handbag on the doorstep (no moonlight, pitch black). I must have looked as if I was praying (I think I was), but she wasn't impressed and I may have to stay in and watch every episode of The Partridge Family on tele!"

In Peterborough Cathedral Precincts.

24th October 1972: No I can't forget this evening or your face as you were leaving..........

"When you are miserable with someone and miserable without them, what do you do? We agreed tearfully that it could not go on and met for one last time at the bus stop so I could give him back his book, 'Lord of the Rings', which I never did finish, and after 2 years it seemed so final. Just as the bus was about to go, I walked away into Chelsea Girl boutique, then turned to see him. He looked so unhappy."

Reader: Ironically this song, 'Without You' by Harry Nilsson was playing in the shop! I never saw him again as he got a transfer with his job but I did hear that 6 months later he was engaged to be married to a former finalist in the Miss Anglia contest! Just pass me the tissues!

2nd August 1973: Perhaps I need a change of job.

"By the time I got to work, I hated the place. Was pleasantly surprised though, as we had a bomb scare and it was lovely weather for it – sunny, hot and not a cloud in the sky. Chatted to Justin who had been out to buy a new radio which was top smart! Quite fancied him but I realized I'd be cradle snatching, after all, he told me he had to get back to school for a butterfly hunting trip! So all in all not a bad day. Managed to avoid Freaky Clive and Tatty Jim on the way home. Jeanette came round for tea in her Dad's new Hillman Avenger and looked far too little to be driving such a big car! Brian phoned and I felt that I'd left him happy. I then went out with Mick."

Sally, Vicky and Lynn in Peterborough Park.

17th November 1973: The Isley Brothers and 'Who's That Lady?'

"Jane took Diane and I to the Bertie Arms in her car, but the battery was flat so we had to push start it, in our heels! Same happened on the way out and when we got to the Riverside Club the atmosphere in there was as dead as the battery. Brian wanted to go to the Flamingo Club, so I went with him, but remembered what a rough place it could be. Brian agreed with me especially when a brick was thrown through the window! The music was good though!"

2nd December 1973: I am fed up with the oil crisis now!

"I tried 6 garages but no petrol! Went to work on the bus to conserve what little I have. No heating or lighting at work but we were told to work harder and faster to keep warm! Charming I'm sure! The shops at lunch time were either closed or only half lit. After tea, Jean, Jane and Julie came over and as I was the one with half a tank of petrol, I drove us all to the Pheasant Pluckers' Party out in a barn. Was a great night and we left at 2 a.m., but as Julie was engrossed with Martyn and didn't want to leave, she arranged a lift with Shady. Got to bed at 3 a.m., but the phone went at 4 a.m. waking the whole house! It was Julie's Dad asking where she was and who was bringing her home. Oh dear, I didn't know his real name so hesitated before saying.... "Shady"! Mum had been angry at being woken, but this creased her up!"

13th January 1974: On the A1, going south, past RAF Wittering.

"We were woken early by Jean, as we had to go and find out where we left the car, and also find Jane, as the last time we saw her, she was with Dave the Rave. Anyway the car was still at Stretton in the Stonehouse car park and written on the steamed up window was 'Pal Gal Sal' which makes a change from 'Barley Wine Queen'. I found one of Jane's earrings, in fact, I think there are more earrings than gravel in that car park!. Then I remembered to my horror that I had invited Keith to tea at home. Last night, dancing to 'I saw the light' by Todd Rundgren, I was watching him engrossed at the record decks helping the deejay. No matter how much I shout at him, walk off, go out with others, he still comes back to me as if nothing has happened. Mum and Dad love him but I don't as there is no spark. Life is mean!"

19th January 1974: Time to leave home and move away.
"Julie and I went to the Tollgate Club on the Whittlesey Road but it seemed deserted so we raced to Spalding to the El Cid. As a rule nobody is allowed in after 11p.m. Anyway we did a lot of grovelling and were let in. What a waste of effort! Everybody was with someone but we weren't! We went home feeling fed up. I started thinking I just have to leave home. Inspired by Jean as she has left Barclays Bank and has gone to Wiltshire to be a farm secretary, and Julie is going to train in London to be a midwife/health visitor. Got the atlas of Great Britain, put a blindfold on, and stuck a pin in anywhere. It landed in Wales – Cardiff. Wrote a letter to the YMCA hostel and will get the address from the Library tomorrow. I can join a temp agency for work and Aunty Doris lives up the road in Newport, if I am stuck. Feel quite excited ."

13th May 1974: Handed in my notice in at work today.
"After working 4 years in the Town Clerk's Department of Peterborough Town Hall, it's time to go. I've had some good times. There were a few raised eyebrows when they knew I didn't have another job to go to but the agencies in Cardiff have plenty of work. I took Jane out in my car, "Buttercup", which has lasted me well, except as I left, the horn went off and wouldn't stop. Ran back to the house to fetch Dad and he just wrenched the wires out.... So, I was on my way with just another thing to add to the list of repairs – the windscreen washer pipe is not attached to anything and the speedometer cable snapped last week, first gear doesn't work, the door lock is broken and the door tends to swing open round corners and bounces back off the bonnet! Had a good night out with Jane and met up with Ric Tic Toc Tic Toc, Cockatoo, and Anne and Ann from Spalding. Stayed the night at Jane's, and she let me have her feather bed....I don't know quite how ancient it is, but it is lovely and cosy."

13th June 1974: Got stopped by the Police!
"My car's front number plate was missing! On investigation it was still there but had been pushed under the car by that wooden box I ran over in the High Street! The policemen were very friendly and I told them I would get it fixed (it's now added to the long

list). On my way to Spalding for 'farewell drinks' I managed to drive the wrong way over a complicated 2 bridge roundabout over the river! At the Red Lion I got invited to a party out at Moulton Chapel. Didn't stay long as I wanted to go home and pack. Unfortunately I drove home in the wrong direction and kept seeing signs to Fleet, Gedney Drove End and The Wash! Being born in the marshy Lincolnshire fens (therefore with webbed feet) I wonder how I will cope with the mountains in Wales. Just as well I am leaving the car behind on familiar territory!"

15th June 1974: Dad and my brother Ian drive the 200 miles to Cardiff.

"It just happened to be the hottest day of the year. When they left me at the YWCA hostel, to avoid my tears, I sent them off with a reminder that I would be back in 6 weeks to be bridesmaid at Helen's wedding. Once they had gone, I felt a bit bewildered and couldn't quite take in the fact that this would now be my home for goodness knows how long! It is a lovely double-fronted 3 storey house overlooking Roath Park – not bad! The place was deserted as the girls were either out or had gone home for the weekend. Found the pay phone and noticed, stuck on the wall, the list of residents – Tegwyn, Sian, Valmai.....I do wonder if I will need to learn Welsh! Wandered down to the lake in the park and got talking to a girl Valerie who took me back to her flat for a coffee and to meet her flat mates, Jill and Andy (wow English names!). They are going for a picnic down by the River Usk tomorrow and have invited me to go with them. Went back to my room so happy that I have met new friends and immediately started writing to my old ones!"

17th June 1974: The Brook Street Bureau (founded 1946) and Green Shield Stamps.

"I woke up feeling as if I'd got flu, but I think it was a hangover. The girls here have been introducing me to all the pubs, bars and clubs in Cardiff. They are all such party animals (girls after my own heart). Serious stuff today though, as I had to go looking for a job. Quite fancied working for the BBC, but when I enquired, it was 'don't ring us, we'll ring you'. Had better luck at the Brook Street Bureau and after a shorthand and typing test (scary), they must have been hard pressed for office staff as they asked if I could start at the Museum of Wales next Monday! (Thrilled). Walked down Albany Road on the way home to buy some food,

YWCA 86 and 87 Ninian Road, Roath Park, Cardiff.

but will do a big shop on Thursday when it is 'double green shield stamps day'. Back at the hostel, Helen and Joyce wanted to go dancing at Mont Morenz. It was so hot in there, yet Helen had amazing energy on the dance floor. I survived until the end when a boy called Tom George introduced himself to me and said we had danced together earlier. I couldn't remember this (probably couldn't see who I was dancing with because of the cigarette smoke and sauna like atmosphere) but he looked rather like the singer James Taylor, so when he asked me out, I said yes! I will meet him next Friday at 8 p.m. outside the Students Union".

24th June 1974: I wondered why the streets were deserted.
"Woke up at 7.45 excited about starting my new job at the Museum. Caught the 8.30 bus and it was half empty, in fact there was no-one about. I thought the clocks in town were obviously wrong as they all said 6.40, but of course, IT WAS 6.40! I had looked at the 'alarm hand' on my new clock from Woolworths thinking it was time to get up! This was bad news considering I hadn't got in until 2.30 a.m. after a good night dancing at the Golf Range Club. I then had to wait until 7.00 for the café at the Bus Station to open! After buying several cups of coffee and a magazine, I went to work at 8.00. The Museum is a beautiful place to work in and I soon forgot that I'd been up for hours. The offices were a bit crummy though. Interesting work, but to my horror I was expected to type the exhibit labels in Welsh! That

rather slowed me down. Back at the hostel, after hearing about the big fight at Qui Qui's wine bar (where Mags works and we got free drinks) and also the fire there, I had a bath. Sian and I went to our ballroom class and met up with Lesley, who is a 25 year old bus conductress. Tonight we learnt the Breakaway Blues."

28th June 1974: A dilemma today, as Mr Roberts at the Museum wants me to take on the job permanently.
"I've been offered a job at UWIST (University of Wales Institute of Science and Technology) in the Committees Section. The deciding factor is that UWIST has Electric Typewriters, so I'll be writing to them to confirm. I was meeting Tom George tonight and it was raining yet again so I caught the bus. I was thinking that if I married him I would be Sally George and I liked that. We went for a drink to the Buccaneer and then on to Titos. I was a bit disappointed really as Tom kept yawning! Although, he then asked me to go to his birthday celebrations next week and he doesn't mind coming to the pictures with me to see 'The Way We Were'. I just hope he isn't bored by the film as he may think it's a load of romantic twaddle. Came home feeling quite confused about Tom. I don't know what his game is as I don't think I've played it! Anyway my room mate 'Ann from the Valleys' was upset as her parents had been to see her and said she looked tired from all the late nights. Poor girl, she has only been enjoying herself!"

8th July 1974: The Twin Tub Washing Machine.
"Not much work once I'd finished typing up the dictation from Dafydd. I bought a quarter of a pound of Welsh mints in the afternoon and ate them all! Annoyed with myself as I caught the wrong bus home from work! I suppose it was interesting to see places I would never normally see, in and around the Llanishen area. Two new girls had arrived at the hostel – Valma and Wenda. I did my laundry in the Twin Tub Washing Machine, but the pipe from the tap to the machine flew off and there was water everywhere! Tom phoned to tell me to meet him and his friends in the Buccaneer for his birthday. I was a bit annoyed as I don't like going into pubs on my own. Anyway I needn't have worried as I saw all Tom's friends and Huw bought me a drink. We were having a great laugh until Tom walked in! After a few more drinks we went to Bumpers night club and we all had a good time."

15th July 1974: IBM Electric Golf Ball Typewriter.
"Raining yet again and I started my new job at UWIST. Met my boss Colonel Martin and across the corridor Major Watkeys and did wonder whether I had signed up for the Army by mistake! Also met Jackie who sits opposite me and is lovely. Upstairs we have the Principal and Registrar. I will have to stand in as holiday relief for the secretary Merle on occasions which I didn't want to think about. Anyway, the best part of the job is my typewriter which is an IBM electric golf ball typewriter! When I got home Tom phoned and I was enjoying the conversation until he said that his friends didn't like my accent at all! Afterwards the girls in the hostel were telling me to finish with him! I walked up Penylan Hill to the Applied Psychology Department as they want volunteers for their experiments in attention and perception. Delivered my letter and I will be contacted – I am intrigued. Gorgeous view of the sea from up there."

19th July 1974: The Principal's Key is no doubt on it's way to landfill!
"The rain never lets up here. Work gets better though. Colonel Martin still shouts and Jackie always has a refined accent. I had some training as acting PA to the Principal and Registrar today. Apart from cutting off a few phone calls and misinterpreting a little of my shorthand notes, it all went well! Merle gave me the Principal's key and I couldn't find it when I left work. I now have an awful feeling that it fell in the waste paper bin which would be emptied into the dustbin by the cleaners! Another thing that happened today is that Ann and I have been getting lots of bites just lately and I woke up last night and saw an insect the size of a ladybird on my pillow. I killed it and put it in a matchbox. At lunch time I took this to the Library and found an encyclopedia of household bugs. Identified the culprit as a 'bed bug'. Gave this information and the bug to Mrs Bradley who said she would have the room fumigated immediately and for now Ann and I would sleep on camp beds in any other rooms that would have us. Well, what a day!"

30th August 1974: The Bed Bug Saga continues!
"I was getting ready to visit my Aunty Doris in Newport when I heard the shocking news that Ann, my room mate, has got to leave (and go back to the Valleys) as her Dad is threatening to sue the YWCA for not burning the beds! Whilst she was packing her

things Mrs. Bradley came and told her it's about time she stood on her own two feet! Her Dad arrived and stormed into Mrs. Bradley's room and we could hear raised voices but he came out looking rather glum! Nobody messes with Mrs. Bradley and comes out unscathed! Phoned my parents, as, out of interest, I wondered what they would do. My Mum roared with laughter and said we are country fenland folk and we've had worse than that – bats, rats, mice, lice, toads and silverfish! She also said we had no fancy fumigators from the Council, we just had to deal with it ourselves! When I put the phone down, I wondered how we dealt with it.....perhaps with advice from Mrs. Beeton's Book of Household Management 1861 and we bashed each individual bug with the book!"

Reader: I wouldn't mind but the YWCA (Young Women's Christian Association) was 100 times cleaner than any student flat. We had a cleaning lady every day. It was a most respectable place until the arrival of Marilyn and then it became known as 'The House of the Rising Sun'. Ironically, it is now a Mother and Baby home!

5th September 1974: We drove home with 8 of us in the car!

"I met Tom at 2pm or rather he turned up 20 mins late! We went round Cardiff Castle, which I enjoyed and I am so glad I have seen it. Tom was acting like a big kid at times. I don't mind being insulted in fun, but this was all the time. We walked into town for a coffee and I wanted us to have our photo taken in one of those photo booths, but he wouldn't so I refused to go for coffee. We stood in the street for 10 mins not talking, then he called me childish and gave in. He pulled a face on all of the photos except one. I was ready to walk off but wanted to go to Keith's 21st party later on and asked him if he still wanted me to go, to which he said 'you were invited'. I took that as a 'yes' and was determined to enjoy myself. When I met him later, he looked so lovely, having had his hair cut and wearing a collar and tie. So it is a shame that, at the party, he spent half of his time playing on the fruit machine and the other half with his ex-girlfriend! I managed to get a quick word with him and he said he didn't think we should see each other again as I tried to organise him! The sad thing is that I shall miss his friends! They took me home – 8 of us in the car – and had been trying to pair me off with another lad. As I got out of the car, or rather fell out, I could hear someone whisper – 'go on ask her out'!"

10th September 1974: I am sure he had no intention of sending a postcard.
"Felt quite melancholy at work today. I knew Tom was taking an accountancy exam next door in the Temple of Peace and it seemed ridiculous and sad that we couldn't meet for lunch. Went out to buy myself a large custard slice – comfort eating again. Saw a beautiful Austin Seven car, Ruby red, parked and was admiring it when the owners (Jan & Harry) started talking to me. I told them about my Dad's Austin Seven and how I loved the cars. They said I should join the Austin Seven club as they go out on lots of picnics in the Welsh countryside in convoy. I shall go to their meeting on Tuesday at the Pantmawr Inn. Walked home in the never ceasing rain! Back at the hostel, ate too much and went up to my room feeling unwanted, lonely and fat! Then my bell went and Tegwyn shouts up 'you've got a visitor'. Shot out of my room thinking that probably someone loves me and sure enough it was Tom! I was so pleased and was rather over enthusiastic with talking. Anyway he's going to send me a postcard from his holidays. After that, I was on top of the world."
Reader: I didn't hear from him again but occasionally saw him in town, usually when I wasn't always looking my best, so I would hide in shop doorways! Whether I received the postcard or not, I've no idea!

18th September 1974: Tipp-Ex - we couldn't manage without it!
"I enjoyed work today and spent most of it checking the addressograph plates. Just as well really, as I'd knocked over a whole bottle of Tipp-Ex and couldn't find a new one. That would mean not being able to correct any typing mistakes. Back at the hostel, one of the new girls Wenda, was in a panic as her friends had decided not to come and live in Cardiff with her. I said she could share my room, although Mrs. Bradley had to explain about the previous tenants – the Bed Bugs! She didn't mind at all. After tea I went out to my new evening class – Folk and Country Dancing! A friendly bunch of about 6 housewife type ladies, 3 men – Cedric, Nigel and Idris – and a Nun! I really enjoyed it. On the way home, I called in to see Helen and Hazel's new flat. It was really grotty, but I didn't like to say. Three of Helen's hairy (male) friends were supposed to be painting it, but were more like messing about. I am so pleased to be living in the YWCA and have

put my name down for one of the bedsits next door. One of the tenants has been there years, so is no longer a "young woman" and the Committee are going through the rules carefully and want to evict her, just because she is 58! I think my name is on that room but I will feel awful if I am given her home and she has to go!"

6th October 1974: Austin Seven Club Outing.
"In the middle of the night, someone opened the door to our room, looked in, then left! It rather scared me. I found out in the morning that Mark had called for Wenda at 12.45 a.m.! I wondered who had let him in and then remembered that Sue and Mags have raised suspicions, when a man was seen leaving their room at 7 a.m. Mrs. Bradley is on the case and biding her time. Rumour has it that she is intending to surprise them at the top of the stairs in the early hours one morning soon. Today was very enjoyable as Jan and Harry came and picked me up in their Austin Seven 'Ruby' and we met the other Austin Sevens at Ross-on-Wye. Had lunch at the Hope and Anchor and it was beautifully picturesque there. I was talking to Roger and his girlfriend Carys....and I wanted to say to Carys that if she ever got fed up with Roger....I would gladly take him off her hands. We went for a 25 mile drive in the countryside and stopped at a picnic place by a ruined castle and tiny village. As we all went exploring, we got separated and I was left talking to this middle aged woman. All of a sudden I realized it was Roger's mother so I started being extra amiable! It was a lovely, still and mild day, so we had our picnic on the grass....just before it started to rain yet again! Coming from the driest part of England, I will never get used to the almost constant rain in Wales."

8th October 1974: Today's Minutes will be pure fiction.
"I had to take the Minutes at a meeting today in the Pharmacy Lecture Theatre, but didn't have a clue whether a thing was resolved or agreed. It took all afternoon, as this bloke Aston argued about everything! I was so bored that I nearly nodded off, and hardly wrote a relevant thing down. When I got back to the office, just as I was putting the kettle on, the stroppy Registrar came storming in, pointing out typing errors. I wanted to tell him that these new Minutes were going to be pure fiction and I might add one or two jokes just to perk up his afternoon! After tea Wenda and I set off to Ty Celyn for night classes and at Wenda's request we hitched a lift! Wenda went to 'Modern Convenience

Cooking' and I went to 'Italic Handwriting'. It was really interesting, much more than I thought and we should learn bookbinding too. Wenda wanted to go on to Tito's, so I agreed and there was a good crowd on the dance floor. I must have enjoyed myself as we didn't get back until 3 a.m."

11th October 1974: Freshers' Coming Up Ball and The Rubettes.

"Woke up late, didn't hear the alarm, and only had time to throw on some clothes and run to work. Just about made it on time and I was needed to cover for the Registrar's Secretary. I was not pleased as I felt really scruffy, so I ate a Danish pastry and 2 custard slices. I then felt like a fat slob! I forgot about it in the afternoon as I was looking forward to the evening and the Freshers' Coming Up Ball at the Students' Union. The Rubettes were playing and Wenda, Joyce and I were quite excited! We had a great time and got invited to the band's dressing room to talk to them and get autographs. We then sat on the floor in front of the stage to watch them and felt like 13 year olds! Afterwards, we were invited by some students to Senghenydd House – Halls of Residence where we had chips and wine. They happened to be postgraduate civil engineering students so we listened to music on their expensive hi fi, and had our photos taken with their expensive cameras. They were fun to talk to and walked us home and one of them wanted me to be his photographic model....but I took that to mean girlfriend. Anyway, Jackie, at work, has got a blind date lined up for me – next week."

14th October 1974: The day I met Marilyn and Tiger Bay.

"Enjoyed work, but it rained all day again. I went to the Library at lunch time and picked a novel called 'Do You Remember England'! This will be a good book to read. There is a new Welsh girl at the hostel called Marilyn who works for the BBC. We went out together in the evening to Bakers Row for the UWIST disco and then on to the Casino on Bute Road. Quite a lot of students in there, and some dockworkers and sailors, as we were in Butetown, on the edge of Tiger Bay. We sat talking to a student called Dai Davies and he lived in our street. He told us to be very careful as Tiger Bay was well known as a tough and dangerous area, there were prostitutes and mysterious unsolved murders. I told him I found that strange, as the singer Shirley Bassey came from here and said the area had a friendly community spirit. He said she would be talking about the gambling dens! We were a bit

Postgraduate students in Halls of Residence, Senghennyd House.

1955 with my Mum and brother Ian in the Lincolnshire Fens.

scared then and left with Dai. We had a coffee at his flat in our Road and I noticed that although it was a tidy place, there was an air of shabbiness, fustiness, damp and cold. Marilyn, myself and the Bed Bugs prefer our warm, clean and cosy YWCA hostel."
Reader: Tiger Bay is no longer an industrial dock area but has been transformed into a leisure and business hot spot. Stunning old and new buildings, a water bus, and Dr. Who and Torchwood were filmed there. It is now the place to be!

25th October 1974: 'Salad Bar' or 'Grease Bar' at the Students' Union?
"Good intentions for a salad lunch go out of the window when we smell the delicious fry ups and roasts, so the 'Grease Bar' it was, with Jackie and her husband Richard this lunch time. They wanted me to meet a certain Rob Davis, law student at a party tonight and would call for me. Went to Vi's the hairdressers on the way home to see if she could do anything with my wayward locks. She wrapped my wet hair turban style around my head and put me under the hairdryer. Twenty minutes later I came out, red faced but with smooth, shiny, straight hair – better than my Mum ironing it under brown paper on the ironing board! Jackie collected me at 8pm but before I could get downstairs the two lads, Chris and (I've forgotten his name) came to take Marilyn and I out. We had forgotten that we met them at Mont Morenz and made arrangements for tonight! I slipped out the back door and Marilyn said she would make excuses for me and entertain them both herself - what a good friend! The party at Senghenydd House was rather good and so was Rob. I was determined not to dislike

him but didn't have to try as we got on really well, and I am seeing him Monday night."

27th October 1974: Coffee and Lime drink?

"Marilyn and I had a coffee and lime juice drink in town and came home via the park. We sat on the swings – my favourite place for thinking – and wondered where we would be in 10 years time. Then, of course, it started to rain so we came back and cooked cottage pie and heated up a Marks & Spencer dessert and coffee. Crashed out on the bed, listened to the radio and I wrote letters while Marilyn read my poetry book. I haven't had such a relaxing and happy Sunday afternoon in ages. It was soon disrupted by Wenda and Jane returning and I felt guilty as I'd been eating Jane's biscuits. Rob phoned and asked if he could see me tonight. I was a little taken aback but agreed. We had a drink at the Criterion and then a walk down Lovers Lane to the Lake. The rain came on again so we went to Senghenydd House, listened to records, talked to his housemates and I can't believe how well we get on."

30 October 1974: Who remembers Joss Sticks?

"Storms in the night – violent thunder, lightning, wind and hail. It kept me awake, as it hammered on the skylight in our room. I didn't particularly want to go to work and when I got there the kettle had gone missing! Back at the hostel there was a furore about Wenda. She is in the habit of knowing when someone's boyfriend or potential boyfriend is in the building. She floats downstairs in an almost see through negligee and dazzles the said young man with her charm into an almost hypnotic trance! Apart from that, she is very kind hearted, as when I'm in bed, she will bring me a cup of tea or coffee and my post. She also teaches me Welsh words. Anyway tonight I walked up to meet Rob rather than him come to the hostel as I didn't want him falling under her spell! We drove out of Cardiff to the Six Bells for a drink but I was a bit alarmed when Rob said he wanted to see me every night, so I gave him a lecture on being possessive and rushing things. I should have felt flattered rather than disturbed. Anyway, his eyes glazed over at this point. Back in Halls, we joined Rob's flatmates, who were sitting around listening to music, chatting, drinking wine, and had lit candles and joss sticks."

1st November 1974: Can you still ask for a 'schooner of sherry?

"I felt better for more sleep. Work was going o.k. until lunchtime when I was searching for a spoon to eat my yoghurt. I turned round to see Richard and Rob! Richard and Jackie wanted us to go straight to their house in Pontypridd, after work, for a meal. That seriously messed up my plans as I wanted to call in on my hairdresser Vi, who is also my agony aunt. Instead Jackie came back to the hostel where we had coffee and an egg custard tart and I had a quick wash and change. I felt a right scruff and yet Rob was beautifully turned out. Anyway after a schooner of sherry at the house in Pontypridd it didn't bother me. Jackie cooked us 'Coq au Vin' with Black Forest Gateau for pudding. The wine and conversation were free flowing. Got back at 4 a.m.! I really am liking this life with Rob and we are going to his friend Tim's house tomorrow night. I almost feel as if it's all too good to be true!"

2nd November 1974: Polaroid Instant Cameras were the latest novelty.

"Had to be up at 8.30 to go to the hairdressers. Afterwards Marilyn and I went shopping in town. We went in all the boutiques but saw nothing we wanted to buy. Had a quick drink in the Buccaneer and called into Senghenydd House. We had coffee and biscuits with Rob and friends. Marilyn had bought a flash for her camera so we now have photographs and just need to use up the film and get them developed. In the evening Rob and I went to Tim's house which he shares with 3 women, one of whom has kids, and the other two who were rather very frosty towards me. Tim was acting weird and rude and Rob was frowning. We went back to Senghenydd house with Trevor and there was a strange atmosphere. Not a good evening, but we are going to the pictures tomorrow night, so perhaps things will go back to normal, whatever that is!"

3rd November 1974: The latest film 'Chinatown'

"Wenda brought me breakfast in bed and then I got up to go out and buy a Sunday newspaper. I bumped into Marilyn in the hall, she was just coming in from a party the night before! We then cooked ourselves Sunday lunch and had a lovely lazy Sunday afternoon. I must adopt Marilyn's outlook on life. In the evening Rob and I went to see the film 'Chinatown'. We both enjoyed it

The Lounge in the YWCA hostel, 86 Ninian Road.

but hadn't a clue as to what it was about! When we got back to his room, his mood changed and he started talking about not seeing me, as he didn't want to get involved with anyone! He then took me home and as I got out of the car, fighting back the tears, he said I would make somebody a marvellous wife! I'm just reeling in shock, that a week ago I had to talk him out of seeing me every night and all of a sudden he doesn't want to see me at all! I was right when I thought it was all too good to be true. Anyway, I got out my italic pen and copied out a poem I'd seen in one of my books. I would like to say I'd composed it myself, but I'm not that clever. It made me feel better though!"

14th November 1974: Ruby Tuesday - diet did not go well today.
"At lunch time I went to UWIST refectory and ate a pizza, 2 beef and cheese fritters, baked potato with sweet corn and loads of butter followed by a dessert of fresh cream strawberry gateau! I felt bloated all afternoon and had to staple and collate papers. At my evening class, after work, I nearly fell asleep. I went out with

Marilyn in the evening to a party in Richmond Road. She disappeared with Roger, the boyfriend of the hostess whose birthday party we gatecrashed last week and where we all ate 5 pieces of birthday cake each. I followed others who were going to a party in the Halls of Residence. That was almost finished so I went to see Jed and Steve who had promised they would tape some L.P.'s for me by Melanie and Free. I apologized for imposing but did their washing up, so then, there were smiles all round. I also got my songs."

5th December 1974: Crazy Christmas Party Season Has Started!

"Colonel Martin had been singing my praises to Jackie, saying that I was efficient in my work and polite and he was worried that I might leave for a better job! Well that cheered me up, especially as I've made quite a few blunders since I've been here. All day we were working on the Admin Handbook as the Principal wanted it urgently. Marilyn, her sister Carol and others were all meeting up at the Students' Union with Geoffrey in the evening for Geoffrey's party. I was talking to Colin who said he was going to the Badminton party upstairs so I thought I would look in on that one first – you can never have too many parties, it is the crazy Christmas party season after all! It wasn't much good so I met the others outside and bumped into Jed, and although I'd told him I just wanted to be friends, he looked rather nice under the romantic street light, so I may have to revise my decision. He wouldn't come to the party, though, as he was off with the lads. Colin turned up later and took me home. He didn't ask to see me again though!"

10th December 1974: Penarth Pier.

"We were given a morning off work to go Christmas shopping – how generous! I did pretty well and managed to find the L.P. my Dad wanted 'Johnnie Mathis – Greatest Hits'. I enjoyed the afternoon at work as Colonel Martin had given me the golf ball composer typewriter to use – £3,000 worth! It was quite fun trying out all the golf balls for the different type faces. When I got home I wanted to stay in and write Christmas cards but the girls had other ideas and I was dragged off to the UWIST disco with Marilyn. It wasn't much good so we tried Bakers Row where a Biology party was going on. Stayed a while, then decided to walk home – in the rain, eating chips. We bumped into Joyce and Valmai who were about to take a taxi to a party at Penarth Pier, so we jumped in too. Well, I enjoyed it, but the others didn't, although we stayed a couple of hours. Whilst waiting for the taxi home, I was watching the waves break on the shingly beach, and I can't believe I live so near to the sea now."

12th December 1974: Mothballs and Bar Morganwydd.
"I wanted to sing Christmas carols, so went to our nearest church – St. Margaret's Baptist at the top of the road. It wasn't a very churchy atmosphere – modern, like a hall. The candle light was not real, and the choir who did most of the singing, were wonderful but my concentration was taken away by the overwhelming smell of mothballs. When I got back, I sat by the fire writing my Christmas cards while Marilyn sat reading my diary. Later, we went to the University Carol service, which was different again – modern verse, different views and jolly carol singing. Afterwards, we sat in the Bar Morganwydd with a drink and saw practically everyone we knew (or had been out with)! A bloke dressed as Father Christmas came in and we had a long conversation on how and why he came to be dressed so seasonally. He was extremely pleasant and he took us home and came in for coffee. Of course, with Wenda there, I didn't get a word in as she wouldn't let his attention wander to anyone but herself."

20th December 1974: Dancing 'The Bump' to 'Nutbush City Limits'.
"Poor Marilyn was changing her mind, several times, in between phone calls about going home for Christmas. At work it was the office Christmas lunch today. We all had sherry in the Principal's office, and I felt very important sitting on the top table next to Colonel Martin, the Principal and Registrar at lunch. The wine wasn't as free flowing as my Christmas lunches with the Town Clerk's Department at Peterborough City Council, but at least I was clear headed to finish my work in the afternoon. I packed my suitcase to go home, but Marilyn and I had one last night out at Bumpers night club. We had been put off a bit by the terrorist bomb blasts in London. Anyway, all bags were searched so we hoped that was enough. We sat drinking upstairs (Campari and Pils Lager) listening to old Beatles records and having a laugh over things. Before leaving we had a good old dance and practiced the latest dance craze –'the bump' especially to 'Nutbush City Limits'. Excited about going home, I have missed my Mum, Dad, brother, cat and dog."

The evening summer sun out in the Lincolnshire Fens.　　Fluffy and Gem.

30th December 1974: Christmas on the East side and no rain!
"I am writing this on the train back to Cardiff after Jean kindly dropped me off at Swindon station, before returning to her Wiltshire farms, animals and accounts. I was so excited to be home for the Christmas holidays, I didn't stop talking, and Mum and Dad say I've developed a 'sing-song' Welsh accent! I watched Mum decorate the Christmas cake and put up the cards – she has so much more energy now, since leaving full time work. I met my old workmates from Peterborough Town Hall and put £1 in the kitty for lunchtime drinks. Went out with Jean and Jane to all our old haunts, and a few people didn't even realise that I had been away! Brian gave me a photo, taken in the Spring, just before I left for Wales. Taken in the Lincolnshire fens, bathed in the evening sun leaning against Brian's Morris Minor. It made me realise that it hasn't rained once during my few days at home. I don't know where I will end up living but I don't think it will be in the rainy West country!"

Reader: I must have wished too hard about the rain as in 1976, I experienced Britain's worst drought of the century and the area most affected was Cardiff and South East Wales! We had water rationing – just an hour a day, I think.....but I will come to that later.

1975

2nd January 1975: New Year's Resolutions.
"A phone call at work from Marilyn to say that a huge Y.W.C.A. sign had been put up outside the hostel and she was horrified. She didn't want the fact advertising that we lived in a Warden controlled, strict Convent type establishment, when really it is more like The House of the Rising Sun! At 11pm, when Marilyn got home from the BBC Newsroom, she was clutching a copy of The Echo to look for a flat to rent. We went to see Mrs. Bradley, the Warden, who leaves the job tomorrow, for a late farewell drink. She is on our side and wanted the sign taken down. In fact now that Mrs. Bradley is leaving, she has become quite human.
New Year's Resolutions:-☼ To get into the habit of changing my mental picture if something depresses me.
☼ Realise that things are often better if they don't go to plan and the unexpected happens.
☼ To see the good in people and not the bad.
☼ To lose one stone in weight.
☼ To join some more clubs.
☼ To be a Professor's Secretary.
☼ To have a proposal of marriage."

9th January 1975: So what did happen to the sign?
"Marilyn phoned me at work to say that Mrs Evans, the Chairman of the YWCA committee says that if no-one owns up to the missing Y.W.C.A. sign, then all the girls will have to pay 50p each! Worried about this all afternoon! When I got home the new Warden, Mrs Hemming thought all this was hilarious. We had word later that the Committee have backed down, as some members think it is foolish to advertise the fact that the house is full of single young women! Felt quite relieved. Wenda wanted to take us all to Qui Qui's Wine Bar in her Mini, as I wouldn't be in Cardiff to celebrate my birthday this weekend. After a few drinks, courtesy of Sue & Mags, who work there, we went on to the Spanish Bodega for the dancing. Wenda put a birthday request in to the DJ who played 'Je t'aime'...... of all things! Not really what I would have requested myself! Oh well, I shall be celebrating my birthday this weekend up in the Welsh speaking North Wales – Dolwyddelan with Marilyn's family – can't wait!"

12th January 1975: When the trains still had compartments.
"Fantastic Birthday weekend. It started when we caught the 5.10 p.m. train to Llandudno Junction. We shared our compartment firstly with railway labourers, then a very friendly woman got on with her 3 dirty, smelly children and after a change at Crewe we enjoyed the company of some very young sailors! It was raining hard when Marilyn's Dad & Uncle met us at the station but Marilyn's lovely Mum had a meal and roaring fire waiting for us. On Saturday woke up to gorgeous scenery and we went to Llandudno. Party time in the evening which started at the local pub, 2 doors away, 'The Gwydyr'. Word spread quickly that there was 'Bingo' at Marilyn's house and quite a crowd came – Micky T., Roger, Butch, Merv, Ginger....We danced in the front room and at midnight everyone wished me a happy birthday. Marilyn was ill though and had to go to bed. We caught the train home on Sunday and she started to feel better by the time we got to Chester. She has gone to bed while I'm writing this but we have just heard that Wenda was rushed to hospital with a suspected appendicitis."

14th January 1975: My salary was £1,500 per annum.
"I need a better job, firstly to increase my salary from the £1,500 p.a. I get now, and also I do have to think about my career! As luck would have it, I went over to the Refectory for lunch with Cath from Printing. She told me that part of her work is to print the Job Vacancies! A good person to know! Called in at the Library and got a book 'Teach Yourself Welsh'. Perhaps it was just a coincidence that it was raining heavily on the way back to work and I got soaked (wonder what the Welsh words are for 'sodding rain')! I still felt damp whilst taking the Minutes of the AUT Exec. Committee but for once started to understand what it was all about! In the evening I went hospital visiting with Marilyn to see Wenda. What a picture of health – full make up on, nails done. I felt like taking the chocolates home that I'd bought for her, or on looking round the Ward, perhaps giving them to one of the poorly old ladies in there! We left and went to the Students' Union but it was packed out, as there was a Group playing, and John Peel (yuk) was the D.J. for the disco. We didn't bother and walked home past the Halls of Residence listening out for parties

and nearly fell in a door when it was opened by some medical students. They had wine, coffee and a sink full of washing up, but invited us in. One of them was telling a few 'tall stories' and before we left they pulled a skeleton out of the drawer!"

19th January 1975: If a mobile phone had existed it would have saved me a 3 mile walk.

"Marilyn had some beautiful green drinks glasses for Christmas and wanted to do some entertaining, so Sunday lunch/dinner it was to be. She invited Peter and I had contacted Bob from Bristol who said he would come, but then he cancelled so I invited Richard. As Marilyn was still in her dressing gown (until 4 p.m.), I said I would do the cooking, it was my turn anyway. I had just put everything in the oven when Richard rang to say he had family problems and had to go home, so I then had to walk to Geoffrey's to get him to come (3 miles in all) and the dinner was 'well done' but edible when I got back. Unbeknown to anyone Marilyn said it would be interesting to tape the dinner conversation, so we did! Peter and Marilyn went out for the rest of the evening, Geoffrey went off to the Union and I stayed in and chatted to Joyce. We also played back the tape.....what polite and idle conversation it was!"

20th January 1975: The Warden was waiting at the top of the stairs at 3 a.m.

"Overslept and just got to work on time then realized I hadn't got my handbag, so no money. Raided the coffee jar which only contained 30p, but that was enough for lunch, so put an IOU note in. Back at the hostel, Wenda gave me the shocking news that Sue and Mags have got until Saturday to get out! Mrs Hemming was at the top of the stairs, waiting for them at 3 a.m. when they brought a man into their room! Also they've been sacked from Qui Qui's! No more free drinks then....but they were lovable rogues, too generous with the Wine Bar's profits so it seems. I can't say we were keen on the unsavoury types they brought back to the hostel! I do wonder if the Young Women's Christian Association was hosting a brothel in one of its rooms! Andy took me out in the evening for a drink and we sat listening to the Juke Box. Met up with another couple and went to the Biology and Chemistry New Year Party at Titos. A few drinks, a few dances and looked in on the Cabaret – Paul Jones - who used to be lead singer with Manfred Mann. There were only a handful of people in there so we felt that we were being serenaded by the singer!"

Senghenydd House, Halls of Residence.

26th January 1975: Pan's People who became Legs and Co. on 'Top of the Pops'.
"We invited Andy and Roland for a meal this time and things were not going too well in the kitchen. The roast potatoes went on strike and I managed to drop the dinner out of the oven! We were thankful for the litre of wine they had brought. The roast chicken with all the trimmings turned out well, considering. Our experiments in cooking, baking, grilling and boiling things to a pulp had never poisoned anyone yet! There had only ever been one occasion when we had to put out a fire and the Warden never got to hear about it fortunately. I think we bribed (or threatened) certain witnesses to keep quiet We then started on the rum but the deep and intelligent conversation kept us fairly sober

although the concentration was exhausting. We were grateful that we were leaving our guests for something more light hearted. Marilyn and I had planned to go and see 'Sons and Lovers' the late night film so we set off and bumped into Richard and Jackie on the way, who were going to see 'Pan's People'. Called in the Union for a drink and poor Joyce, who has such a kind hearted personality was being totally monopolized by Freaky Helen. We sat listening to the Juke Box – Rab Noakes 'A Clear Day' and Sandy Denny, 'Solo'. In the queue for the film we were frisked by security men which caused a few laughs. We walked home, because for once, it wasn't raining."

1st February 1975: Pontypridd then back to the mansion of mayhem!

"I got up at 9 a.m. and made Marilyn some breakfast. We caught the train to Pontypridd which has a great compact shopping centre and market. Jackie met us and took us back to her house for lunch. She is always in a happy mood when her husband is away! She had cooked Spaghetti Bolognese and Cherry Pie with cream. We staggered home from the train station and there was no peace at the hostel. Joyce was in our room so we had our tea in the dining room. It was noisy in there and Wenda was droning on. The phone was going constantly and the door bell. In the middle of Marilyn's tea, Alun came in to see her and secretly I think she was pleased as it was someone to take her out. Luckily Wenda wasn't around to change Alun's mind, as she was soaking in the bath upstairs. The aroma of scented candles and musk body lotion was making its way downstairs. I went to the Union with Joyce, mainly as a bodyguard to ward off Freaky Helen. David kept coming over to dance with me, and he is so sweet, witty and charming with a gorgeous Yorkshire accent. At the end he wanted to walk me home or here, there or anywhere. His friends call me 'SuperSal'. What a shame that he is only 18 and I am 22. Joyce and I got a taxi home!"

6th February 1975: Can you really eat daffodils?

"I have now moved into Marilyn's room on the ground floor next to the front door. Wenda is sharing our old room with one of the new girls. I shall miss the weather beating down on the sky light but have swapped it for a bay window overlooking the park, although there are disadvantages. I was woken at 3 a.m. with Joyce tapping on the window – she had forgotten her key. I now know how my Mum felt back home! Today there was commotion in the kitchen as a few new girls had moved in. Out of the two I met, one was quite brusque and the other dopey. Joyce, Valmai and I had managed to get some free tickets to see John Martyn at the Union, so that is where we went tonight. Afterwards there was a party in Connaught Road. Full of students, friendly enough and one of them was eating daffodils! We walked home in the freezing cold. M. got in at 4.30 a.m. after going out to dinner with Geoffrey!"

9th February 1975: 'Lady Eleanor'
"Marilyn woke me and handed me a cup of strong coffee. She was going off to the hospital to see Geoffrey who had just had his appendix taken out! He had been fine 48 hours previously! I had forgotten we had dinner guests today, so when Marilyn got back we set to in the kitchen. Dafydd and Alun were coming round for Macaroni Cheese only we miscalculated on the sauce, so it was mainly Macaroni! We obviously need more practice and the two lads were not impressed as they sat reading rag mags most of the time! We made them come to the pictures with us to see 'The Getaway', but it turned out to be 'The Man With The Golden Gun' – James Bond! When we came out, the lads went off but we saw Nicki who was going to Top Rank for the Rag Ball. We looked in but there was a loud progressive group playing and everyone sitting on the floor. We danced a little in the small space that there was left. At the Bar we bought a drink and then lost Nicki! Bought some crisps and chips to eat on the way home and as we passed by the Halls of Residence we could hear music playing - 'Lady Eleanor' by Lindisfarne – I do like that song."

11th February 1975: The Rosko Roadshow.
"I was sent into town in the morning to buy 'Doggie Chox' for Colonel Martin's dog. Tried to diet today, but we all had Danish Pastries and Chelsea Buns with our morning coffee and at lunch I had a large portion of Welsh Rarebit followed by Apple Pie and Custard, so really it was a bit pointless. In the evening I went with Marilyn to see Geoffrey in hospital and had a laugh. Poor Geoffrey but I really admire him. Two of his friends came and we left as we wanted to call in at the Union where the Rosko Roadshow Disco was happening. It was an 'emancipation disco' so we needed to ask the lads to dance. Everyone was so friendly, but they were just the babes of the University – all of 18 years old. It finished at 12.30 a.m. and there was a party at 18 Connaught

Road, but after all the dancing and it was so hot in there, I was just too exhausted to go. We walked home stopping for chips."

19th February 1975: My own place at last!
"Someone had phoned me at 1.30 a.m. but the Warden, Mrs. Hemming didn't know who it was! The good thing is that she didn't tell me off. I was getting myself some porridge in the kitchen, half asleep, when Nicki came in crying about all her worries. Oh, poor Nicki, she needs so much love and understanding and I've never been brought up to give such sympathy. Still I helped her to sort herself out, I hope. I was just thinking that there is no peace in this place, when Mrs. Hemming came in to give me the keys for an empty bedsit next door. I couldn't believe it! Went to wake Marilyn up but she was already awake sitting up in bed reading holiday brochures with her sunglasses on! I also needed to find the alarm clocks. Marilyn has 3 clocks to make sure she hears the alarms, but we couldn't sleep with all the ticking so have buried them deep in the wardrobe somewhere. Anyway, when I got home from work, we went next door to my bedsit with coffee and a few things. I rearranged the furniture and moved my food in (what little I've been able to afford). It is beautiful and I can hardly believe that it is mine. It is so good to have somewhere of my own. Nicki wanted to come and have a look but I was looking forward to getting away from her and now she would have more barriers. I was tired, anyway, but couldn't help thinking about the party I'd missed in Senghenydd House tonight."

21st February 1975: Situations Vacant.
"In the post at work, there was a circular advertising a secretary's job in the Pharmacy Department. I made discreet enquiries, and found out it is working for a Professor Cook who has an abrupt manner. Didn't know what to do, so in the afternoon I slipped out to Pharmacy and spoke to Susan who explained the job to me, but I felt she was not telling me everything, and I don't know if I will be any better off. I decided to apply anyway, for the interview experience alone. As I would need a reference, I plucked up courage to tell Colonel Martin and I got a frosty reception "certainly not for another 6 months"! After work, it was great to be in my own room and I loved how the one wall had 3 sets of fold back doors and hey presto, one opened up to a kitchen, the other a wash hand basin and dressing table and lastly the wardrobe. I was admiring all this when my doorbell went. I

Students Union for University of Wales, Institute of Science and Technology (UWIST) and University College Cardiff.

couldn't be bothered to run down the 2 flights of stairs, when I knew it would be Nicki and I would spend the next hour listening to all her troubles, so I ignored it. Ten minutes later I heard just 3 rings, so I knew it was Marilyn. I let her in and she had brought food for tea. She also lent me £5 for the train fare to Dolwyddelan, for this weekend, to celebrate her 21st birthday."

23rd February 1975: The previous tenant told me something which rather disturbed me!

"We celebrated Marilyn's 21st birthday by starting off at the village pub 'Y Gwydyr'. The Martinis were free flowing and although the Wolverhampton Mountaineering lot were not there, plenty of Air Force personnel were! They all came back to Marilyn's parents' house. I did wonder why there were a lack of girls, but as Marilyn quite rightly pointed out, we didn't want any competition! We were dancing non stop in the front room and I think I had one too many drinks, as I couldn't stop laughing when a chap came downstairs from the loo wearing some of Marilyn's underwear on his head! The night ended with me walking down the road with Marilyn, her sister Carol and a Wing Commander! We arrived back in Cardiff today and it was a treat knowing I could have a peaceful evening, in my own place to try and finish my unpacking and sorting out. The previous tenant came to see how I was settling in and she told me something that rather disturbed me. Apparently she hadn't been ill for years until she came to live in this room, and then had colds, the flu, stomach bugs and ended up with jaundice before she left! I developed a really bad sore throat after she had gone!"

1st March 1975: The Best of Bread and Thayer's Ice Cream.

"This is the first day I have felt human again, after being off work all week with a lousy bad cold. I hadn't the energy to put one foot in front of the other and if I did, my head was so heavy, I thought it would roll off! Today I ventured out to the shops for food and as a treat bought some delicious Thayer's Ice Cream. Whilst in the queue I was reading about Cyril Thayer and how he started making this delicious ice cream, all night in the back of the shop in 1940. I was shattered by the time I got back and Mrs. Hemming came round to see how I was settling in and she is just like one of the girls. Marilyn came over and we were listening to 'The Best of Bread' on tape. I ventured out in the evening with everyone to the Union and met up with Geoffrey and friends. After a few dances, Marilyn and I left and walked home in the direction of a party we had been given the tip off about. It was packed out and not all that sociable. I was really squashed at times, but had conversations with David (the baby Casanova), Dave (the long-haired lover from Liverpool), Roland (hell's teeth) and someone whose name I only know as the boa constrictor! I was quite amused in a way, but we only stayed half an hour."

12th March 1975: My boss refuses to let me leave!

"Once again I was working for the Registrar and had quite a bit of work. I made a few boobs but showed efficiency. I still think you need to be a perfectionist to work for him. I was feeling quite happy, until just before lunch when I heard Colonel Martin talking to someone on the phone about me saying that I should not be accepted for another job! I was furious! To make matters worse, he called me in straight after lunch to say that I might be told about another job for a research secretary in Maritime Studies but I wasn't to be interested as it wasn't what I want! It sounded just my cup of tea though and I decided that I would find out more about it when I got the chance. Oh, and how dare he be so controlling! In the evening I went out with Nicki, Val and Allie to the Union. We met Tim in there who has a really good personality- witty and yet serious – pity he looks so out of date. Nicki and I then went to the Law Society disco but there was hardly anyone there. We waited and sat playing 'I spy' for an hour until we ran out of things to look at! I was informed, later, by young David that it was on the Tuesday night!"

14th March 1975: 'Petticoat' and 'Look Now' magazines.
"Jackie is off work with flu. I had to work for Colonel Martin and the Registrar, plus get 300 ballot papers out. I was shouted at by the Registrar, but could forgive him now that I know he is well known in Welsh Amateur Dramatic Societies and is a personal friend of Judi Dench. By a piece of good luck Colonel Martin went to the Registry and I had a good talk to Karen about the job in Maritime Studies and it sounds a fun department to work for. After work Marilyn came over to see me and despite the fact that she had a bad stomach ache, she still managed to chase me downstairs, poking a rolled up copy of the 'Petticoat' magazine in my back! No-one wanted to go out, so I got ready in a hurry and went to the Union. At first, I sat by the Porters Lodge until I saw people I knew and then went to see the group and disco. I was talking to Tom who asked me out! I said I was busy but actually I would like to go out with him on a platonic basis. I started talking to this Architecture student, who was very pleasant, but perhaps not witty and cheeky enough for me! As I walked home with Sue she commented that I would never get married as I need a man who is hand knitted. Maybe she is right. Perhaps I need to be a career woman, but that doesn't look very likely either!"

2nd April 1975: The Building Was on Fire!
"The interviews for the jobs went well, but at the end of the day both Pharmacy and Maritime Studies were looking for an older person – I wonder how much they were influenced by Colonel Martin. When I got back to the office Jackie told me that Dr. Fricke wished he had known that I was looking for a change of job as he had wanted a Secretary to take with him for a year's research in America! What a missed opportunity! I was quite pleased to know that word is getting out about me wanting to move onwards and upwards in the University. At 3.30 pm the fire alarm sounded. As I work on the ground floor, I thought there was no rush.....and then I could smell smoke! Dashed outside

with everyone else and the building was on fire. Huge flames coming from the roof. We were told to go home but report for work in the morning, although we would be without electricity. Sue and I spent the evening at the Med Club over at the Heath Hospital, as she wanted to meet medical students. We decided that although the conversation was keen, the students were very serious and formal. On finding our way back to the Crwys Road, first I stepped into a big muddy puddle about a foot deep, we then encountered a group of skinheads on a lonely road, and when we thought we were safe back in our street, a man in strange clothing was following us. He tapped me on the shoulder and made us both jump! He looked like a guru, and only wanted directions to Richmond Road. I should have asked him to give me some tips on transcendental meditation!"

11th April 1975: ....every trollop and slut from miles around!

"My Mum came to stay for a few days. At work, Colonel Martin bought us all a custard slice and said I could leave work at 3.30 p.m. on account of my 'Ma' being here. He is such a lovely boss, as long as I don't want to leave. He was having a sort out and I helped him clear up the 'dogs breakfast' of a mess in the room. Mum was really enjoying the streets full of shops and the park across the road with its lake, flower beds and hot house plants. She told me to go out and enjoy myself in the evening so I went with the girls next door to Bumpers. Dancing with the men in there, put me off men! We left and went to a party at Sue and Mags......big mistake! Just as I thought, they had all their rough and ready friends there drinking whisky and rum from bottles. Mags looked so butch in her denim suit and must have invited every trollop and slut from miles around. Everyone was being crude except for Quentin and Julian, so I tried talking to them, but they only wanted to talk to each other. Let's hope my next evening out is an improvement on this!"

21st April 1975: I like the idea of being the President's Secretary!

"In the post, a vacancy fell into my hands for a Secretary at the Students' Union. I couldn't believe my luck! When everyone had gone out I phoned and spoke to the Student President and Louise, who is something to do with finance. I was encouraged to apply. Before leaving work I had to take the minutes at the LAUT Exec extraordinary meeting involving a dispute with a pay claim.

I still have this magazine.

The fire alarm was for real!

I didn't want to stay late but in the end didn't mind as there was a lot of arguing, so it was good entertainment value and also I find Dr. Fricke very good looking. After tea I went out with Wenda and Marilyn to a Welsh speaking club – The Conwy. Of course, I couldn't join in, so took myself off to the Union but it was 10.30 when they stop letting people in. I pleaded and it worked. Met the usual crowd in there and they wanted to go to Mont Morenz. It is always so hot and smoky in there but it is the student nightclub and the best people go. I had a babycham bought for me by an Architecture student. We may meet in the building I work in, as the office (Committees Section) is housed by the Architecture department and we discussed the fire a few weeks ago, but the students were away on Easter holidays at the time. His name is Edward Williams from Regents Park, London."

24th April 1975: Marilyn and I get our heads tested!
"I went to work early to ask Jackie what I should say to Colonel Martin about leaving, and my new job. When I told him, he didn't seem shocked and said he was delighted....in a subdued tone. I later found out that the Student President had told him at a Council meeting. After work I went to the BBC to meet Marilyn and we caught the bus to Llyn-y-Grant UWIST Applied Psychology. We were volunteers and tested on reaction to numbers, by the electrodes on our heads. We also had questionnaires to complete and both enjoyed the experience. Marilyn and I went our separate ways as I was meeting Edward at his house in Wordsworth Avenue, in what is now a tatty Victorian street and mysteriously dark because of the trees. I liked Edward's

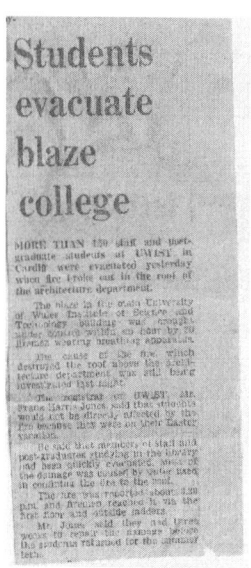

Report from the Western Mail.

Ambrose and I at Jean's cottage in Wiltshire.

room, but was whisked out of there and taken for a drink to Poets Corner, then on to the Pig & Whistle and finally to a beautifully decorated pub called The Bertram and the music was good too. Edward walked me home and I do like his company, but he will be leaving Cardiff at the end of next month."

28th April 1975: I just hope Colonel Martin doesn't put a spanner in the works.
"The job is not mine yet as there are other candidates who have to be interviewed! Louise says she has told them that she expects me to be appointed! I was at the Dentists in the morning and instead of going straight back to work I went to the Students' Union to see Louise and look round the office. If I got the job, I would be the Student President's Secretary! It seemed great, but somehow I couldn't see myself working there although I'd love to with all my heart! At lunch time I took my radio to the Park and sunbathed. In the afternoon, I had to take the minutes at the NPSA AGM and, after the Committee had discovered, and corrected my typing errors I got a vote of

appreciation, through being patient at meetings! Back at the office I had a phone call from the Student President who wanted to see me for an informal interview on Monday. That made me happy and I nearly forgot to go and collect my big cushion (one meter square) from the Company Store. I was staggering home with this and my heavy shopping, as I would never get it on a bus. Anyway this kind man rescued me by carrying the cushion nearly all the way to my street. After dragging it up to the top floor the cushion is just the job to make my room more homely."

30th April 1975: ...unless the other candidates have thigh length leather boots and a whip, I should get the job!

"I had my interview with the Student President and Vice President today in the lunch hour. By what they say I stand a very good chance of getting the job, because apparently, Louise has taken to me. They do have to interview outside candidates, but unless they have thigh length leather boots and a whip, I should get the job! After the last two interviews I've had, I'm not all that confident. I walked back through town and got accosted by the 'Children of God' – they flattered me, and I gave them 10p, I don't know why. I then got kissed and told 'I love you' – I admired their technique as this happened 3 times. I had read about the Moonies though, and how they make you feel so special and loved, then whisk you away so that you are never seen or heard of again, so I did my best to avoid them. We had to work 15 minutes late to get 'Links with Industry' information sent out, which was annoying. When I arrived home, my new candlewick dressing gown had arrived. It fitted perfectly and made me look like a film star!"

4th May 1975: We took turns in sitting on the floor in the back of the Mini Van.

"Jean stayed the weekend and thankfully left Ambrose, the Labrador, at one of the farms she works for. I just remember Jean's Mum sitting in the back of the mini car pushed up against the window, with Ambrose sprawled across three quarters of the seat, despite putting her handbag between her and the dog as a shield. She emerged from the van smelling of a 'canine' variety of perfume! This time Jean had arrived in her mini van, complete with good old Wiltshire mud, and Marilyn and I piled in, taking it in turns to sit in the back. We set off for the mountains, stopping at the Traveller's Rest for a pint of cider and a packet of crisps. We went to Caerphilly Castle, which was delightful, had an ice cream and I finished up the film in my camera. We got back and I cooked my Dad's favourite "mince and tatties", and for dessert - ice cream, chocolate sauce and hazelnuts. When Jean left, it was a beautiful evening so I went for a walk in the park. This photographer turned from flowers to me and took 20 photos. I got suspicious though and felt uneasy, so ran back to the hostel."

13th May 1975: New job and New Boyfriend - Edward I.

"Louise phoned when I got to work to say that the President had contacted the Bursar and asked him to offer me the job! I was so happy to think that it was all sorted and I will be the President's Secretary. Then I remembered about Colonel Martin, what he would say now that it is final and what the consequences would be. When he came back from a meeting he had bought us sticky buns but was in a sarcastic and cheeky mood, so I wondered if perhaps he knew! At lunch time I went over to the Union to see Louise but the office was deserted. I studied the notice board to see if I could learn something about the job, but it was full of everybody's holiday postcards and photographs! In the evening I met Edward at the Union and we were watching everyone from the balcony. He says that I am always a happy girl. I like him because he is so easy going. No doubt, I will find something that I don't like about him. He is only staying around until he gets his degree results and then he is off back to London to look for a job. Perhaps that is it!"

16th May 1975: 'Pinball' by Brian Protheroe.

"I was up and ready for work, earlyish, so I went next door to wake Marilyn up, but she had just got in! At work I felt quite enthusiastic but poor Jackie, everything was going wrong for her. Even Colonel Martin was being beastly to her whilst praising me! I can't understand it, as I am the one who is being disloyal by leaving. In the evening Marilyn was going to meet her new man and I went to the Union alone. I was having a laugh with Geoffrey on the dance floor, he is such a warm and loving person. When he was going out with Marilyn's sister, Carol, I was always envious that she would run up to him and he would lift her up and swing her round. If anyone tried that with me they would buckle under the weight! Anyway he told me that Edward had arrived, so I went and found him. At the end of the evening Edward walked me home and came in for coffee and was most impressed with my rather chic bedsit. We were listening to music and chatting away when I noticed it was light outside and the time was 4.30 a.m.!

He left and when I got to bed I couldn't sleep for the birds singing. I did wonder whether Marilyn had arrived home yet! Thank goodness it is Saturday tomorrow. I was humming 'Pinball' by Brian Protheroe - another record I must buy."

17th May 1975: The wonders of Tiger Bay and the Docks, from the safety of the car.

"A bit annoyed that I didn't wake up until 1.40 p.m.! I took Marilyn and Joyce a cup of coffee, and as it was a beautiful warm sunny day, Marilyn and I went off to the the lake in Roath Park, across the road. It was definitely sunbathing weather. We were reading magazines and writing poetry. In the evening, at 10.45 p.m. we went to the Casino. The usual sporting and drinking mad crowd were there. Dai was looking for a nibble of the female ear, and goodness knows why he picked on me. I got rid of him, and for the first time started talking to the 'boa constrictor' and I found out his name is Aneurin. He was extremely pleasant and was keen to tell me about the time when he and his friends 'streaked' down Queen Street and got put in a police cell for the night! I had a feeling he thought I would be highly impressed by this and immediately attracted to him! It was about the sum total of any intelligent or meaningful conversation I had all evening! Joyce's friends drove us home via the Docks and Tiger Bay which was probably the most interesting part of the night out!"

22nd May 1975: Emotions run high in Mont Morenz.

"Jackie had been off work 'ill' for a few days and I'm not surprised with the raw deal she has been getting. Colonel Martin is still very nice to me but I'm sure he is trying to get rid of Jackie and she will be having a nervous breakdown at this rate. I wonder if he thinks that she is the reason I'm leaving, which is totally not true, I just feel I can aim higher than the work I'm doing here. It didn't get any better, as a nurse was summoned for Colonel Martin because he was feeling dizzy and was then taken home. After work, I knew it would be a different sort of evening. I had been seeing Edward almost every night but tonight we agreed that he would be with his friends. He was at Monty's and so was I and I just couldn't help watching what he was up to out the corner of my eye. Marilyn went downstairs, to the other bar, with someone she had met and I was left to the lions. By then Edward was dancing with other girls so Geoffrey was being amorous (only to let Edward see) and we were messing about and decided to break the record for non-stop snogging for 15 minutes. Edward didn't see this as he was chatting to a girl and bought her a drink. I was furious and upset at the same time! He came over and was so nice to me, that I just forgave him. If he wasn't leaving Cardiff then I wouldn't have been so stupid!"

31st May 1975: Wiltshire born, Wiltshire bred etc.
"Woke up miserable as Marilyn and I were spending the weekend at Jean's in Wiltshire. We arranged it ages ago but now I would be missing going to a party with Edward and his friends. I told myself, he is leaving, so what is the point and was determined to enjoy the life in the countryside. Jean and Jane met us off the train and after putting our luggage into Jean's farm cottage and being licked to death by Ambrose the dog, we started off at the Vale pub. We gave a handwritten note to the DJ to read out – 'Party At Jean's – All Males Welcome!' Jean was not pleased and it did backfire on us because the party was just full of Blokes and Booze! I ended up going to bed early at 2.45 a.m.. Today has been good as we went to Westonbirt Arboretum in Gloucestershire – a beautiful place. Back at Jean's cottage we had dinner by the fire, but she had put too much pepper in the mince so there was a lot of coughing. On the way back we missed the train and had to wait two hours. Marilyn and I started discussing holidays, and we can go and stay with her brother at his flat in Bournemouth for a week. By a strange coincidence, his name is Edward too".

5th June 1975: Drama at the Y.W.C.A.
"When Marilyn and I got home last night at 2.30 a.m., Sue one of the snobs next door, where I live, had been caught by her boyfriend with another man! It appears there had been an argument. We went to Marilyn's for coffee at No. 86 and after a while, a policeman appeared at the window. A disturbance had been reported at No. 87 and Sue's window had been smashed in! All the parties concerned had left though, and we made the policeman some coffee and helped him with his enquiries. Got to bed at 4 a.m., and of course it was light, so today I was a little tired at work. It was my last day working with Jackie as she is off on holiday. I can only think that there is a clash of personality between Jackie and Colonel Martin, as to why they don't get on, and she is hoping to move back to London when Richard finishes his Law degree. On the way home I did my shopping and voted YES in the referendum to join Europe. I slept for 2 hours when I got in! Edward came round, we went to the Union and I had a bacardi and coke. Quite a few drunken celebrations with people

Marilyn and I at Caerphilly Castle.   Sunbathing by the lake at Roath Park.

finishing exams. I was told by some of Edward's friends, that he really likes me. I forgot to mention, so why is he leaving Cardiff, for London, without me!"

7th June 1975: I need a book on 'Easy Cooking to Impress'.

"Set my alarm for 8 a.m. and the sun was up and hot outside. Marilyn and I sunbathed in the back garden. At noon, it was too hot so I came indoors, and Edward phoned to say he was coming round for a walk in the Park. What a lovely afternoon we had. I took a photo of him and the lighthouse on the lake. Decided that, as the way to a man's heart is through his stomach I will cook a few meals for Edward on his last weekend here. I will go to the Library and get some books on easy cooking to impress! Going on my recent track record it might be better to get a takeaway in and pass it off as 'home cooked'. Anyway, I successfully (and with the confidence not to poison anyone) cooked us steak and chips for tea tonight and then we walked in the warm evening breeze to the Claude. They had no beer or lager due to a brewer's strike. Walked into town to a great pub called 'The Rumner Tavern'. Carried on to the Union and everyone was out on the balcony in the late evening sun. Soon all the students will be gone for the summer break, including Edward, only he will not be coming back!"

16th June 1975: A Challenging First Day in My New Job.

"I started work at the Students' Union today in a thunderstorm, so I looked a bit like a drowned rat. Louise took me round and introduced me to everyone. Apart from that there was nothing to do! I liked the fact that all the young people kept coming in, although some of them were full of themselves - or rather loud-mouthed yobbos! Met Edward in the park outside the University buildings at lunch time, as it turned out to be such a lovely hot day and no rain clouds on the horizon! In the afternoon I was told I would be taking the Minutes at the SUC meeting. I was a little surprised especially with everyone staring at me for my reaction. I soon got into it, and after a while of sloppy shorthand notes, carefully missing out the swear words, I had a note passed to me. I opened it up to find a message asking me to go to a party, signed Jeff. He was the one who could win 'the most swear words in a sentence' competition so I tore up the note and left it on the table. I was beginning to think that I preferred working for all the old, kind and absent minded professors in Committees Section. I got back to my desk and things were happening too fast. At 4.30, Matt wanted me to take down the Minutes of the 2 previous meetings, 2 letters and have them done by 9.00 in the morning. I said I couldn't stay tonight but would come in early tomorrow. After work whilst drying my hair I drafted the Minutes in longhand and was glad that I had Marilyn to talk to about it. Also had to clean and tidy as Jackie was coming round tomorrow. What a hectic first day!"

17th June 1975: I felt as if I was being laughed at!

"I was in work at 7.15 a.m. and as it is rare to see a student before noon I was able to finish everything by 9.00 a.m. without interruption, but I felt as if I was being laughed at a little. I think they had been rather mean to me on my first day! Phil Reid, who runs a 'Nightline' office could see what was going on, he was really good to me and took me to his room to give me coffee. It was a kindness I valued and I do feel that I am going to have to 'toughen up' working here! At least I have the summer recess to learn about the job slowly before madness begins when the students return September/October. I had more dictation today, to do at my leisure, and then Mike whisked me off to help him in town. I met Jackie at lunch time and we didn't need to come back to my flat after all, so I needn't have bothered getting the place ship shape. Edward came into the UWIST Students' Union office to see me twice! Not many students around now, only the ones who haven't quite finished partying in celebration of their results, or drowning their sorrows because they haven't done as well as expected!"

23rd June 1975: Send in the Clowns - Judy Collins.
"After a weekend of cooking meals, I have not poisoned the two of us. The recipes I used were 'Carbonnade de Boeuf a La Flamande' (Belgian beef stew cooked in beer), Moussaka, and Pork with tomato and pepper sauce. I really surprised myself, and Edward was under the impression that I always produced these sort of meals.....I will not enlighten him otherwise! Anyway tonight I was walking to Wordsworth Avenue for the last time to meet him. His street will always look beautiful to me even though it is practically a slum. It was lovely to be with him and we went to our favourite pubs, the Bertram and the Poets Corner. It wasn't even raining when we walked back and we were both humming that song 'send in the clowns'. I was to catch the bus home as Edward needed to finish packing. He said he would write every two weeks and would even come and visit some weekends. We were both happy, no tears.....that is.....until I got on the bus."

26th June 1975: Propositioned by the Deputy President.
"Not many at Mont Morenz but the vice-president was there and bought me a drink. We were chatting about the job at the Union, but it was noisy and smoky so we left and stopped off at his place. I went in for a drink to continue our conversation, or so I thought. I was enjoying his company until he said it was getting late and I might as well stay the night! I knew exactly what he meant and was so taken aback I just mumbled something about, no, not in the mood and take me home. Looking back I Wish I Had Said - 'Nice try Mr. Deputy President.....casual sex is not one of my hobbies, but obviously it is one of yours, so I hope you have visited a clinic lately!' This is the man who chose me for the job at the Students' Union and I do have to work with him so how could I tell him that I wouldn't lower myself! You're damned if you do and damned if you don't! I've known girls who think they can keep a man by sleeping with him, but then they are discarded and labelled 'easy' and the man in question gets another notch on the bedpost! As I fell asleep I had two thoughts - 'nice girls don't' and 'spinster of the parish'!"

27th June 1975: Hells Bells - can it get any worse!
"First person I bumped into at work, of course, was the vice president. To make matters worse, Louise was humming the tune 'In The Mood' by Glenn Miller.....she said she overheard a conversation! In the afternoon there was a student meeting in the

bar and I had to take the Minutes. Of course, guess who I was sitting next to and he asked if I was in the mood? I ignored it, but revenge is sweet and I will think of something. I spent the rest of my time filing the mounds of paperwork which I am sure has accumulated over the years. The vice-president said we would go through the files together and an evening would be best. I didn't cotton on until Louise said that, of course, we would be alone! Oh hells bells, can it get any worse! One interesting things was that the solicitor would be in tomorrow -something to do with issuing a Writ about the takeover by University College Cardiff. Not sure what it means, but anything to take my mind off my 'new girl in the office' image and its implications. Went for a drink with Dai Jones in the evening and we went to a quaint village called Drope and a I had 3 babychams and a sherry in the Greendown Inn."

6th July 1975: What a year it has been!
"Another bad thunderstorm in the morning but the sun came out and Marilyn and I got some sunbathing in before she cooked us a delicious dinner of cheese omelette, roast jacket potatoes and peas followed by strawberries and ice-cream. Louise joined us for this and then we went down to the Lake and for the first time went on the rowing boats. To start with I was scared, but was soon roaring with laughter, as all the people on the lake, seemed to be in hoots. I couldn't tell if Louise was enjoying herself or not. As it got dark, we went back to Marilyn's and wrote letters and watched tele. We also tried on the bikinis we bought from British Home Stores yesterday. This caused shrieks of laughter. There is hardly anyone left in the hostel over the summer so the place did need livening up a bit. I have been here for just over one year now and have met some lovely people and made loads of friends. I have also met lots of Mr Wrongs and no Mr Right! My career is moving in the right direction though as I am now the 'President's Secretary'!"

10th July 1975: Graduation Day - the best day ever!
"Today has been the happiest day ever! I was an Usher at Graduation Day. I had to wear a cap and gown, have a formal portrait photo taken, and a free lunch on UWIST in the Main Dining Room. There were so many students and lecturers who spoke to me and said how nice I looked. I felt a bit of a fraud dressed in academic gowns mixing with all these intellectuals, when I haven't even got an 'A' Level! It was a hot and humid day and yet still it was raining. Nothing could dampen anyone's

spirits though as the atmosphere was overwhelming. When I got home I encouraged all the girls to go to Monty's as everyone would be there celebrating and also the Writ had been called off....so a double celebration (still not sure what the Writ was all about, but any excuse to celebrate). It turned out to be a great night and the champagne was free flowing. The last thing I remember was on the way out on the steps I gave my phone number to someone called Ewan or was it Euan or Iwan? No idea what time it was when I got to bed".

12th July 1975: Holiday Destination - 'Faulty Towers'!
"We set off on the coach to Bournemouth for a week's holiday to Marilyn's brother Edward's flat at Boscombe. We got there in the pouring rain and no-one was in. This very elderly couple told us we could wait in their flat and gave us a treble whisky each! Edward arrived with arms full of bed linen he had just bought, as he only moved into the flat/bedsit last week. Despite being hungry and the whisky going straight to our heads, we managed to arrange furniture and put things into some sort of order, but there was no crockery, cutlery, pans, or food in the cupboards or drawers! We set out again in the rain to Boscombe shopping centre to buy these for him and grabbed a beef burger to eat on the way! We didn't go out that evening as we were rather tired. Edward went out to the pub and Marilyn fetched in some fish and chips and said we would start our razzling tomorrow night!"

13th July 1975 : The bath taps were rusted on tight and linked by cobwebs.
"When I woke up, I decided to explore Edward's room and also to see what was down the corridor. The big bay french window, in his spacious room, had seen better days when it had once been a grand house, and opened out on to grass which was knee high. There was a shared toilet, in the corridor in rather a dirty state! Upstairs was the only bathroom - for all the flats, but the bath obviously hadn't been used for years as the taps were rusted on tight and linked by cobwebs. We intended to go to Southampton to see the QE2 sail out, but instead went into Bournemouth. Had a tour on an open top bus and lunch at the Pavilion. Went round the shops and I found a phone box to give my Mum a call who thought my holiday so far was hilarious! In the evening we went to Tiffany's night club. Nothing to write home about and I left there with my woolly hat on and Marilyn's sunglasses."

15th July 1975: We seem to spend our lives being involved with the Police (as innocent bystanders of course)!
"Yesterday whilst buying a cotton headscarf, gypsy earrings and sunglasses in Bournemouth I realised I had £5 missing from my purse. We reported this to the police as my bag had been "looked after" in Tiffany's cloakroom last night. At the police station they were very friendly. We spent the rest of the day on the beach in our bikinis. Had to take my sandwich back to the shop as there was a piece of wire in it! On the way back to Edward's flat we saw a car backing into a van and our details were taken down as witnesses. Went to a club called 'Adriane's' which seemed quite international, but was small, hot and dark. As for today, not beach weather as it was much colder so we explored some of the area by bus and on foot. Back at the flat I was in my dressing gown, drying my hair, Edward was at the sink, with his shirt off having a wash and Marilyn opened the door to a policewoman. She had come to take a statement about my missing money, but I could see she was checking the place out and seemed to have a permanent grin on her face at the set up! After she had gone, Edward took us for a drink to the Salisbury Bar and Marilyn and I left him there and went to Bournemouth for a meal at Curry Corner - I particularly liked the banana fritters. We looked in on Whisky's nightclub, but it was a place where you could easily fall on to the dance floor!"

17th July 1975: The Police were round again - What will the neighbours think!
"Our legs were aching from all the hills in Bournemouth. Yesterday was the hottest day so far and we ran along the beach from Bournemouth to Boscombe pier and I so enjoyed letting the big waves splash over me. At night we went to the '81' Club but didn't stay long. Instead walked back eating fish and chips. A long walk of 2 miles but later found out that there is a short cut! Today we sat in deck chairs listening to the brass band. We shouldn't have looked round the shops as I am now overdrawn at the bank. I bought a 'cut price' portable typewriter. We were back early and whilst waiting for Edward to come home from work there was a knock at the door. This time, there were 2 policemen wanting to take statements about the car incident we witnessed. I got up to make them coffee quickly hiding Edward's 'Vibration' and

'Forum' magazines under the cushions. The policemen were enjoying every minute and we were doing a lot of giggling in between answering questions. In the middle of it all, Edward came in and wondered what we had been up to. When all the laughter was over and the policemen had gone I suddenly realised that I was quite attracted to Edward!"

19th July 1975: Edward II.
"Marilyn and I went on a boat from Poole to Brownsea Island yesterday. It was so hot and deserted there, apart from the red squirrels. We had to leave to go back at 3 p.m. to pay the rent at the flat. In the evening Edward dressed up in his suit and looked very dashing. We all went out together. We did a bit of a pub crawl, nearly falling over some morris dancers in a car park and ended up at Boscombe Pier where we almost got involved in a talent contest! Finally we found ourselves at Tiffany's. I lost Marilyn but found Edward and we danced, rather romantically, to 'Knights in White Satin'! We were all very merry when we got back to the flat, but on opening the door Edward shouted for us to keep out in the hallway. He had seen a rat running around in the room! It scuttled away...., so that was all right then and the laughter continued! Today we had forgotten about the rat and Marilyn and I went to our favourite cafe for our full English Breakfast. We had just started eating when this Irish tramp came in, sat next to us. He said 'yer don't want that do yer', and in a split second, grabbed our food with his hands and stuffed it into his mouth and left! We sat there in stunned silence and then both burst out laughing! We bought cleaning materials on the way home to give Edward's flat a good clean before we left. In the evening we were getting well known in the Salisbury Bar (and at the police station!) We sat with the Newcastle girls and a Thai boy called 'Cerf'. Marilyn was having a conversation in Welsh with Edward asking him if he liked me to which he replied that of course he did! On the way home he pinched some flowers from a garden and gave them to me. I disowned him!"

21st July 1975: We took photos in the overgrown garden.
"Yesterday was the last day of our holiday in Boscombe. We went to a different cafe for our breakfast, keeping an eye open for Irish tramps. The Launderette was nearby so we took Edward's washing......he really does need a woman to 'do' for him. Our coach left in the afternoon to go back to Cardiff. We hacked our way through the long grass and took photos in the garden. The

journey back was enjoyable and we stopped, as usual, at Aust for something to eat. We had promised Edward that we would try and make some weekend visits, and would do some housekeeping chores for him! Today at work I was in a daze so had no resistance to remarks and couldn't laugh anything off. I decided that I would put my mind to work tomorrow. The new sports administrator started work - a 50 year old ex army man called Glan. In the evening we had to get to grips with the twin tub washing machine, which dances round the kitchen, in order to have something clean to wear. Edward II phoned and then I wrote a letter to Edward I."

25th July 1975: **His filing cabinets were filled with bottles of whisky.**

"The huge mountain of filing does not go down but surprisingly the vice-president shows such kindness in helping me with it. Glan, the new sports admin, tried to give us his private letters to type up but was told that due to pressure of work we couldn't do this! Of course, I then sat with nothing to do all afternoon, but that wasn't the point. Louise and I noticed that his filing cabinets were filled with bottles of whisky! He brought us flowers and then announced he was taking the men out to lunch. Louise asked if we needed to change our sex in order to be taken out to lunch as well. So in the afternoon he bought us cream cakes. He was trying hard! I was leaving work early to catch the coach for Bournemouth. Marilyn and I had a good talk about this and the only way to know if I have a future with her brother is to go and find out! She wished me luck."

27th July 1975: **Summer Breeze on Bournemouth Beach**.

"I am writing this on a swelteringly hot coach on my way back to Cardiff after a lovely weekend. Edward was so happy to see me and we met his friends at the Salisbury Bar. While he was at work on the Saturday morning I sunbathed and read my book in the tall grass out in the back garden/wilderness. The only thing that unsettled me was the old man from Flat 4 who kept asking me to sit on his knee! Edward was home at lunch time and we did some shopping in Boscombe and ate steak at the Hamby Bar. As the sun was setting we were walking hand in hand along the pier. Today, we walked through Boscombe Gardens to the beach and also went on the rowing boats. He is such a kind, funny, easy going and warm hearted person, but is that enough....time will tell I suppose!"

I was an Usher at the Degree Ceremony.   Edward I at the Lighthouse in Roath Park.

3rd August 1975: Beach Boys - Sail on Sailor.

"I am writing this at Aust. It has been a week of leaving parties for the retiring President and Deputy. On Thursday we had cream cakes then lunchtime drinks in the Bar - Louise and I both had the same - 3 brandies and 1 babycham. She was as sober as a judge and I was good for nothing - far too sleepy to do anything. Everyone was at a meeting, despite lunch time drinking, so Louise sent me home. When Marilyn came home she gave me pro plus tablets! I walked it all off in the park and went on the swings vowing to stick to fruit juice at lunch time and will put up with being laughed at! I was really looking forward to seeing Edward this weekend and we went to the same places as last week. There seemed to be hundreds of grasshoppers in the garden when I was trying to sunbathe and read. When we went rowing in the sea I got scared as the waves seemed to be of the surfing variety. I have bought the Beach Boys record 'Sail on Sailor' which I thought was very appropriate."

10th August 1975: "The Students' Union new President and Executive Committee take up Office.

"The new Student President Frank, and Deputy Tim, moved into their offices this week. We had a drink with Frank to christen the arrival of the order for his cocktail cabinet! Lunchtime drinking again, so I looked for a plant pot to pour my babycham into, but we have no plants. I am thinking of buying one for the office, but which plant would thrive on alcohol I wonder. Met Jackie for lunch and my successor Susan. It has been a week of thunderstorms and for 2 nights I slept on top of Marilyn's spare bed, fully clothed, as the storms were lasting 5 hours. There have been reports of 50% humidity in London. I caught the train for the first time to Bournemouth, and had 3 changes, but it was still faster than the coach. I was very pleased that Edward was there to meet me as it was lightning viciously when we walked out of the station. Weekends in the Bournemouth area are full of life, being in the middle of the holiday season, whereas Cardiff is a bit flat without the students. Oh, but I tell a lie as the Students' Union building is hosting the Brass Band Festival this summer!"

17th August 1975: I would prefer a seaside residence without a rat!
"Another hot week at work and I am beginning to see daylight with typing the budgets. When Frank came in I was eating an ice lolly and he started grilling me about the work, but I managed to change the subject. We have started up a swear box and I had to pay 1p, just for saying 'damn'! Tim gave Louise a little reprimand about her cheekiness as Glan had been complaining about it. After this, for two days the atmosphere was rather subdued. Marilyn and I had been out to the pictures to see 'Tommy the Rock Opera', and while she went swimming I entertained Helen and Linda. They were most impressed by my 'flatlet' and we sat drinking wine, eating crisps and popcorn and listened to records. I related my holiday capers which had them in stitches. Marilyn joined in when she came back and it seemed like a party with the joss sticks burning. Another good weekend with Edward at my seaside residence! I spent Saturday looking for better accommodation - a place without a rat, and a bath that works, would be nice! Marilyn's sister Carol said that her Aunties are choosing wedding outfits for 'Edward and Sally's' wedding!"

18th August 1975: The Union host the Brass Band Festival and it was rather good.
"Louise seemed much happier at work this week but said it was just an act, as she was unhappy! Anyway she enjoys fathoming out my shorthand outlines when I can't read them, which is quite often. I'd be lost without the radio on all day at work, keeps us up with the latest tunes and brings back memories with the 'golden oldies'. At lunch time I went out and bought Steely Dan record 'Do It Again'. When I got home it was quite a rush as we had be at the Union for 6.45 p.m. for the Brass Band Performance. When we arrived, everyone from the office was there to greet us with the

news that they had secured tickets for the open air performance at the Castle afterwards. We enjoyed the Australian Band in particular. The rain, as usual, caused the cancellation of the Castle open air performance, so Frank and Tim showed Marilyn around the office."

NB. This must be the first time that Marilyn had met Tim, and guess what......Reader: she (eventually) married him'!

25th August 1975: The last time I stay in the family home.

"Spent the Bank Holiday weekend with Marilyn at Mum and Dad's. Edward was invited, but got cold feet and said he would come during the Christmas holidays! We packed a lot into our time there. Mum and Dad took us to see the chalet bungalow they are moving to, in Deeping St. James which we liked, plus the village was pretty. I felt sad that I was staying in the family home for the very last time - the bungalow in the village of Eye that I had grown up in, even though Eye came 2nd in the 'ugliest village' competition! The next evening the bus to Peterborough didn't turn up so we hitched a lift with a young lad from Great Yarmouth market. I showed Marilyn around all my old haunts and met up with old friends. Dad and my brother Ian took us to Hunstanton, 'sunny Hunny', our nearest decent seaside town. Marilyn swam in the sea, we sunbathed in the sand dunes, had 3 goes on the Waltzers, ate hot dogs, toffee apples and ice cream and came home with red faces from the wind and sun. Normally we would watch the sun go down over the Wash whilst eating fish and chips, out of newspaper, on the sea wall, but Mum had a roast dinner waiting for us at home."

4th September 1975: Do offices still have the Tea Trolley?

"I was at a meeting all morning taking minutes and enjoying it, feeling quite important until I was asked to read a proposal back. I couldn't read my shorthand so guessed by making something up and got it completely wrong! I spent my lunch hour ringing around the Professor and Chairman, to find out what they actually did say, as even Louise couldn't work out my shorthand notes! I was quite pleased to go to the Registry in the afternoon to type out addresses for Freshers' mailing so that I didn't have to think! It was good timing as I arrived just as the tea trolley rolled up! In the evening Marilyn and I went to the pictures to see 'The Boyfriend' starring Twiggy. I wasn't that impressed and much preferred the film we watched on tele, just before going to bed. 'Goodbye Columbus'. Loved the song from the film by The Association....such a happy, feeling good song."

14th September 1975: There was a loud bang and the lights went out!

"Several meetings at work and I had to take the minutes. The weather is colder and my brain doesn't work well in cold temperatures so I didn't get many notes made. Marilyn is coming down with flu and Charles called by unannounced which annoyed her - she wanted to look her best. Edward I came from London to see me and we had a drink at the Claude. He had nowhere to stay and wanted to sleep in my floor but I said 'No'. He then wanted to know all about Edward II and when I told him, he made jealous remarks! Despite all that, it was good to see him and he is going to continue to write. My train journey to Bournemouth was a little unnerving. The signals in the Severn tunnel were not working so eventually the train proceeded through, very slowly with the whistle blowing. All of a sudden I heard a loud bang and the lights went out! There was a scream.....I think it was me! We carried on in the dark and it must have just been a fuse that had blown. Nevertheless I had to have a Rum and Pep at Bristol Station to calm my nerves. The train was 2 hours late and Edward was still there waiting!"

21st September 1975: Cardiff comes alive with students while Bournemouth is shutting down for the season.

"We complained to Tim that it was cold in the office so he brought us some Cherry Brandy in to drink, and yes it did warm us up. I spent lunch time in Chelsea Girl wondering whether to buy trousers or a maxi skirt. There are a lot of new girls in the hostel and Marilyn was worried about who will sharing her room. Her sister Carol called and told us that there were wedding bells for herself and Robert. On Thursday night we stayed in to watch 'Top of the Pops', 'The Two Ronnies' and 'Man About The House' and then decided to go out and try 'Montys'. I hadn't seen so many people there since term finished. A lot of students were back for 're-sits'. The trains to Bournemouth were cold on Friday night. In fact the resort is much quieter and it is fairly obvious that the season is almost at an end. When I think of Cardiff, the season is just coming alive again with students. I am beginning to wonder if Edward is just a holiday romance, but then I have quickly put that out of my mind for now!"

28th September 1975: Never had it so good and felt so bad.
"Work is getting more interesting now that the whole of the Executive Committee are in and out of the office all day. The Entertainments Officer Steve Gordon, has a bedsit in the Union Building and we all went up to see it and it has its own balcony. Later, Frank opened his cocktail cabinet, yet again, and we had a drink. I had to take the minutes for the Working Party after this and nearly fell asleep. They must think the Minutes are appalling! Frank wants the meetings to be held in the evening.....I told him I couldn't possibly! Went to Vi's the Hairdresser on Thursday night, and although I didn't want any advice, I got some on my so-called romance with Edward (the 2nd). Saturday in Bournemouth was cold and wet. There is no t.v. so I bought a Monopoly set. Sunday was dry and warm but we had a difference of opinion about how long to stay out walking. As I caught the train home, I kept thinking of that song by the Chi-Lites 'Never had it so good, and felt so bad'!"

2nd October 1975: Itchycoo Park.
"These last two days have been very hectic with student enrolment, after which the students all come to the Union, as it is next on their list! I seemed to be giving out NUS cards to millions of students. Marilyn and I have had two contrasting nights of entertainment. Last night we enjoyed the film 'The Paper Chase' at the Sherman Theatre, which is a gorgeous place. Tonight we went to the Union to see 'Steve Marriott'. When we got there, Tim was on the door, so we got in free. After buying a drink, Steve Gordon took us backstage to see Steve Marriott. He was quite polite, but every second word was a four letter one! We left and went to the Bar upstairs and came across Steve (can't remember his other name) who is NUS Secretary on the Exec. Committee and I do rather like him! We sat with his friends talking for ages, then went to see Steve Marriott on stage. Well, in between songs, he was knocking back a bottle of brandy and spitting. He has gone down in my estimation from when I admired him in the Small Faces singing 'Itchycoo Park'!"

6th October 1975: 700 students at the General Meeting and my sherry-fuelled shorthand notes!
"I was writing up Minutes on the train to Bournemouth as I needed to transcribe my shorthand notes before it was completely

gone from memory. The General Meeting was in front of 700 students and I felt very important up on the stage. The Sports Administrator had been round with the sherry bottle beforehand, so I didn't get many decent notes down but I'm sure I can make it up! Edward met me and we went to the Salisbury Bars but didn't have a lot to say to each other. The highlight of the weekend was a visit to Lulworth Cove. It was beautiful there but I felt that Edward didn't appreciate it as much as Marilyn would have done. I suppose it would have been more fun with Marilyn rather than her brother! I stayed over an extra day as I'm staying in Cardiff next weekend. Edward was at work in Southampton building a bridge. I caught the train there and he was waiting for me with his work mates. He got some time off to take me over on the floating bridge to see the QE2 depart. He was so happy showing me things and bought me coffee from a vending machine. When I got back to Cardiff, Marilyn and I had loads to talk about, as she had spent the weekend in Wiltshire."

12th October 1975: Georgie Fame and the best party ever.

"The week started with Phil Perryman's birthday (Finance) and we had cream cakes. Frank opened up his cocktail cabinet and I had a Snowball. Georgie Fame was playing in the Union that night. We were taken backstage to see him but as he was late we didn't get time to talk , although he signed Marilyn's autograph book. Next morning I went in to see Marilyn, but she hadn't been there all night! That evening we all met in the Dyfed Bar before the Barn Dance which was fast and furious, so didn't stay long in case we ended up with broken bones! Caught the train to see my brother in Bristol yesterday. So pleased I wasn't in Bournemouth for the weekend as I got back to Cardiff in time to go to Stuart's party at Fitzhamon Embankment, Riverside. It turned out to be the best party I've ever been to in Cardiff so far! The basement was set out for dancing. I knew most people there and spent most of my time with Steve George, the NUS Secretary, who was very attentive. Whether that was anything to do with Louise 'putting in a good word' for me, I don't know. We were dancing to Fleetwood Mac's 'Albatross' when I looked at my watch, and it was 5 a.m.!"

15th October 1975: I have a dilemma and I'm not sure what to do.

"Yesterday, nothing was said about the party, but Louise was in

19 The Crescent, Eye, Peterborough, the family bungalow 1956-1976.

Marilyn and her brother Edward at the flat in Boscombe, Bournemouth.

an excellent mood. By the end of the afternoon, Steve had not called into the office, so I thought that I obviously didn't live up to his expectations and oh well, I still have Edward. In the evening I was sewing my skirt over at Marilyn's and took some baked jacket potatoes. The phone went, and it was Steve - well I was so surprised and he said he would see me at lunch time the next day. Just put the phone down and it rang again, this time it was Edward! He was so looking forward to seeing me at the weekend! I realise I have a problem! Today, Steve came in at lunch time wearing his Aston Villa scarf. Louise did her usual 'Up the 'Ammers' (same colour as Hammersmith!). He sat next to me. Tim kept bringing receipts over for me write, much to Louise's annoyance, so we went down to the Bar and we were chatting to Bar Manager Bill. As Steve left he didn't mention seeing me again, but just at the door, he turned round, looked back at me and said he would call in tomorrow! Marilyn and Babs (the office typist) made me feel bad about Edward. What am I going to do?"

19th October 1975: I felt as if I was being introduced as the prospective bride!

"I had arranged to go to North Wales this weekend and meet Edward at his parents house. The night before Marilyn and I had been out with Steve and his flatmate Dick. We were all dressed in our finest, but they took us to their 'local' pub 'the Romilly' and we looked out of place! Went on to Monty's and back to Marilyn's for coffee and it was getting late, 3.45 a.m., when Marilyn and I were on our own talking by the window. Marilyn saw a 'Peeping Tom' which really scared her, so much so that she called the police. She stayed at mine the night after a very nice policeman had been round to take a statement. This weekend has been too busy for me to think about my predicament. Edward took me round the village to introduce me to all of his family. They are such lovely people and it would be wonderful to be part of them. We had an alcoholic drink in every house and wine at dinner. Later we were watching Bette Davis being interviewed on t.v. and she was drunk and slurring her words, but so was I! I finished reading my book 'South Riding' on the train home, to take my mind off my predicament with Edward and Steve!"

26th October 1975: Hot Chocolate, the band, and too much chocolate, the diet.

"Steve has been in the office every day to see me and taken me out two evenings. He drove me in his car over Caerphilly mountain, through Machen to a lovely small and quaint pub. The other highlight of the week was that Louise, Marilyn and I went to see 'Hot Chocolate' at the Union. After the show, we went backstage and stood with all the Cardiff 'townies' to meet the group and get autographs. The lead singer has the most beautiful personality. By Friday I was in turmoil but fortunately I didn't have to go to Bournemouth this weekend although I do really have to make a decision. When I got home I ate a whole family size caramel dessert, finished off the chocolate cake, felt sick and fat and panicky, so washed it down with a drink of cider. I must go on a diet, or go insane! Steve went home to Birmingham for the weekend but came into the Union to see me before he left. Edward phoned and said he couldn't bear to be without me now and was looking forward to meeting my family at Christmas. I hit the bottle once again!"

1st November 1975: Steve asked me why I was going to Bournemouth, so I had to tell him.

"Quite an emotional week. Steve took me to a gorgeous pub on top of a mountain at Rudry. He asked me the real reason why I was going to Bournemouth at the weekend! I told him the truth. I went on the coach to Bournemouth for old times sake and when I met Edward, he put his arm around me and it felt like an iron arm. The atmosphere became very strained and I told him that we did not have a future together and I could only think about him as a friend. After that he didn't say a word. The next morning he went to work looking incredibly sad. I went into Bournemouth and felt as if I was there under false pretences. I sort of said goodbye to everything. I ate some sandwiches on the pier and bought the Bee Gees record 'Nights on Broadway'. I didn't want to go back to the flat and when Edward got there, he was bitter. He said he had spent 2 hours at work discussing it all with the foreman and another workmate. I told him I was truly sorry but I had to leave. I gathered my belongings together and left. I didn't want any emotional 'goodbyes' so just left. I said I would send on the Post Office savings account book I had set up for him. At the coach station I phoned Marilyn and she was very understanding and it was good to have someone to talk to but I felt awful for Edward. I never ever wanted to break anybody's heart, but I think I just did."

7th November 1975: Stencils and the Gestetner duplicating machine.
"A Stationery Rep parked his caravanette in Park Place and Frank, Andy, Louise and I went in it for a glass of sherry. We were there about an hour and did not discuss much about office equipment! Steve has been in at lunch times and we often have a walk in Sophia Gardens or go to The Bungalow cafe in town, otherwise I have been going to the Bib and Tucker for a salad with Louise. Steve and his flat mate Dick collected Marilyn and I and took us to the Star at Dinas Powis on Wednesday night. Edward phoned Marilyn and she said he sounded as if he was having a 'whale of a time'. I really want him to be happy but I doubt if what he makes out is true. Friday was Andy's birthday so we all went out at lunch time for a meal - roast turkey, wine, apple pie and custard. Glan bought french coffees afterwards. Back at the office he bought 'After Eight' mints and Andy came round with cream cakes! It is impossible to diet in this place! Frank is being exceedingly nice towards me and wearing some quite overpowering spicy aftershave. Ten minutes before we were about to leave the office he brought 7 stencils to be typed and run off on the Gestetner duplicating machine. I was about to explode but he realised, and said 'leave it'! I have never known him so considerate!"

12th November 1975: There were lager cans strewn all over the floor.
"'Circles' in Howells for afternoon tea on a Saturday is something Marilyn and I could get used to. Dai had seen us and asked if we were going attacking men in town! Sunday morning I went over to Marilyn's and found lager cans strewn around her floor…I

didn't get chance to ask. We were cooking Spaghetti Bolognese for Steve and Dick and it all went quite well. Afterwards we went to a pub past St. Fagan's but didn't stay long as Steve accidentally spilt his pint of beer all over Marilyn. All was not lost because we came back, she got changed, and we went to 'The Inn on the River'. Louise had been off work at the beginning of the week, but when I walked in today, I could tell she was back as all the windows were wide open! It must have been the coldest day of the Winter too! Steve came over in the evening and took me for a drink to the Forge and Hammer. He was talking about solar radiation and the management of the Students' Union. We came back to mine and he wanted me to listen to his favourite singer Tom Paxton. I can't say that I liked his music at all! Steve was reading some of my poetry and took 2 of the poems with him as he liked them. I wish I could have said the same about Tom Paxton!"

17th November 1975: A crocheted dress without a hint of lingerie underneath.

"While the four of us were in the Butcher's Arms at Llandaff, Marilyn came out with a lateral-thinking problem which Steve and Dick were discussing for 30 minutes. I was pleased when it was time to go and see a group playing at The Quebec down Bute Street. That is until I realised it was down a back alleyway, dark and seedy with dubious people around and prostitute type ladies of the night! Once I got over that, the group and music were really good and we enjoyed ourselves. Tonight we were all out again at a party, but only three other people turned up. One was Hilly (Hilary) who used to share a flat with Dick and Steve. She arrived on a very loud motorbike and was dressed in denim and leathers. I couldn't help notice the black grease marks on her cheek. Her language matched her appearance but she didn't sound offensive, in fact she had rather a posh accent. Apparently she would make an entrance like this in the middle of one of her parents' cocktail parties. I couldn't help but like her. I was told that the only time she ever wore a dress - it was crocheted - without a hint of lingerie underneath!"

21st November 1975: He disappeared with Jackie Rothery, my biggest rival!

"Steve had a meeting with Frank and the Principal about Union matters today. He came into the office looking very smart.....I wish I felt sure he was mine for keeps. It was lunch time when he came back so we had a drink in the Bar and he told me that he hasn't the money to keep going out. I tried not to read too much into that. We had the General Meeting in the afternoon in the hall. I was on the stage pen poised to take the Minutes. I saw Steve on the balcony, deep in conversation, with no other than Jackie Rothery, my biggest rival! The General Meeting could not take place as it wasn't quorate, but Steve had disappeared with Jackie Rothery! A discussion followed with some rather awkward students who had come for an argument. I was in a panic and didn't write any notes down. I was expecting Steve at mine in the evening and bought beer, cider and crisps on the way home. If he comes round to tell me it's over then at least I can drink all of it to drown my sorrows! I braced myself and he did come round. He told me that he would rather not go back to Birmingham next year after his degree, but would prefer to stay here with me and get involved with the Cardiff Housing Association! So how wrong can a girl be, and I never dared ask where he went with Jackie Rothery!"

30th November 1975: Mrs Hemmings shot out of her room with a carving knife.

"I was over at Marilyn's in the evening and we were drinking coffee and listening to old records. I was just about to go when we heard a lot of screaming coming from Tydfil Place. Marilyn and I were scared and, the Warden, Mrs Hemmings shot out of her room with a carving knife! She had called the police. Next minute there were ten police vehicles of different kinds all around the place. We didn't see anyone, but heard afterwards that it was an hysterical wife in the flats in the vicinity of Tydfil Place. This weekend Steve had gone home to Birmingham so I was invited to Louise's parents in Abercarn. They were lovely and after tea Louise and I went to Tiffany's nightclub in Newport where the age group appeared to be 'Twenties'. After socialising with students, these people seemed really old, but then so I am I! We got back and the house still has an outside toilet down the bottom of the garden! Louise said she would come and shine the torch into the gap at the top for me, which was most kind! Today we went for a drive around the beautiful countryside, visited Louise's very lively 93 year old Granddad and had a roast dinner back at her home in front of a roaring fire. Her parents took me back to Cardiff and we hit dense fog."

6th December 1975: The balance was altered which caused untold sulking.
"The Economics and Politics Party' and the 'Blue Jays' concert caused a lot of bad feeling this week. I was going to both with Marilyn and Louise, but Steve wanted to come. It altered the balance of things so took the edge of their enjoyment and it caused untold sulking. I have decided that it is the last time I make arrangements with friends. In future I go places with Steve and they are welcome to come too! Anyway, Steve says he wants to take me to Paris in June, so on Thursday lunch time I bought a book on French, and the single by Ace 'How Long Has This Been Going On'. The town has Christmas decorations everywhere so I bought a blue jumper for Steve as a Christmas present. We went to a fancy dress party on Saturday. Steve dressed as an Aston Villa football supporter, Dick just looked as if he had forgotten to put trousers on and Marilyn looked really good as a schoolgirl. The party was great and really funny with everyone dressed up!" NB. I failed to record in my diary the outfit I was wearing!

13th December 1975: Mandy put the mistletoe up - over my desk!
"On opening the Swear Box we had the sum total of £2.83, so that was enough to buy some Christmas decorations for the office. We went off to town and bought sherry too, I couldn't keep up with Louise, she moves so fast - tazzing through town as if there was no tomorrow! The office looked very Christmassy and Mandy put the mistletoe over my desk! Most people were leaving to go home this week, including Steve, but he would be phoning every day and meeting my parents at Christmas! In the Salad Bar, these 2nd year Architecture students bought us a drink and asked us to help them with their survey on the Union building. It just so happened that the survey was to do with the whereabouts of the parties this weekend! We had to laugh. In the evening I went with Marilyn to Vicky's flat as she will be moving there, to the other end of the street, in the new year. I shall miss her being just next door. This morning we were watching The Addams family in our dressing gowns. Marilyn was tormented by packing and I wanted to go to church, so I went to the chapel at the top of the road. Sang some Christmas carols which was how it should be."

17th December 1975: The Office Christmas Dinner.
"I stood by the Christmas tree in town, listening to the Christmas

carols and watching the hustle and bustle of the shoppers, thinking how lucky I am. Back at the office I phoned my Mum to let her know when I would be travelling home. Felt guilty when Frank called me in to take down a memo on 'metering of phones'! Louise came home with me, we had a snack, then got ready to go out. We were early and Louise was very restless so I've decided that she likes to rush through life. I suppose we were apprehensive about the staff Christmas party. Three hours later - Christmas crackers, party hats, a delicious meal, dancing till we dropped, well for me anyway - Louise and Tim had endless energy! We gave Tim a lift home and had a bit of a discussion on marriage. Tim said marriage is part of society's pressures and we should fight it! I actually wanted to say that I would like someone to marry me so that the world knows of the love and commitment and people could be happy for you, but he was out of the car by then." Reader: - all three of us got married!

19th December 1975: The Office Christmas Lunch and the Strip Club!
"We wore our party hats all day at work on Wednesday and ate practically nothing but cake and biscuits. Marilyn came round in the evening and was a bit downhearted. I helped her take a few boxes round to her new flat and I felt I should stay with her until she goes home, but I've booked my train ticket. Yesterday was the office Christmas lunch and all the men came to work in suits. We all piled in the minibus and went to The Lantern for a slap up meal. From there we went to the Le Mans Strip Club! I didn't seem to mind as I was in such a giggly mood, but Louise did, and I don't know whose idea it was. After a while we were called horrible names by the women and so quickly left. We forgot about this back at the office when all the fun and games started. Boxes of chocolates went round and Frank's cocktail cabinet was raided. The mistletoe was well used and Tim announced that it was "free sex" in his office (of course it wasn't), so we all piled in there in shrieks of laughter. Louise took a whole film of photos. Marilyn came and joined in. We left her with Tim and all piled in Frank's office. At 7pm we must have sobered up as we went to see The Messiah at The Capitol. What a day! This morning Louise went round the departments apologising for her behaviour. I just thought it had been a normal office Christmas party, and rather jolly. I did have a bit of a hangover though, and was glad that this was the last day, and I would be going home tomorrow for a rest!"

21st December 1975: Like Santa Claus, you're almost too good to be true.
"I had to get up at 6.30 a.m. in the darkness. Went to Marilyn's at 7.30 a.m. for coffee and she bid me farewell. As I'd missed all the buses, I had to get a taxi to the station. Mum and Dad met me at Peterborough and took me to the new chalet bungalow in Deeping St James which I liked. The best surprise of all was a Christmas card from Steve which said 'Like Santa Claus, you're almost too good to be true'! I went for a walk and explored the local shops. In the evening I went out with my brother Ian on a pub crawl to give all 6 pubs from Deeping St. James to Market Deeping a star rating. By the time we got to pub No. 6 we couldn't remember the first one! Today I took the dog for a walk to Frognall and had a tomato juice, with Worcester sauce, in The Goat. The country lanes were beautiful and it felt like a summer's day except for the pockets of snow. We walked on to The Rose where the landlady was behind the bar doing her ironing as trade was far from brisk!"

25th December 1975: Gaudete (Rejoice).
"Saw my old work friends at Peterborough Town Hall yesterday. We went to the Norfolk Inn and after several glasses of cider and much merrymaking Helen dropped me off at my Dad's CCS office. (Commercial Cleaning Services). He took me to Jean and Jane's house to take their presents and I did hint that I couldn't go out with them as I had no transport! In the evening Sara collected me and we started off at The Crown and ended up at Annabels which is a great place. Got home at 2 a.m. and there was a huge spider the lounge! Well today we opened our presents and collected Great Aunty Violet from the home in Holbeach. We all ate too much Christmas lunch and Aunty Violet wouldn't sit still, she kept wanting to do the washing up! They all went off to Grandma's and I was watching Swan Lake on t.v. and practicing my ballet moves when Steve phoned. Later cousin Jill, Aunty Lil, Angela and David arrived and the Christmas partying continued."

31st December 1975: I wasn't quite ready to give up this life of luxury.
"Steve was here for a glorious 2 days, met Mum and Dad and what a great success! Before he got here I was convinced I was coming down with flu but it was all in the mind. We drove into Peterborough and Steve was fascinated by the Cathedral. We met

a few of my friends in the Bull Hotel and we used the phone in there to call Steve's Mum, as she wanted to speak to me! Today we drove out to the Wash and stopped off at Crowland Abbey on the way back. After Mum cooked us an evening meal, Steve left, to go home to Birmingham, saying that he could give me a lift back to Cardiff, whenever I was ready to leave! Well I felt so honoured but wasn't ready to give up this life of luxury at Mum and Dad's too quickly and I had accepted quite a few party invitations for New Year's Eve. Also it is Mum's birthday on New Year's Day - she was born 1 - 1 - 31. Great to feel wanted though, and I just hope it continues!"

1976

1st January 1976: A terrible hangover and I'm convinced my drinks were spiked!

"I was sick in the night and woke up in my cousin Shonagh's bed with a pounding headache. I was perfectly o.k. at the first 2 parties I went to, but when I got to Uncle Angus' hogmanay dance in his living room, I was given lots of mixed drinks by people with wicked smiles on their faces, so goodness knows what I was drinking. I phoned Dad to come and collect me and he hadn't realised I was still out! I decided that I was never drinking alcohol again but I didn't quite get round to adding that to my New Year's Resolutions:-

1. Write some short stories and some more poetry.

2. Learn some more French.

3. Do routine things much more quickly to leave time for worthwhile things.

4. Look at all the advantages of a situation and NEVER the disadvantages.

5. Not to let things bother me.

6. Do at least one good deed a day for someone else.

7. Get a barmaid's job for two evenings a week.

8. Try to achieve goal weight of 8 stone 3 pounds.

3rd January 1976: Last night was quite frightening!

"We had gale force winds which smashed the glass in the garage door and roof tiles were ripped off. We were concerned that the chimney might topple over and smash through the roof. Mum went to bed fully clothed and I kept the bedside light on. Woke up in the morning and heard the news that at least 10 people had

Steve and I met at a party here in October 1975.

Office Christmas Lunch at the Lantern, Cardiff.

died in this area alone because of the storm. I had 2 hours to pack, look at the damage and find out if the trains were still running. Caught the train which was 1 hour 20 mins late and Steve was still waiting for me at Birmingham New Street Station. We went back to Cardiff in his car. I did wonder when I would be meeting his parents, but then again, it was a scary thought - would they like me? It was great to be back in Cardiff together. As we had no food in, so dinner was produced out of tins. We went out for a New Year drink to The Discovery, where we have never been unhappy yet!"

10th January 1976: Steve was rather alarmed when I took him to the Jewellers!

"We are getting into a routine, even shopping together at the Supermarket like a married couple. I have done the cooking - highlights were lamb chop and welsh rarebit - and Steve has washed up, tidied my flat and tried to fix my record player. In return I have been doing all his course work typing. I do like this life but there is no guarantee that it will stay this way. Marilyn, Louise and I went to the Nalgo dinner dance. The food was o.k. if you like rabbit food and we were rather bored, as we didn't know all the old folk there. As it is my birthday in 2 days, my hairdresser's assistant Bobby called me in for a birthday drink - 2 varieties of her Dad's homemade wine. I thanked her and staggered back home....that stuff is so much stronger than shop bought wine! Steve wanted me to choose a birthday present, so I took him to the Jewellers. He looked rather shocked until I explained that I only wanted a silver locket to put his photograph

4 Hereward Way, Deeping St. James in winter - my parents' house.

in!"

17th January, 1976: 'Starry, starry night, paint your palette blue and grey.....'

"I didn't exactly wake up to loads of cards on my birthday. I felt like an orphan, still, I had 8 phone calls wishing me a happy birthday. I bought cream cakes for everyone at work and we drank Cinzano and lemonade, with bacardi and coke chasers at lunch time with all the Executive Committee in the Bar. Steve took me out in the evening to the Maenllwyd Inn at Rudry. I had a wonderful birthday. The next day, he came round to give me a lift to work as he had a meeting first thing. I was worried people would talk, so nearly climbed into the glove compartment to hide! Had to take Minutes and Agendas over to the main building and was bothered by a bad cold sore on my face but thought it wasn't really noticeable until Jackie shouted it out all over the office! Had lunch with Louise and Sue Harding (from Battered Wives). Today there was a book sale at W.H. Smith. Steve and Dick came out with books on architecture and cars, and I bought 'Lady Chatterley's Lover'. In the evening we went to Cold Knap at Barry and sat on the pebble beach in the moonlight. It was a still and starry night."

24th January 1976: The Wedding Party when I sneaked off down the stairs.

"Louise was bubbling over with excitement on Tuesday as she

was meeting a fella for lunch, but wouldn't say who! Steve had shut himself away to get down to some serious work, so I spent my free time practising positive thinking, nurturing strength of spirit and looking out my passport for when we go to Paris. On Thursday I went next door to watch Top of the Pops before Steve and Dick came to take us out to the Post House. Marilyn was playing the 'femme fatale', in a subtle way as usual, which she does so well. Yesterday, I was looking forward to the disco at the Union. When I got there Louise was worn out after playing badminton for 3 hours! It didn't matter as the music was only occasionally suitable for dancing. She stayed the night and I was up early and went off to the shops. When I got back she was lying on my bed reading 'Lady Chatterley's Lover'. We went to Mike John's wedding and helped with the food for the party afterwards. Marilyn came along and we were eating more food than we were putting out on the table, washed down with cider. Steve and Dick were confined to barracks with course work so I just had to get on and enjoy myself. I was asked out by Pete Seaward and he wanted me to go on to another party with him! I sneaked off down the back stairs and came home feeling rather foolish."

31st January 1976: Louise's birthday this week, so cream cakes at our desks, and drinks at the Bar.

"Birthday cakes and birthday drinks made Louise more lively and me just sleepy. We went to the Postgraduate party and people kept asking where Steve was and Louise wondered whether he was fed up with me, but I hadn't finished all his typing yet. That brought on some negative thoughts! The next day at work I took in the chocolates I'd won and offered them to Rob Johnson and the Sailing Club who had made an appearance. I don't know if it was the Sailing Club or the chocolates, but Louise and I were in fits of giggles and hysterics all afternoon. By the evening I was back in the Union to see the film 'A touch of Class' with Steve - it should have been 'If' but we went to the wrong Film Club. Yesterday went to Birmingham on a railway 'together ticket' to see Aston Villa play at home. Wore plenty of clothes, to keep warm, we had lunch at Rackhams Department Store and I actually met Steve's old school friends for a drink in The Cabin. I couldn't get over the massive indoor shopping centre - I bought some sticks of rock for work. The worst part was the crowded bus and the cold and windy walk to Villa Park. Once in the stands I was quite warm. There I was, in Steve's home city and still I

First meeting with my future in-laws en route to a 'tart's party'!

My birthday present from Steve which I chose from the Jewellers.

haven't met his parents. Scary thought!"

7th February 1976: I meet the Parents!
"Met Marilyn Monday lunchtime at the Lexington for a snack and chat. I went along with Louise to the Badminton Club Dinner in the evening at the beautiful Victoriana Bar of the Continental. I had to tell Graham, the Captain of the Club that I was spoken for, which boosted my ego! We had a fire alarm at work in the morning so Louise and I took ourselves off for coffee at the Lord Sandwich. Tim was being funny about time keeping, but we put it down to Hustings and Rag. Louise didn't notice as she is so happily wrapped up in her new world. Most important news this week is that I met Steve's parents! We went to Birmingham on the train and Steve's Dad met us. Back at the house I sat, with a tea tray on the table in front of me (best china), and Steve's parents and brothers in a semi circle around me, asking questions, but in a friendly way! A bit like an interview and I wonder if I've got the job, although they say that no woman is good enough for your son! That evening we were going to a Vicars and Tarts party and we dressed for the part. We met more of Steve's friends there, but I couldn't help feeling that the girls didn't like me. I decided to join in as much of the conversation as possible rather than being a shrinking violet, which would have been rather difficult dressed as a wanton woman!"

15th February 1976: Ventura Highway and Queen Street Chaos!
"Steve's flatmate Dick has pneumonia and I went round to tell

Marilyn. Tim called in and told me that Steve had been seen in the Pantmawr Inn with another girl. It rather upset and disturbed me. This had me thinking and I realised that since Christmas I had only missed seeing him on a couple of Mondays or Tuesdays. The next day Steve made an announcement in the office saying he was fed up with people upsetting me! I bought two L.P.'s this week - Bob Marley and the Wailers Live for Steve and America's Greatest Hits for me. I could have gone to St. Mellon's yesterday where Steve was surveying his site to make a model and drawings for buildings. It was a good opportunity to catch up with Marilyn so I caught the bus to Llandaff and we had a drink in the BBC club. On the way back the bus was held up and I was amazed by the circumstances. The Bishop was being ordained, the Rag Procession was mixed up with the clergy and officials, plus a railway bridge was being demolished! I was surprised I got back at all! I was just in time to go out again to see 'Return of the Pink Panther' with Steve. Hilarious film!"

22nd February 1976: Duck a L'Orange in the Coal Exchange Building.

"I have only been out 2 nights this week - to Steve's local pub where Dick and Euan were playing darts and the jukebox was playing....oh and it was so warm in there compared to everywhere else - a lovely atmosphere. Marilyn turned up and left early with Dick "to look for the cat"! Last night was the Architects' Dinner Dance at the Coal Exchange Building in Mount Stuart Square, Tiger Bay. A most beautiful building in all its architectural glory, paired Corinthian columns, oak balcony and rich wood panelling in the Trading Hall. The only problem was, the freezing temperatures. We all sat with our coats on eating 'Duck a L' Orange', which was cold by the time it had been carried piping hot from the kitchen to the dining room. I was drinking rum, cider and wine which didn't warm me up! Eventually industrial sized hot air blowers were brought in. Today the chairman of SAWSA (Student Association of the Welsh School of Architecture) came in the office. I phoned the solicitors to make an appointment for him."

29th February 1976: Our quilted dressing gowns and my very comfy, pink fluffy slippers.

"Louise was full of enthusiasm after a day in London with her mystery boyfriend David which seems to have made them! There was a bit of trouble in the office with me ordering a mini bus for

the Women's Aid dance and Tim cancelling it. Frank had got
bronchitis so we sent him to the Nurse. He came back with
antibiotics and a temperature of 101.8 but was determined to go
to the Court dinner and speak to Roy Jenkins MP. In the evening,
we were all at the Students' Union and so was the Principal of the
University. After the Court dinner and rather a lot of drinking, he
was very merry. For once when I spoke to him, he didn't frighten
me! Later we met up with a few others and had a great time at the
'Wild Night at the Commodore'. This morning Joyce gave us the
photos she had taken in the hostel and Marilyn and I look very
fetching in our quilted dressing gowns, my fluffy pink slippers
and only 2 heated rollers in my hair. I kindly loaned my heated
rollers out and they seemed to have been distributed - a few in
each room!"

10th March 1976: Hustings and voting for the new President has taken up time this week.

"I was on ballot box duty which was interesting at times. Monday
was St. David's Day (1st March) and I am in Wales! Louise went
out and bought us all daffodils to wear. Tim was sitting with his
feet up on Louise's desk shouting orders! We all ignored him and
I made sure I was back from lunch early which annoyed him
intensely as he was in the mood for asserting his authority. Today
was exciting. We all went on a coach to Twickenham to see the
University Rugby finals between Cardiff (UWIST) and Swansea.
We met Marilyn who was waiting for Tim, she was in tears
strangely enough, but soon cheered up (we must have a talk). The
coach journey was great as on board we had Colonel Martin,
Major Watkeys and most of Steve's tutors. The match was quite
exciting at times and in the last 5 minutes we scored to win over
Swansea, although as people admitted Swansea was the better
team! We got back to the Union at 9pm, happy and tired. The
Kinks were playing and I desperately wanted to see them, but
hadn't the energy to wait until they appeared on stage. Can't say I
like rugby, but I've had such a good day."

11th March 1976: Frank opened his cocktail cabinet and gave out whisky, gin and brandy.

"Work was mostly General Meeting papers. Babs the typist
helped an awful lot. I met Marilyn in Asteys for lunch as we had
lots to discuss, but I couldn't stay long as we were really busy at
work. I was duplicating papers on the Gestetner machine non-
stop all afternoon. The Rugby Team came back, straight to the

office and wanted attention, congratulations and booze! We were just too busy and I didn't know what to say to them. Frank opened his cocktail cabinet and gave them whisky, gin and brandy. A few got really sloshed and the language was quite embarrassing. They gave me a brandy, but I didn't drink it all as I didn't want the General Meeting papers to be printed upside down! Pleased to get home and after tea, picked up my Daphne du Maurier book to read and promptly fell asleep. When I awoke my bookmark had fallen out - a picture of Julie and I at Hammersmith Palais in 1974. That prompted me to answer a few letters to make sure I keep in touch. I love getting letters and by the end of the night my hand was aching and my pen nearly out of ink."

20th March 1976: A vacuum in your pocket, can only mean a car!
"Steve was sorely distracted from his course work and contacting Trading Standards, the Council and his Dad's solicitor. The garage were demanding payment for work to his car that hadn't been agreed. They were then going to charge storage if the bill wasn't settled. To make matters worse, when the car was driven away the brakes didn't work, well only the handbrake! I had a problem with my record player as most L.P.'s I buy, jump all over the place. After having it "repaired" and paying several times, I eventually got to see the owner of the shop, Rex Morris, who told me that the record player is too cheap to play records with a loud base! So, I suppose, budget record players should come with a warning that they are selective as to what they will play! The end of the week made up for it as we caught the train to London for the Ideal Home Exhibition at Olympia. I secretly wished we were looking for ideas for our own house instead of for "architecture degree course" purposes. After 3 hours we went to Dick's friend Susie's bedsit (the size of a small garage, but cosy) in Earls Court (the Australian quarter) and had pie and chips."

28th March 1976: The terrorist bombs in London yet again!
"Babs the typist said something which bothered me. She mentioned, that as Steve will be leaving Cardiff, when his course finishes, to go home to Birmingham in July, he will become a weekend boyfriend, as was Edward, and that relationship didn't survive! So I obviously have 4 months to make him recognise that he would like me around back in his home city of

Quilted dressing gowns before the more fashionable candlewick styles.

Louise and I at the office Christmas lunch.

Birmingham! Well, we were having a drink at the Water's Edge in Barry when Steve announced he would cook me dinner. I hadn't realised that being a student he bought 'pet's pieces' at the butchers, so although I felt honoured that he was cooking me a meal, I sat at the table, trying to dissect all the pipes, fat, gristle and offal related stuff, to try and find the recognisable meat! I didn't like to say anything. After that, we went to the Sherman to see 'The Great Gatsby' and I ate plenty of crisps and ice cream, to make up for what I didn't eat at the dinner table. Today Marilyn and Tim were at the Ideal Home exhibition and we heard the news that a bomb had exploded in the exhibition hall. I was so relieved to see them walking down our road at tea time.....they had missed the explosion by just one hour!"

4th April 1976: The week started with an afternoon out in 'Splott'

"I do enjoy Noel Edmonds on the radio, in the morning, especially as the programme was coming from a plane on April Fools Day! The week started with an afternoon out in 'Splott'. Photos were required for Architecture project purposes, it was very interesting with the steel works looming up against the sky. Back at the student flat, I decided to help out whilst Steve and Dick were trying to write up a sociology project, and clean up a bit for them. I always dread the kitchen there, as it seemed beyond help - 10 mould ridden milk bottles on the window-sill, a cooker encrusted with years of baked on food, and the bin which was overflowing topped by a layer of crawling maggots! I don't know how they stay so healthy....must be the pets pieces they eat! The bathroom is

Hammersmith Palais, London with Julie.

Steve and car outside his flat in Romilly Rd.

At my parents' house in Deeping St. James.

generally cleaner, but you tend to come out of there with dandruff, but it isn't really, just bits of flaking plaster from the ceiling! I decided it needed an industrial clean by a company who have specialist power cleaning tools to blast the dirt. So, instead, I offered to type up the sociology projects and fire reports. As a reward, Steve stuck my green stamps in the book for me, and took me out to Ogmore-by-Sea and Merthyr Mawr, a place of stunning sand dunes used in the filming of Lawrence of Arabia."

15th April, 1976: I'm told I need something more solid in my relationship such as gold!

"The last day at work before the Easter holidays and Louise and I were drinking snowballs and Frank bought us all Easter eggs. Before going home to pack, we went to the Chapter and saw 2 really hilarious films - 'Smile' and Woody Allen's 'Love and Death'. Steve took me to my parents and stayed so that he could see some more of Peterborough Development Corporation's new town - overspill for London. I wasn't prepared for all the comments we were going to get. First of all my mother who mentioned 'settling down' and 'you're not getting any younger'! A friend in town asked me if I wanted something more solid in my relationship - such as gold! As not many people know me in Spalding, well only the nightclub owls, we went there and Steve was intrigued with the Odeon cinema (Regal) and would have loved some pictures of the light fittings for his project. Then we saw Brian in his car, so I flagged him down. He told us he was getting married and asked when we were tying the knot! This morning, just as we were all packed up and leaving to go, my Uncle Angus called by and asked the same thing!"

20th April,1976: Singing solo to impress - I don't think so!
"Spent the second half of the Easter weekend at Steve's parents in Solihull and I was hoping no-one would mention the 'M' word. We were out that evening at the Star, for the folk club night (it is also the IRA HQ!). Met Steve's friends in there and it was all quite friendly until Carolyn walked in and she just took Steve over and looked straight through me. Any words I spoke were disregarded! I don't know which I prefer, being pressured into marriage plans or ignored as if I don't exist! Anyway we left her behind, and went to Snobs but it was too crowded so went for a kebab at a Greek restaurant which was very romantic. The next day went out for a heavenly walk in the Warwickshire countryside. Back at the parents house, a few Aunties, Uncles and cousins came round. We were all sitting cosily on the sofas looking at family photographs when Steve's younger brother (aged 11) came in with a microphone and insisted we all take turns in singing. It was viewed as endearing behaviour, but I could have cheerfully strangled him with the wire. Next the subject of houses came up. I thought we were talking architecturally but Steve's father was asking what sort of house would we be looking for! There is no escape from embarrassing questions!"

30th April, 1976: Vicky's friends were from Oxford University and all posh.
"The pressure is on for the students now and this year I have been drawn in! Luckily there is not too much work or meetings going on at the Union as every evening I've been typing for Steve and Dick. One night I was typing until 1 a.m. and they were both still working away into the night. I was going to get a taxi home but drifted off to sleep and woke when I heard voices - I made out I was asleep as I thought the conversation would be more interesting! It wasn't. Next thing it was 7.30a.m. and I needed to get to work but only had the clothes I was in! Just as well it was quiet and nobody of any importance in the office. No going out for a drink in the mountains this week but there was a party at the weekend. Marilyn's house mate Vicky invited us and we met everyone in the park coming up from the lake. All the food was home made, even down to the bread and the freshly squeezed orange juice. Vicky's friends were from Oxford University and all

posh - there were some awkward silences. After a few drinks we all went down to the Claude and got on famously!"

8th May 1976: Very strange that it hasn't rained for 2 weeks, but my ceiling has developed bulges full of water

"The garden was a jungle and every time you opened the back door it tried to get in. Steve hacked away and made a clearing and tied a hammock between 2 wild bushes for me. I could read and sunbathe in between producing meals, typing projects and fetching beer from the off licence.The Students' Union is quiet and Louise is happy having spent a weekend with David - without any unfinished arguments! It was Frank's birthday so he opened the cocktail cabinet. Then he disappeared so we celebrated without him. Louise and Tim weren't speaking but David came in and whisked her off to lunch, and Marilyn came in for Tim, so it was just me drinking to absent friends. The General meeting was inquorate, so cancelled. Instead Frank, Ian and I went to give a pint of blood in the Temple of Peace. Strangely enough we all enjoyed it, especially the tea and biscuits. Good news that Steve's Odeon project has been put on display. The ceiling in my room has developed bulges filled with water which I reported to the Warden. As they got bigger, we burst them and drained all the water out. My room now smells damp as if water is seeping in."

22nd May 1976: I was destined to be Max Boyce's Muse!

"I have spent this week helping with typing, meals, washing and ironing, as final hand-in dates loom. There was a panic because building plans needed reducing so that I could type on them but the printers were all snowed under with work. I amused myself in the evenings at the New Theatre to see George Melly, the Rag Ball with Louise and Marilyn and the highlight of the week dinner with Max Boyce! He was the after dinner speaker at the CAB - Cardiff Athletics Board dinner and dance. I was selling raffle tickets and someone told Max Boyce I was the prize! By this time he was well away with drink and chose me for a slow dance, and was rather amorous by then, whispering in my ear about wanting to take me to Qui Qui's Wine Bar! He certainly had the charm, but I wasn't fooled by it. Did my disappearing act and got a lift home. What a good night and I felt rather flattered!"

1st June 1976: The flat hadn't been burgled but it appeared that way!

"The Sandhurst rep. called this week and Tim and I were taken to a luxury yacht worth £362,000, docked in Tiger Bay. It was fitted out with shelves stocked with stationery, office supplies etc. We were given sherry, and after being shown around the boat, we put in an order for paper (foolscap, quarto - bond and copy), carbon paper, envelopes, tippex, typewriter ribbons etc. Louise was away camping with David this weekend. Panic was the situation in Steve and Dick's flat again and the place looks as if a bomb had hit it. I was typing until 1 a.m., woken at 6.30 a.m. to finish before I went off to work. My portable typewriter was overworked and every so often kept typing 2 letters in one space. When all the work was handed in at midday, the two of them came into the office with roses for me! Nobody had ever bought me flowers before! On further inspection they were the wild roses from their garden/wilderness and were full of greenfly - but it's the thought that counts!"

5th June 1976: Joe and Maggie's wedding at Cleveleys
"Arrived in Solihull to pick up Nev to take with us to the wedding. Only Steve's brothers were at home - Malcolm in the front room with girlfriend Hilary and Richard in the garden making a tent. Today we had a fab time at Joe and Maggie's wedding at Cleveleys Register Office. The only thing that went wrong was when my hat flew off. I had to chase after it and dropped Steve's camera! The evening party was great, only marred by Carolyn, talking very loudly about herself and Steve and all the good times they had! I was playing the perfect girlfriend and must have overdone it, as Steve asked me what sort of wedding I would like! I wanted to ask, if that was a proposal or just a general question - but thought better of it!"

15th June 1976: The final coursework countdown!
"Tim came in and announced that his father had died. We all felt sad for him and then heard that Bill the Barman had been sacked! The office atmosphere was rather subdued. Louise was back from her camping trip and was telling us about her stormy love life. Later we wandered over to the College of Music and Drama Bar, where Bill was now working, to see him. This week, in the evenings, I have been making the trees for Steve's model - the final part of the coursework. Today I was in the School of Architecture helping to pin up all the work and it was quite an exciting atmosphere! The models looked great, and I felt I had the edge on the trees! Fish and chips for tea and then we all went to the Duke of Clarence to celebrate the end of the course. I have

An evening with Max Boyce, Louise, Marilyn, Tim and Tim's brother.

now lived in Cardiff for a whole 2 years, and it just gets better!"

20th June 1976: Will I be moving on?
"The week started with Louise and David having a bad row. I spent evenings making a huge 'congratulations' card for Steve, hoping he passes and gets his B.Arch. On Tuesday, it was a year since I started work at the Students' Union and I saw one President and Deputy out, have worked with Frank and Tim, and soon will have John and Maggie - I wonder how often John will be opening the President's cocktail cabinet. Steve has been for interviews in Birmingham and is expecting a salary of £3,000 p.a. As soon as he gets a job he wants me to move there and will help me find a flat and a job. Well, perhaps I will not get to work with the new President and Deputy after all. This week Dick was staying in London with Susie and asked us to go. We had a good time, but I can't believe how expensive it is. In Hyde Park a hot dog is 25p and an ice cream 15p. We went to Thursdays nightclub - £2 entry and the cheapest drink is 30p!"

25th June 1976: Public Schoolboy to Dustman's son - the diverse backgrounds of our Presidents!
"Louise plonked her wedding dress pattern on my desk! Work and evenings are more relaxed now, and we have even been able to spend the odd evening driving to the mountains for a drink. The Lamb and Flag at Llantrisant, overlooking the common, was an excellent choice for a summer's evening. We parked on a grass

verge under which was hidden a ditch and the front car wheel went into it! Some kind villagers pulled us out! The next day, the car kept stalling so we used our legs instead, and took a picnic down to the lake in Roath Park, watched the ducks and the rowing boats. The new President and Deputy came into the office to sort out Freshers' Week and I soon realised that it would be a rough year. We have been spoilt by the manners of Frank and Tim who are ex public schoolboys. Today the course results were out and Steve was rather nervous about it. Anyway, he passed, Dick got a distinction and Euan failed. We had our last drink in the Duke of Clarence."

27th June 1976: Moving Day, but not for me!
"Steve's parents want him back in Birmingham and the lease on the student flat has ended anyway, so his Dad came with a van. It must have been the hottest day of the year and me, Steve and Dick had to sit in the back on the floor of the van, with all the luggage as there was only one seat - for the driver! It was a hot journey to Streatham, where Dick's parents live but I soon forgot my heat exhaustion when I saw their house. It was huge and the hall was so big, it had a fireplace, a large staircase, and doors leading to other rooms. A bit like Hollywood only English style. We had drinks, dinner and ice cream on the balcony. Set off for Solihull at 8pm when it was much cooler. This morning Steve was up at 6.30 a.m. to help his Dad. Tears kept filling my eyes as I realised that he had moved back home and wouldn't be with me anymore in Cardiff. The next thing I heard was Steve's Uncle and his lively daughters arriving. More family arrived for Malcolm's birthday party and Steve and I arrived back in Cardiff at 2 a.m. Opened the door to my flat and water was pouring from my ceiling!"

28th June 1976: It was raining in my flat!
"I had to go and wake up the new Warden, Mrs. Foreman to tell her that my room was flooded. She went up into the loft with her nightie on and then phoned an emergency plumber. The other problem was that she saw I had Steve with me and I explained that he was good enough to drive me back from a family party after I'd missed the last train (all lies), so I was offering him my floor to sleep on before he drove back in the morning (more lies). She seemed convinced, and as the hostel was almost empty, she found us a room. The next day we found out that someone from outside had walked into the hostel and into Mrs. Foreman's room

and had stolen her purse plus other things. We went into the office to explain to Frank and Tim and that I would need the day off. They didn't seem perturbed by this, in fact, I think they were suffering from sunstroke, and they looked rather burnt. By tea time, we had sorted things out so drove off to Nash Point on the coast, and made our way to the rocks, and then back up the cliffs along the grassy coastal path. Bought fish and chips in Llantwit Major and forgot about the chaos back at the YWCA."

4th July 1976: The temperature stays at 84°F all week and no rain.

"Every night we have been to the beach to cool off - Llantwit Major and Southerndown, apart from one night at the cinema to see "The President's Men". The cinema has just been made into a triple so tickets now cost 95p each! Friday night we drove to Jean's in Wiltshire and there was a note on her door to meet at the Vale. There, we sat outside around the lake drinking dry cider. Before going to sleep at Jean's that night, I had to get all the moths out. The next day was another scorcher and we left to go to Steve's Grandfather's bungalow in Hampshire. This was the first time that I have met him, and when we arrived, he was in a great state of anxiety which I later found out is quite normal. More family arrived for me to meet, but I could hear raised voices in the garden and a big argument was going on. We took ourselves off to another village to a pub for a drink and left them to it. All was calm and quiet when we arrived back and no-one had been murdered in a fit of frenzy that we know of!"

5th July 1976: Transvestite tendencies!

"I walked into the office and Louise and David had been quarrelling again. That evening we were meeting them both at Castell Coch. We were delayed as the YWCA committee were in my room discussing the flood damage and apparently had noticed men's clothes around! Wondered if I could just tell them that it is a hobby of mine! The next day I had rather a disturbing phone call from my Dad saying he wants to leave my Mum! That evening I took some time off to go and see my brother in Bristol for a discussion on the parent crisis. He said Mum is stubborn and Dad has been too tolerant. We then forgot about it as I was intrigued by my brother's new flat. It is rather ultra modern, as the living room has a suspended platform upon which there is a bed with stairs to get to it. It all seemed unfinished though. We went out with my brother and his friends to 3 pubs and a party.

Back at the hostel I had been locked out, as someone had marked me "in" when I was "out" so the chain had been put on. Steve climbed through an open window to let me in. Just shows how secure the place is!"

8th July 1976: Graduation Day 1976.
"Had a rushed letter to type at work and then went with Tim to do my marshalling at the degree ceremony. We got our gowns on and it must have been one of the hottest days. Steve's parents and brothers waved at me, and after Roy Jenkins' speech I went outside to meet them, by the fountains, and we had our photos taken. The heat was getting to me and we went to the Architects Department for sherry before getting into the hot oven of a car for a quick lunch at the Traveller's Rest. A ham roll and bottle of coke was all I had time for and I was on duty for the afternoon degree ceremony. Saw lots of people I knew and they all spoke or waved - such a happy time. I didn't notice until later but I had a bright pink lipstick mark on my cheek! I needed a cold bath to revive myself when I arrived back at the flat."

10th July 1976: Steve leaves Cardiff - not a good day!
"Steve's last 2 days in Cardiff and yesterday we roamed around the Roman ruins in Caerleon and on to Tintern Abbey. In the evening had a drink with Marilyn and Tim in Llandaff at the BBC club and joined in a party back at the hostel. I cooked us a meal and felt as if it was The Last Supper - tears in the gravy! I was convinced we would start to lead separate lives in different cities. Everywhere I went and everything I did I was almost bursting into tears. I waved Steve off from the window and the last thing he said was that I have to believe in us. Went to work today with puffy red eyes and Louise was the same as she had had a very bad weekend of rows with David! What a pair we are and what a sight we looked! I wandered aimlessly at lunch time. The place seemed so empty without the students and without Steve. I had a phone call from him in the evening, and he hasn't had time to miss me because in between applying for jobs, he's been working for the company where his Dad is Area Manager - cleaning toilets at the motorway services for £28 a week! With two degrees I wonder if he is their most over qualified member of staff!"

16th July 1976: The place had been ransacked!
"Went to McIntosh Place and sold my cassette recorder for £7. I had to temporarily move out of my flat as it was being

redecorated after the flood damage. That morning I had forgotten my umbrella so dashed up the stairs, rushed through the door and knocked the painter off his ladder! The new President at work said he was going to run off with his secretary and literally did - scooped me off my feet and ran! The evenings have been so quiet and lonely and when I phone Steve he is all happy and going out! I started looking to make new friends and then got all upset. This morning, when I arrived at work, the CID were there taking fingerprints. The place had been ransacked. This evening I should have been happy as Steve arrived for another weekend but was a bit uptight as his Dad had wanted him to work all day Saturday, then just as he was adamant that he was setting off to see me, his brother needed help with fixing his car - I feel that his family refuse to let go!"

20th July 1976: A piece of wood came smashing through the window.
"It was great having Steve back for the weekend and he asked if I'd mind if WE had to go to Hong Kong, as he was applying for a job there. I didn't mind at all! It seemed most appropriate for us to have coffee in town at the restaurant in David Morgan's department store. There is a plaque on the wall stating that the University of Wales Institute of Science and Technology started in this room of the building over 100 years ago! We went to Penarth in the afternoon and it was such a clear day that we could see Weston-super-Mare. Penarth is such a quaint Victorian place and walking along the pier was like an old fashioned romance. The rest of the week was quite dull, although I was invited out with Tim and Marilyn and Louise and David but felt like a spare part. I was going out with Helen last night and we were to meet outside The Claude. Just as we got there a piece of wood came smashing through the window! We went in anyway and it was all quiet and relaxed, so we never did find out why!"

22nd July 1976: Dad phoned to say that Mum had left home and was on her way to Cardiff!
"I was happy today buying my Birmingham Coach ticket but when I got back there was a phone call from Dad to say that Mum had left him and was on her way down to mine! Actually Dad sounded quite relieved but my stress levels went up! She arrived at 11pm and I let her have my bed and went to sleep in the hostel. She was talking about divorce, but apart from that seemed fine. At 8 a.m. she was tapping at my window, bags packed and going

home again! Apparently, she couldn't stand the noise my fridge makes, and the traffic on the road! Tried to phone Dad, but no reply. Still, I didn't want to spoil his day! When I got in from work, I had the phone call from Dad and he didn't know Mum was home. He asked my advice on what he should do, and I just didn't know. I felt as if I have a big weight on my shoulders. To make matters worse, Steve's parents asked why he has to see me every weekend. At that point, I wanted us both to run away, and wondered how the job application for Hong Kong was going!"

25th July 1976: I could get lost driving in Birmingham - I just have to think about spaghetti junction!
"I was looking forward to a weekend in Birmingham to celebrate Steve's 24th birthday. First there was the bad news that he would have to alter our plans to transport his brother to and from work each day and the good news was that we would get a flat together as soon as a permanent job came up, and I could give my notice in at work and look for something in the Birmingham area. That would be great except that the parents would not want us 'living in sin' and they would have to be told, but it wouldn't be easy. The weekend turned out o.k. but at the pub with friends, I couldn't seem to change the topic of conversation from olympics and fishing! I was helping with the job applications on Sunday and scrutinizing the Architects Journal. After a walk and a drive to collect brother Malcolm, I drove all the way back, through scary Birmingham. It was hair raising for everyone else in the car and on the roads, as well as for me!"

30th July 1976: Everyone is in a couple except for me!
"Back to work - Tim was playing his 'little Hitler' tricks and annoying me intensely. I was walking home when a Biology Technician started talking to me. I quite enjoyed the conversation and realised he wasn't chatting me up as he talked about his wife. Yesterday, after collecting the sweatshirts in the minibus from Penarth, we had an office outing to lunch with the retiring and new Executive committee with partners. Of course, I was the only one without a partner, so when they all disappeared afterwards to Barry Island funfair, I stayed behind. Also, the new President has taken a dislike to me as I put a stop to his childish behaviour in the office. In the evening, when Steve phoned he said his parents were annoyed at the huge phone bill! To make matters worse, he had been out with all the girls and everyone, not arriving home until 1.30 a.m. I was so upset, as everything he

enjoys without me is my enemy! Fell asleep on my bed until my bell woke me and it was Graham the Biology technician. We chatted for ages then I went to see Geoffrey, who wasn't in, but his flatmate Rashid gave me a cup of tea and sympathy."

7th August 1976: Our two weeks fixed holiday from work.
"Spent the first week of my holiday with my parents and brother. We had trips out to Cambridge and Hunstanton. Did some shopping and bought the record 'The Continental' by Maureen McGovern. Mum was being extra nice all of the time and Dad was looking sad. Steve had collected me in Cardiff and taken me to my parents' house and stayed for a meal. His Mum wanted to know why I couldn't have a got a coach or a train! Anyway he came back at the end of the week and we were off to spend a few days down south. Stopped off in Andover for a cup of tea with Steve's Aunty Nancy, then went on to Poole to stay on a small boat in the harbour at Parkstone Bay. The boat belongs to Steve's father, a 19 ft cabin cruiser. I was rather apprehensive about staying on a boat but I was distracted by the boatyard. I bought a sailor's hat and some sailing daps from the Chandlers Shop and so felt ready to go! We rowed out in the dingy to the boat and it was smaller than I expected. We changed for dinner, rowed back, went into Poole and ate fish and chips on the quayside. I was really enjoying the seaside life! After a few drinks we rowed in the moonlight to the boat and it felt as if we were smugglers!"

13th August 1976: Poole Harbour
"What a glorious week on the boat. Just one scary moment, just before sunrise one morning and the tide was out. The boat had tipped over on its side in the mud and we could hear the water coming lapping round the boat and the tide coming back in. We both sat on the one side hoping it would right itself and thankfully it did! The weather has been so hot. We hired bikes, played crazy golf, explored Swanage, Brownsea Island, saw Hilly in Brixham on our way to Dartmouth. In the evenings, we visited all the places I had been to last summer and I would have ordered the steak in the Hamby Bar but the price had increased from 99p to £1.75 in just one year. We had the gammon instead. Couldn't believe we saw Edward II in the Salisbury Bars and he called over to me. Thankfully he was with a very sweet girlfriend and they were both very friendly. I think Steve was a bit jealous, so we didn't stay long! Today we visited Steve's Grandfather in Abbott's

Ann. He was full of moans but commented 'Haven't you got your engagement ring yet?'."

15th August 1976: Water rationing had started in Cardiff!

"Yesterday morning we took our luggage ashore and sat on the front of the boat waiting for Steve's parents to arrive for their holiday. I was wondering if the boat was ever put to sail out of the harbour. Apparently it has, but once the mast fell down and broke, hitting Malcolm on the way down and they were left drifting towards the Isle of Wight until another boat came to the rescue and towed them back! It was assumed that the 3 sons would take after their father and not only want to sail but at least know what to do in an emergency! The seafaring enthusiasm must have missed a generation much to their father's disappointment. The parents came with a message that I need to phone my parents. Found a phone box and Mum informed me that Dad had left home! Luckily my brother was on his way there to see if he could sort things out! Today we travelled back to Cardiff and the car was like an oven. Water rationing had started, but luckily we got back just before 7pm which is when the water went off. Well, what a fantastic holiday, the saddest part was Steve going back to Birmingham. Marilyn rang so I went straight over and we talked until midnight."

19th August, 1976: Water from 7 a.m. to 2 p.m. only, each day, and the next stage will be standpipes!

"First day back at work and it took 2 hours to open all the post. Louise was back from a busy holiday of 'wedding preparations'. John and Margaret were in and John is so different to Frank, wanting to get things done straight away instead of spending time thinking, so that he could go off where he wanted. He stayed in all day though, rewriting the Constitution for me to type up. After work I went to Marilyn's for dinner. She is rather upset as Tim's mother does not like her and certainly doesn't want him spending weekends in Cardiff. We commiserated together. As I left the office for lunch, Wendy, John's girlfriend was on the phone to him shouting. He had gone out with Glan and the sports people all day and we all knew they would be drinking well into the night! I was at Tesco's, grocery shopping which was heavy and the day was hot! I went to the hairdresser's on the way home as the water rationing from tomorrow means the water will be cut off from 2pm and not on again until 7 a.m. the next day. I don't

The pressure was on

while I sunbathed!

Wedding at Cleveleys.

know how Vi keeps a hairdressing business going. I did notice she had a few gallon containers full of water in the salon. I never thought I would say this in Cardiff, but I wish it would rain!"

22nd August, 1976: There have always been barmaids in our family!
"Caught the coach to Birmingham on Friday night with 2 dried up sausage rolls and a can of lager and lime for tea and 'The Lost Girl' by D.H. Lawrence to read. At the Aston Villa football match on Saturday there was a lot of jostling, shouting, bursting of balloons and I couldn't see. An evening at the Hare and Hounds made up for it as I love the music in there. I was confronted with the news, when I returned to Cardiff, that if it doesn't rain soon, there is only 2 weeks water supply left! It annoys me that Birmingham's water comes from Wales and yet they have no restrictions! I cooked dinner for Marilyn and I and we had lots to talk about - do we take a chance and follow our hearts which means leaving our jobs and friends in Cardiff? I wrote off for 2 jobs at Birmingham University. Also when I was taking my old clothes to 'War on Want' I noticed a sign in the window of the Gower pub around the corner. They wanted a barmaid for 3 nights in the week. That would stop me being lonely in the week and I could earn extra money. Went in to see the Landlady, and I could tell she is the sort of person you wouldn't want to cross. It is a Brains real ale pub and I have no experience with pulling pints but told her that I am eager to learn. She will let me know on Friday." Reader: Photo taken in 2009 and The Gower has survived when

82

other pubs are closing at the rate of one a week! It used to be a railway building!

30th August, 1976: Spent the night in an AA van!
"I have been collecting money for Louise's wedding this week and Pam in Lear's Bookshop wanted to chat about parties and events when the students return. Wonder if I will be here then? Later this week Maggie and I went out and bought Louise a Fondue Set and cookbook for a wedding present. The Bank Holiday weekend was far from uneventful. The car broke down on our way to my parents and we had to contact the motorway police to get in touch with the AA. They finally arrived at midnight then we whizzed down the M6 in the AA van at about 90 m.p.h. to get a new regulator and dynamo. The car was repaired by 3 a.m. and we arrived at my parents at 5 a.m.! Woke up at midday and my Dad took us for a tour around Perkins Engines, from the factory floor, to the Managing Director's office. Went to see my Grandma who Steve really likes because she is cheerful! We all had an evening out at the George Hotel in Stamford to celebrate my brother Ian's 21st birthday. Dad said he wasn't going back home but now has a solution and would discuss with Mum tomorrow. This worried her! I'm back in Cardiff now and, at last, it is raining!"

2nd September, 1976: My new evening job is Barmaid at The Gower!
"Well, I got the Job at The Gower pub around the corner and I'm working 3 nights a week. I felt a bit uneasy about it and had to learn how to pull a pint of Brains Dark. A new barman called Tony started with me and the other bar staff seemed friendly enough. I wasn't sure about the customers though. Some had their own glasses on a shelf above the Bar. These glasses had a nude woman printed on the inside, so the more you drank, the more you saw. One man comes in after his tea every evening, sits at the Bar on a Bar stool, and just drinks pints solidly all night and his only other activity is chain smoking cigarettes. His wife comes to join him about an hour before closing and is more sociable. What an existence! All the prices of the drinks have to be added up in my head and then the total rung through the till. I can see I'll not always get it right! At the end of the evening the bar staff sit down and are given a free drink, I really wanted to get home to my bed."

5th September, 1976: Louise gets married and Steve's trousers are stolen!

"On Tuesday we all took Louise out to lunch at the Lexington to present her with a wedding gift - fondue set and cookbook. Tim came and John, the new President gave a speech congratulating Louise on her 21st birthday! Yesterday was Louise and David's wedding. Steve came over on Friday night and the next morning went to his car to find it had been broken into! His leather jacket, wallet and trousers had been stolen! After getting over the initial shock I rang the Police with the details. We rushed off into town and I bought him some trousers and off we went to Louise's house and got there just before she left. After explanations and a quick drink we followed Louise to the church and had to rush in quick ahead of her. With all that had happened I couldn't enjoy the service as much, but started to unwind at the reception. On returning home, Steve was quite happy because the Villa had beaten Ipswich 5 - 2!"

12th September, 1976: My days in Cardiff are numbered - mixed feelings!

"My two jobs went well this week. Tim came in at lunchtime to give me instructions on 'student handbook distribution'. I was working with Brenda and Kitty at The Gower and apart from one or two mistakes I had two drinks bought for me by the customers! Steve heard unofficially that he is to be offered a job in Urban Renewal at Birmingham City Council. He was now busy looking for a flat for us and his Mum on overhearing, suggested we buy one. She had to be reminded of the 'no money' situation. On Friday I nearly broke all my nails tying up the Freshers' mail into bundles. Met Jackie for lunch, but we didn't get much gossip in as Mr. Bendall sat with us. The very good news was a phone call inviting me to an interview for a job at Aston University next week. On Friday night, I caught the coach into Birmingham and Steve met me, but we had to drive off to Felixstowe to collect his Aunty who at least, bought us a meal. We were too tired to go out Saturday evening after all the travelling. Steve's Dad was in a bad mood and not talking to anyone. We busied ourselves writing off for flats to rent and I came back on the coach having made a decision that I shall give in my notice at work tomorrow!"

14th September, 1976: The Interview, against all odds!
"At work yesterday, I handed in my notice. They didn't take it badly at all. At first I was pleased, but then it bothered me! Today I went for my interview in Birmingham, at Aston University. The day didn't start too well, as the first bus into town, didn't turn up, and the second one was very late. I got to the railway station with 4 minutes to spare. I went straight to the train, but I wasn't allowed on without a ticket! Eventually after much pleading I was allowed on just before the whistle blew. I thought the world was against me, sat down and felt like bursting into tears, but got myself a can of beer, instead of coffee and relaxed. It was pouring with rain in Birmingham, so I arrived at the interview resembling a drowned rat. I think it went well, but it's hard to tell. When Steve phoned at night he said his parents had taken it badly that we would be living together and he didn't want to upset them! The thought of living on my own in such a big city and not knowing anyone, was not what I had in mind."

19th September, 1976: A proposal of marriage!
"I had to take down 3 pages of shorthand notes with numerous swearwords for 'Impact' the Students' Union Magazine. I so miss the refined manners of Frank and Tim! John wanted it typed immediately but I said 'no chance' as it was 5pm. When I got home I went to see the Warden, Mrs. Foreman to give notice to leave the flat and asked for a reference. She said I could write my own reference and she would sign it! Such a nice lady! Steve phoned to say his Mum had come round to us living together but he still has to face his Dad that night, and I wondered what he would say. My parents had taken it for granted and were happy for us! He came with an ivy plant for me on Friday night - poor boy has learned that I'm ready to jump down his throat whenever I see him! Apparently his parents want a compromise, for us to gradually move in together, they need to talk to me and bring me into the family! Can love conquer all - he could see I had grave doubts, so got down on one knee and asked me to marry him!"

26th September, 1976: I have a new job in Birmingham, but nowhere to live!
"Back to work, with a lot on my mind, so much so that at lunch time I went out to go shopping but walked in the wrong direction. We had been to see Louise and David in their house at Llanbradach, and they have everything they could ever want or

Graduation Day for Steve.

A summer's day on Penarth Pier.

'Dogrose' in Parkstone Bay, Poole Harbour.

need. The good news was that Mr. Nicholls phoned from Aston University offering me the job of Postgraduate Secretary in the Business Studies department! Great, so I have a job but no flat, and that was giving me nightmares. This weekend I have been to Birmingham looking for somewhere to live. Each flat I phoned for, out of the newspaper seemed to have been taken as soon as the paper was hot off the press! I was beginning to despair. Steve met me and we looked at a flat in Smethwick which seemed suitable for demolition only! One flat was all boarded up and the only half decent one was in Rotten Park Road, Edgbaston, complete with a cracked pane of glass in the front bay window and plaster falling off one wall! Stayed with Steve's parents, his Mum in bed with flu and his Dad playing the martyr. Nothing was said and nobody 'talked' to me about the living arrangements."

3rd October, 1976: At last I have a flat, but the area is on the edge of the 'red light' district.
"Everyone at work was out meeting Freshers at the station. When I went to the Bar at lunch time it was lovely to see the place filled with students again and good music on the jukebox. This week I was invited with the Union Executive Committee to have lunch with the Vice-Principal and Registrar. It was a delicious meal but we had to rush back for the General Meeting. The meeting was a good laugh and also the most docile one I've known. These Freshers seem so quiet and harmless, but I suppose they haven't found their feet yet. I was determined to go to at least one Fresher's event so went

downstairs to see young Pam in Lear's bookshop. She is only 18 and comes from a sheltered background but is so keen to get involved with the student social life! We bought tickets to see Fred Wedlock on stage, and really enjoyed ourselves, it was like old times! Steve phoned to say he had taken the flat in Rotten Park Road - yes! I had somewhere to live. Then I started thinking about how I might have to stay there on my own. An additional problem was that I needed to tell Trish, the Landlady at The Gower, that I would be leaving. I couldn't do that tonight as it would look suspicious.......... there has been a confrontation about stock discrepancies!"

10th October, 1976: Countdown to my new life!
"Went out to the shops at lunch time to look for curtains and bought a tape measure! Can't relax at work with the new President and Deputy. In fact John was sitting at my desk with his feet up on my typewriter and when I asked him to move he told me to "p*** off". There are some things I will not miss! Work in the evenings was o.k. apart from one regular who ordered a round of 13 different drinks which I had to calculate in my head and keep a running total. The figures were different the 2nd time, when he ordered the same drinks and he made a lot of fuss complaining until Trish the Landlady, with hands on hips put him in his place, and she said nothing to me! Edward I came in for a drink which was a lovely surprise. He will be spending the year in Cardiff, just as I am leaving! Pam and I went to see Linda Lewis at the Union who didn't appear on the stage until 11.15 p.m. I had packed half of my belongings to take to the new flat at the weekend. Once we arrived there, it was great making it feel like home, with Steve wall papering to keep the plaster in place and I cleaned out all the drawers and cupboards. There is a possibility we will be working evenings, office cleaning. The money will come in useful for a better flat and furniture, but the thought of it made me feel tired! We had a relaxing drink at the Garden Gate. Caught the coach back to Cardiff for my last week. Met Marilyn on the bus, she came in for coffee and we talked until midnight."

17th October, 1976: Cardiff - it has been a pleasure!
"A Swan automatic kettle and huge leaving card were plonked in the middle of my desk at work! No presentation but I loved the comments on the card! Work at the pub was slow at first, but Geoffrey and Graham came in which made a change. The Darts Team were being really crude and revolting and I was scared to

The Gower pub, Gwennyth Street.

Back pulling pints 33 years later

Louise and David are married

walk home, so Terry took me and said it was a shame I was leaving as he could do with a good barmaid when he gets his own pub! Kitty and Sherlene gave me a Brains ashtray - I wonder if this was part of the stock discrepancies! On my last day at the Students' Union, we all went to the Lexington for lunch and I had to collect my salary and documents from Finance and saw Colonel Martin who took down my new address and wished me well. Vi and Bobby at the hairdressers gave me an ornament and told everyone I was getting married! At the Gower I went to collect my wages and was asked if I could work 2 hours that evening as they were short staffed. I did with pleasure and then went home to pack. Today Steve and I loaded all my belongings into the car, down 3 flights of stairs. I wondered what this new chapter of my life would be like, living and working in Birmingham, the second largest city. As we drove away I looked back over my shoulder one last time to look at the YWCA hostel where my Dad and brother had left me all of two years and four months ago. What an adventure! I really wanted to say, thank you Cardiff, you have been so good to me!"

Our flat, middle floor, Rotten Park Road, Edgbaston.

Studley Castle - our evening cleaning job.

Birmingham

19th October, 1976: The flat appears to have original Victorian electric wall sockets for two pin plugs! "Spent the weekend unpacking in the flat and more decorating and fixing up the stereo. I noticed to my horror that the wall sockets are for the old round two pin plugs! I did wonder how safe it all was! Started my new job at Aston University Management Centre Postgraduate Office, in the centre of town, above Maples Furniture Store. Mr. Nicholl's secretary Phyllis took charge of me, introducing me to everyone and explaining the work. I was feeling lost and all the information seemed to be bouncing out of my head again. I had retained quite a lot though - finding my way out of the building was the greatest achievement! Everyone was nice and friendly towards me but I hadn't met my bosses yet, the course leaders. Back at the flat I cooked dinner and then we were out for the office cleaning job! We had to call at Steve's parent's house as well so that he could tell them he was staying in the flat with me for the first week to help me settle in!"

25th October, 1976: Settling into my new life in Birmingham!

"My first week at the day job went well and I'm getting to know everyone, my work and the way around the offices and lecture theatres. The evening cleaning job at Clutterbuck's offices - a company who make lights, lamps and lampshades was o.k. - they have a huge skip full of rejects and imperfect light fittings ready to go to the dump. It might be worth a rummage through! We had to call in at Steve's parents' house. We also had to spend all Saturday afternoon and evening there for Richard's 11th birthday party. They want to meet my parents, so I shall arrange Sunday lunch at our flat, which will mean cooking for 8, Steve's brothers will no doubt have to be included. We went to Birmingham to see the largest collection of pre-raphaelite works in the world. Bought a print from the Icon Gallery and this will always remind me of our first flat in Birmingham. Phoned my parents who are coming over Sunday to meet the George family. My mum is most concerned that it would not be right and proper to serve anything other than a Sunday roast. I explained that the archaic oven in the flat is not very reliable, so tradition will have to go out of the window!"

31st October, 1976: The two sets of parents meet!

"I was covering for Phyllis again as she had taken a week's holiday. I felt there was something fishy going on and found out later in the week that she and Mr. Nicholls had been having an affair for 2 years! I hadn't much work, the office was cold and I was feeling lonely. I phoned Louise at the Students' Union but she was too busy to talk. I then worried that the phones were monitored. By the end of the week I'd been over to the Chemical Engineering building and met course leaders and although I was still in Phyllis's office I felt I knew what I was doing and even gave advice to students who came in - I hope it was the right advice! In the evenings we have an additional cleaning job at Studley Castle - a computer and training centre. Steve said he can clean them himself if I find it too much! We managed a night out in between the cleaning at Birmingham Town Hall to see Tom Paxton and Barry Dransfield (folk music). We then had to clean Studley and got home at 12.15 a.m.! Today both sets of parents met at our flat and we put the framed pre-Raphaelite print on the wall. On the archaic cooker I produced chicken in mushroom sauce, jacket potatoes, sprouts, peas and sweetcorn, plus trifle for 8 people - my parents, Steve's parents and his two brothers. They all got on well apart from Steve's Dad who stayed quiet as he doesn't approve of the situation! After they had gone we went out with Steve's friends Pete and Gail to the White Lion and they bought me a Davenport Super Deluxe which I don't think I will have again, as when I got home I tried to write a letter to Louise, but my words were all over the place ."

7th November, 1976: Aston Hall by candlelight was a treat!
"Phyllis's husband phoned me today and took me into his confidence. He said Phyllis had left him and he didn't want her to resign from her job and I was to tell Mr. Nicholls that. I have only been working here for two weeks and find myself in the middle of marital drama, it is not the usual sort of message I expected to be passing on! The evening cleaning saga continues. Steve said we would go straight from work cleaning the offices and be back early to have some time to ourselves, but we still had to go to his parents, to sit with them in front of 'the box' as they had made us sandwiches and Ovaltine! Studley Castle is interesting though, built in the 19th century as a house on the site of a medieval castle. It is now a training centre owned by British Leyland and before that was a horticultural training college for ladies. On Saturday, Steve went to see the Villa match with his friends and in the evening we had a tour round Aston Hall by candle light and a drink with Pete and Gail in the Garden House. On Sunday a walk around Rotten Park Reservoir which took just under an hour." NB. Photo is of Studley Castle in 1976, now a Best Western hotel and I want to go back and have the luxury of staying there as a pampered guest!

14th November, 1976: Stopped by the Police!
"We didn't have to call in on Steve's parents this week, just cleaned the offices and sometimes went for a drink afterwards to The Boot. At work I had a laugh with the Course Organisers and had a few 'odd' postgraduate students in - these people make the day interesting though. Otherwise I've been really busy, struggling to keep my head above water. Organising meetings

and typing lots of tables so had a lot of working out and calculations to do with the tabs on the typewriter. The one night when Steve went cleaning on his own, he also had to take his Mum somewhere so was late back. On Friday night we were stopped by the Police as one of the car headlights wasn't working. We were being booked for this, so no doubt paying the fine will take care of a whole week of cleaning wages! On Saturday, I was impressed by Birmingham's ultra modern huge Central Library on four floors, but the Lending Library was not as good as the one in Cardiff. Have been out with friends for a drink but we always need to get back for Gail to watch Parkinson on t.v. - I suppose I prefer it to Match of the Day!"

21st November, 1976: **The consequences of living on the edge of a red light district!**
"I'm now back in the Postgraduate Office, after covering for Phyllis and her emotional stress leave! I work with Val who is about 17 years older than me and fun and interesting when you get to know her. Still having to call in on Steve's parents before or after cleaning, so we never have enough time to ourselves to relax. The good thing is that in the past year I have lost one stone in weight without even trying.......living life in the fast lane! Anyway we had a little bit of Cardiff nostalgia this weekend when we collected Tim and Marilyn from the New Street station, and on the way bought a copy of the Brum Pub Guide! Marilyn and I were walking back to the flat after the boys had gone off to the football match, when a man in a car was driving very slowly next to us. To my horror I realised that he was a 'kerb-crawler'! One of the consequences of living on the edge of a red light district! I made a mental note for us to look for another flat somewhere else! Soon forgot about it, as in the evening we all went to the Jazz Club. The entrance was through a plain black door at the back of the building. I almost felt we had to knock and ask for Luigi!"

28th November, 1976: **We are to be married next year!**
"We only called once this week to Steve's parents as we can leave work at 5pm, clean the two places and be back home for 8 p.m. and finished dinner by 9.15 p.m. to relax before it all starts again the next day! Some good news is that we have been offered a Council staff flat above the Birmingham Municipal Bank on

Rookery Road in Handsworth. It is unfurnished, and needed a cooker, gas fire, carpets, bed etc. On Saturday night we had to go to a Masonic Lodge Ladies Night with the parents. I had never been to one of these before and didn't really know anything about the Masons, but I am told that it is not a secret society! We had to be announced and presented to the Worshipful Master and his wife. We had an 8 course meal but all through it we were constantly 'upstanding' to toast something or other! The dancing afterwards was all ballroom and everyone else seemed to be about a hundred years older than us. Steve's father would like Steve to join the Masons to inject some new blood, but he is not interested. Today my parents came over and we took them to see the flat in Handsworth. Dad liked it but Mum wasn't keen on the area. Anyway, after they had gone, Steve suggested that we take the flat and get married in July, after his 25th birthday! Apparently the married man's tax allowance is coming into force which will save us money - how romantic!"

5th December, 1976: We seem to be packing such a lot into each week - on a roller coaster!
"Lunch times have been taken up looking for a cooker, gas fire, carpets and a bed. Steve visited his parents one lunch time but hopefully the evening visits have stopped to give us a bit more precious time. At work had a telephone engineer and typewriter engineer in the office at the same time. I have been trying to sort out student lists and everyone has told me that the records were in such a mess, they didn't envy me! I decided to walk home from work one night and it took 55 minutes! Made a note of the interesting shops along the route and at Five Ways, which I must revisit. Steve was very late home Friday night and I was getting rather worried. One of his 'Urban Renewal' houses had caught fire! Had a great weekend Christmas shopping and out with friends to the Irish Harp. Today we took a drive out to the Black Country which looked beautiful in the sun and frost. I was fascinated by Ironbridge. We stopped in the freezing fog to take a photograph of the disappearing sun in a country lane around the Black Country."

12th December, 1976: Buying a portable black and white t.v. was a treat!
"Had a rather generous refund cheque from my Superannuation payments. Much needed for furnishings, but as a treat we went to 'Domec' to buy a black and white portable t.v. Also Steve's Dad

came with us to the Carpet Warehouse, one lunchtime, because he could get a discount, but we were not impressed with the selection of floor coverings. Val gave me a green shield stamp book which was full and was a generous gesture, as we had a lot to buy. We were being given an old armchair and a deckchair for the living room as a temporary measure. I tried to concentrate on my work and appreciated the warm office when it is so cold and frosty outside, but pretty though. I had a Christmas lunch with the Course Organisers and I noticed they were all older than me but it was good to be included. Friday night we rushed with the cleaning and managed to see a film at the Midlands Arts Theatre - 'A day in the death of Joe Egg' starring Alan Bates. Shopping in the Bull Ring at the weekend was hot and crowded. At one point we were all walking four abreast at a snail's pace. Last night we went out to a Wine Bar in Edgbaston for a change, but Steve wasn't keen as he said it was full of 'trendies'! Still freezing cold outside, so we were pleased to get back, in time for Gail to watch Parkinson!"

20th December, 1976: Christmas celebrations begin in a more sedate style compared with UWIST Students' Union!

"Not a good start to the week. We had to have our dinner at Steve's parents' house and take his brother cleaning with us and when we took him back they wanted Steve to measure up their house for central heating, so it was a very long day and we were home rather late. To make matters worse, there was a 'personal' letter to Steve from Carolyn! The rest of the week was better. I went to a Christmas lunch at work - all 18 of us in the Management Centre Admin - 16 women and 2 men :-) . Delicious food and wine and I could have done with an afternoon nap instead of trying to concentrate on work. Partners were invited to the Management Centre Staff Party in the evening at Wake Green Road, and our only disagreement was, which records to dance to! Great weekend, snowing outside and we put up Christmas decorations in the flat. At the Hare and Hounds last night, Sue and Fred announced they were getting engaged. As we are getting married next July, I asked Steve why I was missing out on a sparkly engagement ring. He felt it was too conventional to get engaged!! I am pleased to report that he has changed his mind, so it's off to the jewellers!"

24th December, 1976: Subdued Christmas celebrations compared to Cardiff!
"I have been looking at rings in my lunch hour but haven't found anything different, unusual or unconventional. The best one was very plain with a large diamond and cost £108 and we need the money to buy something to sit on at the flat! We had Wednesday night off from the cleaning and Steve's two brothers stepped in, as it was Steve's office Christmas dinner at the Hosteria Italian Wine Bar down Hurst Street. I'd heard stories of people dancing across the road after a night out here. All was tame and quiet though and we walked through a rather romantic courtyard. I ordered Lasagne for starters, then steak, followed by pineapple gateau. It was a bit pricey at £4.40 for the three courses, but apparently the place is frequented by professional footballers, who don't need to think about money! The food was very filling and I was quite pleased that we missed the last bus so that we could walk it off on our way home. I have just been sending prospectuses out at work and on the last day, the only sign that it was Christmas, was a glass of sherry instead of coffee! I bet they were having a whale of a time at the Students' Union in Cardiff! We met the usual crowd in the Cabin in the evening, but it was too rough in there so we went to the White Swan which was too quiet! Sue and Fred came in and were talking about engagement rings until they started arguing about football! We all went to midnight mass at the Cathedral, which was the best part of the evening."

28th December, 1976: We have an appointment at the Vicarage.
"We had Christmas lunch with Steve's family and he proposed a toast to his future wife! I nearly choked on the brussel sprouts as I presume he meant me! His parents wanted to discuss arrangements and wedding plans straight away. We drove to my parents and had another Christmas dinner with them. They were really happy about the wedding but then went on to discuss the topics on the BBC news! One set of parents all keyed up and ready to go and mine all laid back, 'we will sort it out later'. True to form two days later we were round at the Vicarage and when I got inside the stone wall and saw this beautiful Georgian mansion in its own grounds, I wanted to ditch Steve and marry a Vicar! I did mention the delightful house whilst we were discussing wedding plans and apparently it is a difficult building to keep

warm and is very draughty. It didn't take long to sort out dates, times and Banns and when the Vicar wrote down my parents address he was most keen to know all about the wild American parties, held there by the previous tenants. We explained that it is all quiet at this former party house now, apart from the t.v. turned up rather loud, due to my Dad's slight deafness, after years of working in the Perkins Engines factory!"

31st December 1976: Only the footprints of the postman and a fox could be seen in the snow!

"BRMB radio in the morning announced that it was the coldest winter for 21 years. We are paying for the long hot and dry summer, no doubt. After work we have been going shopping in the Sales and the traffic has been bad, due to the rest of Birmingham having the same idea. We bought a bed, curtains and curtain rails and then had to rush off to clean Clutterbucks. We had a nice surprise though, the offices hadn't been used - only the footprints of the postman and a fox could be seen in the snow! Instead we went to the new flat in Rookery Road, Handsworth and we painted, and scrubbed out the pantry. A very industrious evening. I have been full of cold since Boxing Day and when I got to work I felt fine, it was just getting out of bed in the dark and cold, which was the hardest part. I had just yawned and my eyes watered when Mr. Nicholls came in and said I looked dreadful and should go home! I was tempted, but had more Sale shopping to do after work and this time we bought a round melamine table and 6 black chairs in the Lexington style for £129. We cleaned Clutterbucks and then did another hour's work at the new flat. Yesterday was New Year's Eve and we were allowed to leave work early so I went to the Jewellry Quarter and was impressed. I couldn't linger as we had we had a date at the Old Boys Club (King Edward's Aston). I was looking forward to New Year celebrations here - drinking and dancing without being in a sleazy nightclub. I wasn't disappointed and I'm really looking forward to the year 1977!"

1977

1st January, 1977: Two old armchairs and a fan heater will have to do for now.

"1977 New Year's Resolutions:-
To enjoy what I've got and not to think about what I haven't got.
Do things for other people more.

Our new flat above the bank in Rookery Road, Handsworth.

Deeping St. James Vicarage to see the Vicar and arrange a wedding.

Discipline myself to concentrate.
To see our parents' side of things.
To be more cheerful and not 'go on about things'!
We were supposed to be getting up early to move out of the old flat, and some Australians were coming to look at the accommodation. Had to buy a fan heater for the new flat, our only source of heating in the coldest winter for 21 years! Hoping the Bank beneath us will generate some heat which may rise up into our rooms. The thought that we are sitting and sleeping on all that money below. I am now thinking about armed robberies etc.!
We moved everything in and borrowed two armchairs from Steve's parents. Left ourselves some time to go and see the new Pink Panther film."

9th January, 1977: A Revolving Stainless Steel dance floor is something I needed to try out!

"I was painting the window frame in a cream gloss and Steve was hanging our 'Gazette Newspaper' wallpaper, but he was becoming harassed, as it wouldn't hang straight. The day carried on in that way as we had to go and clean the rooms at Studley Castle where we had difficulty getting the tiled floor to dry, to apply the polish. The next day we went to clean but had a lovely surprise - the place hadn't been touched, so we ate our fish and chips in there and talked about British Leyland. Then it was off to the Old Royal Hotel in Sutton Coldfield to celebrate Brian's 25th birthday and Gail was flashing a brand new sparkly engagement ring! I was allowed an evening off cleaning this week to go to the Laundrette and was rather keen to use the dryers too as it saves on ironing.

We overslept yesterday - the clock radio forgot to come on and it was nearly 9 a.m. Such a rush and I was o.k. as no-one saw me enter the building, but poor Steve has to walk through an open-plan office! Good news was that our dining table and chairs had arrived and the brown gingham table cloth. The weekend was good as we went to the Canal Shop for information about our canal barge holiday and then appropriately had a drink in the Longboat. Last night we found a dance place called The Barn with a revolving stainless steel dance floor. I am beginning to enjoy living in Britain's 2nd City!"

16th January, 1977: The Flat Warming Party Despite the Snow!
"I wanted a slinky silk dress for my birthday but came home from shopping with a flat packed rocking chair instead! We have been to cousin Angela's 21st birthday party at a pub, and on my birthday this week, it was the usual cream cakes in the office and then drinks in the pub at lunch time and an evening birthday drink in the Towers (couldn't afford a meal). I have had 3 days holiday this week. Instead of buying a slinky silk dress I bought a cream flimsy one in C & A's and also a cream beret for the 'French look'. It has snowed heavily too and we had arranged a flat warming party here this weekend, with friends coming from all over the country. I was panicking a bit as 33 people were arriving and I felt responsible for their entertainment and amusement, having invited them! I needn't have worried as it all went well, they all turned up and everyone enjoyed the music, food, dancing and conversation. My friends were quite lively (rowdy), whilst Steve's friends were sedate and cliquey! Two couples with babies left at midnight and the rest left at 2.30 a.m. Seven people stayed the night. Jean and Steve were up first this morning while Jane and I were last up. For lunch I made spaghetti bolognese for everyone but there wasn't enough to go round. They were all quite happy to fill up on 'butties'!"

23rd January, 1977: Holidays and Hard Work.
"Val appeared to have 'bad nerves' this week at work, but then she does seem to have more work than is humanly possible! I was enjoying the involvement with the DIA students and pleased that it wasn't my problem when they didn't all fit into their classroom. I booked the canal barge holiday but on returning home realised it was on the wrong canal! I hadn't particularly wanted the Llangollen Canal in North Wales. I started to feel really tired

when Steve said we had the chance to work all day Saturday with his Dad and brother scrubbing floors in Stoke-on-Trent! On Sunday we were going to be cooking lunch for his parents and brothers too. Overcome by exhaustion, I started day-dreaming about holidays, rest and relaxation! So yesterday we were up early and off to Century Oils to scrub off and seal the office floors. It was a hard slog and I felt shattered but so pleased that I managed to keep up with all the men and I'm sure they were impressed. I fell asleep in the car on the way home and then again after tea. I was rudely awoken by Steve's loud shrieks of laughter whilst watching 'Parkinson'."

30th January, 1977: The Habitat House Book.

"Lots of meetings this week with Course Organisers and Dugald from Admin. Evening cleaning is taking much longer at Clutterbucks with having to buff the floors, but Studley Castle seems to have a less messy group in at the moment so it doesn't take long. The neighbourhood where we live is proving to be quite multicultural. Loud reggae music on one side and strong curry smells from the terraced housing on the other side. Oh, and I was ill at work on Wednesday with terrible stomach cramps. It was so intense I went to Phyllis to beg someone to take me home but no-one was around. I was slumped in Mr. Nicholl's easy chair, which he uses for visitors to his office. He walked into the room and was shocked to find me there. He opened the cocktail cabinet to give me a (medicinal) sherry, I managed to croak 'just water'. After half an hour I felt much better but was taken home. The next day, apart from my stomach feeling as if it had been kicked around the room, I was fine and went to work. This weekend Steve went to Sparkbrook to buy some timber to make a centre unit for the living room instead of the conventional 'three piece suite'. After much consultation of the 'House Book' he enthusiastically set to work and I thought I would do the same with my flat packed rocking chair. I was struggling and thought I would need a saw until it was pointed out to me that I had got the seat on back to front!"

6th February, 1977: New Homemade Centre Unit Furniture.

"In the Course Organisers' meeting on Monday morning, all I could focus on were the words 'Sally do this, Sally can do that'. My face was getting longer and longer. Phyllis voiced concern over my workload, so as a solution, a bigger office and a temp was

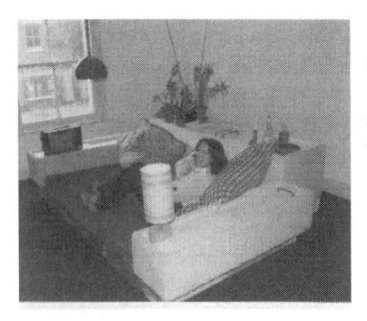

Above the Bank in Handsworth. Centre Unit furniture from an idea in the Habitat Housebook.

mentioned. Felt tired when I had to go out cleaning offices after work but luckily Studley Castle hadn't been used. On Friday the Student picket - objections about high University fees was called off, so I wasn't prevented getting into work. After shopping in West Bromwich we were able to flake out on our new centre unit furniture thanks to Steve's expert craftsmanship, although not quite finished, it is useable for relaxing. It has top sliding door to open up where the stereo is neatly stored. Mum and Dad came to visit on Sunday and were most impressed at how we are transforming this flat above the Bank. Mum appropriately gave Steve a 'Mother in Law's Tongue' plant as a present!"

13th February, 1977: The Wedding Plans are going well so time out for a party in London.

"I was quizzed by the Georges about the wedding plans this week but I couldn't really answer all the questions. My parents had booked the local photographer, florist and wedding car company along with a wedding breakfast for 50 at The Deeping Stage. We were choosing wedding invitations in the lunch hour at a stationers in town and rather liked the 'art Deco' style in cream. My two best friends, sisters Jean and Jane were to be bridesmaids in green floral Laura Ashley style dresses, and Brian my cousin was to be page boy, in a kilt. I was going to look for a cream lacy wedding dress, when I had a minute, in my lunch hour. Val at work was making us a cream and peach wedding cake. It all seemed to be sorted, or so I thought! This weekend we were in London for Julie's party, stopping at the Design Centre and a wander around where Crystal Palace once stood. It was great to

Art Deco wedding invitation.

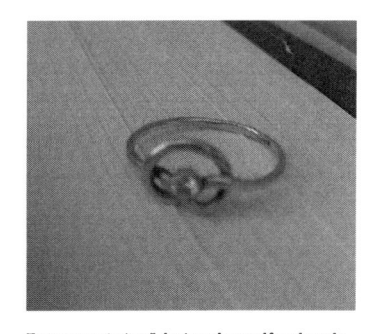

Engagement ring I designed myself and made by Rings 'n Things.

catch up with everyone at the party and that night we all slept on mattresses, on the floor. This morning I couldn't get out of the room because of the mattresses! Also Dick had lost his wallet and we found it later, out in the garden with £14 missing, but whoever had stolen it had left a £1 note......how considerate of them!"

27th February, 1977: A Trip to Henley-in-Arden to buy a Ring.

"The Estates Dept. were round at work negotiating a move to a classroom for Val and I (Postgraduate Studies) in order to have more space. While they were measuring up I needed to change the typeface on my machine and accidentally dropped one of the golf balls and ruined it. I've heard that they are quite costly to replace. Midweek we had to arrange for the evening cleaning to be done by someone else, so that we could go to a Handsworth General Improvement Area meeting - hoping that improvements will stamp out vandalism. This weekend we took a trip out to Henley-in-Arden to a shop called 'Rings and Things'. They have a workshop and will make a ring to your own design. I have designed a half tied knot in gold with a diamond, as an engagement ring. We called in on Steve's parents and discussed having an engagement party in a pub so that we could have music and dancing. The conversation then changed to a heated discussion on trade unions so we left."

7th March, 1977: 'Top Hat and Tails' appears to be the fashion for weddings.

"I have been enjoying the large space of our classroom turned office but miss watching the weather formation beyond the round tall office block that is The Rotunda. To find a venue for an engagement party, we picked up a list of pubs with dance floors, from Ansells Brewery on our way to Cardiff. We were back in South Wales for Rhys and Linda's wedding. We had a good time seeing everyone again and the reception was in Bill the Barman's new pub 'The Three Horseshoes'. We had a really comfortable night's sleep at Louise and David's new house, otherwise it would have meant sleeping on the floor at the newlyweds house. Our own wedding plans had hit a problem as Steve's parents wanted an additional party in the evening for friends and also wanted the men to hire 'top hat and tails'. My parents were not happy about this, especially my Dad......'top hat and tails' was just a bit too fancy for him. I just wanted to please everyone! The good news was that we had found a venue for the engagement party - The Elizabethan Days at Stirchley on the Pershore Road/Dogpool Lane." NB. This pub/hotel, which is Listed, has reverted back to its previous name - The Dogpool Inn and is currently up for sale for £395,000 (8 bedrooms).

25th March, 1977: I have four months in which to find a wedding dress.

"Shahram, Medhi and the rest of the postgraduate students really do make my day sometimes. This week they wanted me to have lunch with them and to go and see a play! Bought the Lesley Duncan LP on one of my lunchtimes out and about - it is great having all these shops on my doorstep. On Mothering Sunday we took Steve's parents to see my parents and to look around the wedding venues. We had booked an evening party at the Bell - buffet and disco for 80, and my Dad had come round to hiring 'Top Hat and Tails'. Mum cooked Sunday lunch and afterwards, I spent an hour in the kitchen, clearing and washing up. I didn't seem to be making much difference, so went and sat down to read a copy of The Bride magazine. This week I've spent all my lunch hours looking for a wedding dress in all the city centre shops. All I can find are gowns of white nylon, dotted with daisies. Last night on the way home, a drunken Irish man got on the bus and was swaying from passenger to passenger, sitting next to each one in turn and singing very loudly in their ear. Fortunately he staggered, off or rather fell off at a stop before he got to me. The hazards of public transport!"

4th April, 1977: White Nylon and Daisies or a Crochet Jumpsuit.... that's the wedding dress choice!
"'Cod Lyonnaise' was my experiment in cooking this week but we didn't like it. Sallie Bees bridal dress shop in Yardley was the place I was going to find 'the dress' but no luck and I have tried many wedding dresses on in the city centre to no avail, probably because I have my heart set on cream. At work a lot of the postgraduate students were going home for Easter and were coming in to say 'goodbye'. Mr Daryarow asked me what present I would like him to bring back from Iran. Mr Tan came in with Asian magazines for me to read and learn about his country and took my address to send me back copies! At the weekend we were invited to Bewdley to stay with Steve's friends Pete and June. It is a beautiful area and we went on many walks. Lots of bungalows and holiday chalets for miles along the river banks. I didn't see as much as I wanted, as June, as lovely as she is, was talking 'nineteen to the dozen'. We must revisit on our own! We called in on Aunty Marj on the way back and saw Rob and Sylvia's new baby, Zoe."

7th April, 1977: A trip to London to buy a wedding dress.
"I decided that the 2nd city has let me down by not providing me with the wedding dress I want, so this week I took a day off and caught the train to the capitol. I met Mr. Bennett, one of our Nigerian students on the train. Once I arrived in London, I went to Regent Street, Sloane Square and Fulham for the shops Mexicana and Laura Ashley. I had seen these in the Bride magazine but I must say that the staff were rather 'snooty' in Mexicana. They must have thought I wasn't seriously looking as I didn't have an entourage of women with me, making it an occasion. Eventually, I found the exact dress I was looking for in Selfridges, Regent Street - cream cotton tiered with cream lace. The shop manageress agreed to have the hem taken up and would post it to me for a total cost of £39 - dress including alterations. By this time I was rather weary and hadn't eaten since breakfast at 8.30a.m. so staggered into the nearest eating place which happened to be a Wimpy Bar. Arrived home feeling quite pleased with myself until I noticed the message from the jewellers. The engagement ring is at the Assay office waiting to be stamped but there is a backlog due to the Queen's Silver Jubilee with all the silver that needs hallmarking for that occasion. It looks like I will not have the ring back in time for the Engagement Party in 10

Wedding Dress, bridesmaids Jean and Jane, page boy cousin Brian.

Mum-in-laws hat alone cost more than my dress!

days time."

12th April, 1977: Fashion Icon of the 70's.
"The jewellers will make up a temporary replica of my ring for the engagement party so we could relax for the Easter weekend. We drove to Peterborough and met Jean and Jane to choose a pattern for bridesmaids dresses. I quietly congratulated myself on my choice of friends - those who are good with a needle and thread! (I'm not - my dressmaking teacher at school would constantly sigh in despair). We were successful but found no suitable pastel green material. Bought Steve a dark brown velvet jacket for the engagement party next week and he looked dressed in the height of fashion! The rest of the time we were out and about, particularly enjoying a day out in Cambridge. We were taking advantage of Mum and Dad's real fire in the evenings and the luxury of watching COLOUR T.V.! Uncle Angus, Aunty Cath, Shonagh, Wendy and Brian came round one evening and Steve was very quiet until he had a 'hot toddy' and a pint of beer and then became very talkative!"

18th April, 1977: I have Tupperware without having to attend a Tupperware Party!
"I asked the Porter at work, if I could go on to the roof at lunch time to sunbathe as the weather was becoming sunny and warm. He said nobody usually went up there, but I could if I liked although it might be dangerous! Decided I would risk it. On Wednesday evening sat in the Laundrette, not a soul about, dreaming of the day I would have the luxury of my own washing

machine. The Manager at Studley Castle had kindly bought us an Engagement present - some Tupperware. The Engagement Party on Saturday night at the Elizabethan Days was a great success. Ten friends were staying with us at the flat and my parents staying with Steve's parents. The next day Mum was staying with us for the rest of the week. As usual the traffic kept her awake at night. Coming from the countryside I suppose it must be considered noise pollution and it does tend to blend in with the reggae music and the barking dogs!"

25th April, 1977: I refuse to have a Hen Party.
"A new hair style was on my mind so I've been into Lewis's to look through the magazines for some ideas but haven't seen anything that would be practical. On Tuesday night I was supposed to be going to Sue's hen party and nearly didn't make it as my hair was still wet in rollers and I couldn't find my handbag. We went to the Pen & Wig which was very smoky and packed to the doors with under age teenyboppers. So we went to Snobs which was such a contrast - full of women who looked as if they had just walked out of a Vogue magazine. That left me feeling like the wild woman of Borneo, so I must find a hairdresser. Exam results at work have caused a frenzy as we were not allowed to give them out until they became official. The office was becoming crowded and for those who had passed I was able to give a smile and a nod - I hope that was taken as exam results only! Mr. Basij shook my hand and said I'd made him so happy, Hackam Singh wanted to take me to lunch there and then, even though it was still only 11 a.m., and Mr. Daryarow came in with presents for me - pistachio nuts and a carpet bag containing many trinkets! I do love my job!"

2nd May, 1977: It seemed a good idea at the time!
"Lunch times have been so hectic with the postgraduate students wanting us to celebrate their exam results but I needed one lunch time to go to the Chemical Engineering Department so see Sue's wedding dress. When I did, the Course Organiser announced to everyone that I was betrothed to be married in July. I felt as if I should bring my wedding dress into the office for admiration! Steve had been to a meeting about the changes to jobs in the Urban Renewal Department making the staff into general dogsbodies. He was feeling quite militant about it all and after quite a heated meeting, at the Birmingham Civil Defence bunker, under the garden of 8 Meadow Road, Edgbaston, he came home,

ate his dinner, drank a pint of beer and fell asleep! Yesterday, we both went to a new hairdressers in town called 'Heads' and I was persuaded by the salon experts to have my hair cut much shorter and dried by infrared lamp to bring the curls out. I thought I quite liked it, but Steve was shocked! I didn't want to go out that evening as I started to feel scalped, so instead of meeting Steve's friends at the Cabin we went anonymously to Edgbaston Wine Bar. I was surprised to meet 3 of my students in there - Mr. Shahroodi, Medhi and Fara. It took them a while to recognise me!"

9th May, 1977: Hair extensions hadn't been invented!
"I woke up for work hoping that having my hair cut short was a bad dream, but it wasn't! Not many people commented at work, but those who did said "wasn't it pretty when it was long"! Sue got married this week in the lunch hour and we all had an office outing at the Register Office. I think she had the rest of the day off, but we had to go back to work! Bought a steam curler for my hair in desperation, but I think it was probably a waste of money. We ventured out one evening this week to see Steve's friends and not one of them, not even the women mentioned my new hairstyle, so I don't know which way to take that. This weekend we have been at my parents to see the Vicar, the bridesmaids and the page boy. Not long now.....just hope my hair grows quickly!"

16th May, 1977: I didn't know there were so many shades of cream - my veil has a pink hue!
"Everyone wants things at lunch time and all I want are my sandwiches and to escape. Managed this week to find a cream lace veil for £70 in a hat shop in the old arcade, so put a deposit on it. Hectic at work, but we have been speedy at cleaning the offices in the evenings. Tuesday night I went with Steve to one of his Residents' meetings to decide what to do with their back gardens. Wednesday night we were out at Wyndley Castle for the Urban Renewal 5-a-side football tournament. It just left the weekend to look for a much needed fridge/freezer as the 'cold slab' in the pantry is only adequate if you grocery shop every day. Also I'm not keen on the silver fish crawling around in there. We also met Steve's parents in Rackhams Department Store to look at the beautiful mint green - mother of the groom outfit and just the hat alone cost more than my wedding dress!"

22nd May, 1977: The Charter Ball - I just love the University life!
"A seven mile walk around Kenilworth last weekend, in the unusually hot sunshine, quite exhausted me, which shows how unfit I am. It was lovely though, walking through fields, farms and past manor and farm houses. We stopped half way at the Tipperary Inn. Everyone at work admired my tan, so in case we get no more sun, I must go and buy some 'Sudden Tan' to keep it going. I was given free tickets for the Charter Ball and wasn't quite sure what it was. We decided to go and I was in for a nice surprise - so much going on in the main building and the Students Union. Dressed in our finery, we saw films, bands, exhibitions and danced at several themed discos etc. My favourite place was the postgraduate disco - I could have stayed dancing in there all night. I was drinking Southern Comfort and Lemonade but lost count. Woke up feeling not so good this morning. By 4.30pm we decided on a short walk around Meriden - reputably the centre of England."

29th May, 1977: Too much sun!
"Just one day at work and then four days holiday this week, so I was looking forward to my only day at work when I woke up with a swollen mouth. I could hardly eat or speak. Got an appointment at the Doctors and I have sun blisters - too much sunbathing. I will need to go out in the sun with a piece of paper stuck over my mouth! I phoned in sick to the office, but still had to meet Steve in town to go office cleaning. I was worried in case I saw someone from work, as I had rather a glorious tan, or if I should bump into one of the students who I might scare with my unsightly mouth. The swelling and blisters got better and the fridge/freezer arrived. Steve managed to drag it up a flight of stairs - I was a useless helper. So Tuesday we went to Bejam for frozen food supplies. The living room is looking good, now that the rocking chair has been assembled and the Dewars whisky mirror is on the wall above the gas fire. We took a picnic to eat in the grounds of Studley Castle after cleaning. So good to get away from the concrete jungle of the city."

7th June, 1977: The Queen's Silver Jubilee.
"All seven doors in the flat needed painting, so we set a day aside, radio plugged in, paintbrushes poised and set to, with a large tin of 'sea spray' gloss. In the lunch hour the next day I came across

the ideal 'going away' outfit for after the wedding - a pink cotton skirt and white broderie anglaise top. The Queen's reign over the country for 25 years resulted in everywhere being decorated with bunting, flags, banners etc. Dick and Susie came over for the weekend and we were joining friends for a celebration picnic. We met Pete, Gail, Brian, Tony, Basher and Sharon in the 'Swan with Two Necks' in Shirley. We played dominoes until the sun came out and it was warm enough to picnic at Castle Ring, an iron age hill fort on the southern edge of Cannock Chase. Afterwards Susie and I went collecting bluebells until the cold wind got the better of us. Street parties everywhere and at dusk, all the beacons were being lit on the highest points throughout Britain. We saw the flickering light on Barr Beacon."

14th June, 1977: The Green Shield Stamp Shop which eventually became Argos.
"On one of my lunchtime shopping expeditions I bought Steve the Cream album 'Goodbye'. On Tuesday I was late back from lunch and the excuse, that there was a huge queue in the Green Shield Stamp Shop, sounded a bit feeble. At work Val was in tears as someone had complained about our untidy office. It didn't really bother me, and while this was going on, a young Persian student called Zohreh came in and she lives down the road from us in the Hamstead Hall campus, halls of residence (an 1880 Grade II listed building). She was lonely, missing her family, not knowing much English and taking anti-depressants. I said I would go and visit - I have always wanted to know someone on that campus - it is historically intriguing. Today, we went to church at St. James in Shirley to hear the banns being read and no-one had any objections but then nobody knew who we were. Mum and Gem, the dog came to stay in the flat and Mum had cooked our evening meal which was a treat not to have to organise."

21st June, 1977: Zohreh and the Iranian way of life.
"I have called in to see Zohreh twice this week. She was showing me photographs of her home and explained to me about her parents arranged marriage back in Iran. Her father met her mother when he was nine. A baby girl was put into his arms who was eventually to become his wife and they had a very happy marriage. After telling me that, someone knocked on her door - some students inviting us to a party in the bar. We both went and I eventually got Zohreh to dance. She was so grateful for the company - I am hoping she can throw away the anti-depressants.

The campus accommodation is very much like a monastery and may have been a theological college at one time. Today we were up at what seemed like the crack of dawn - 8pm to go with Steve's parents, to meet mine in Deeping St. James, Lincolnshire, and hear the Banns read in church. I helped Mum with the Sunday roast and while it was cooking, I joined everyone at the pub. They were discussing Einstein's theory."

27th June, 1977: I just want to avoid the office pre-wedding ritual.
"I had great difficulty getting up as I thought it was still the weekend. It bothers me that I still haven't told anyone at work that I am getting married in six weeks. I am worried in case they dress me up in 'L' plates, a veil and make me parade in public! Only Val knows, as she is making the wedding cake. Sue came in and started talking about her wedding and I wondered how and when I could mention it! The weekend has taken my mind off work problems as we went to Jean's in Wiltshire. She now lives in Lower Upham Farm Cottages which is an improvement on Grittenham. We had a great walk on the old ridgeway apart from the stinger nettles and walking through a field of cows who nearly licked Jean's labrador Ambrose to death!"

30th June, 1977: All Work and No Play!
"Lots of rushed jobs at work, lunch time the food shopping at Asda and worse was to come - we had an extra set of offices to clean in the evening. The company was Perryform in Redditch who make plastic moulded windows. It wasn't a difficult job but we didn't arrive home until 10 p.m. and I was shattered after cooking dinner. This carried on for the week and by the end of it I was like a zombie and Steve was irritable. I really wanted to go to the staff end of term party but needed a new dress and I could hardly go out partying when Steve was out cleaning. At work Mr. Nicholls kept sending me out of the office on errands which normally I'd be annoyed about, but I didn't have the energy to care - only enough to walk in the right direction. I kept bumping into Batool and Bejat Shahroodi - 2 of the postgraduate students and they made me laugh and lifted my mood out of the exhaustion!"

4th July, 1977: The Street Parties continue in Jubilee Year.
"The car needed expensive attention so Steve had to be up early to take it to Val's husband and they would fix it between them, although he wasn't hopeful or enthusiastic. I had loads of housework, laundry etc. to catch up on, but after such a busy week I decided to set up the hammock on the balcony and sunbathe, only stopping for strawberries and cream. Steve arrived home at 7 p.m. covered in oil, but happy to have successfully finished the job! We went out to a street party in Solihull and there was 'dancing in the street'. Today we were back to just the two office cleans after work. As I drove back to the flat, the gears had been tuned differently and crunched more than ever. I got really cross and Steve shouted at me. There was a good late night film when we got in to calm the mind!"

15th July, 1977: A chance of getting on the property ladder.
"Birmingham City Council were on strike due to a dispute in connection with the closure of the Construction Department and Steve couldn't get across the picket line to work. Instead he went off to investigate buying a flat. There are perks to my being employed by Aston University. I can buy one of their staff flats on campus and obtain a 100% mortgage! I met Sue at lunch time and we sunbathed on the grass outside the VD Centre (Vauxhall Dining). Many students were leaving to go home - some never to return. Zohreh came in to tell me she was going back to Tehran for 5 weeks holiday to see her family. My future mother-in-law's birthday was yesterday, so we went out to the Strawberry Bank in Meriden and I had Steak Diane. Overslept today so I was late for work. Fortunately Phyllis was in deep discussion with Val about her divorce, so I got away with it as she didn't even notice."

23rd July, 1977: Does anyone still use a pressure cooker, I wonder.
"Wedding rehearsal this weekend and after going through the service with the Vicar, he then gave us a talk on the 'Importance of Marriage'. After that we had a look around the gravestones and I found one for a Reverend George and for Anna Martin, who is Mum's next door neighbour and very much alive! We arrived back in Birmingham on Sunday evening to look at a flat on the Hamstead Campus - the grounds of the old hall/friary in

Handsworth Wood, where Zohreh lives. We may only be able to obtain a 95% mortgage so would need £450. Spent all evening looking at our finances and can only scrape together £380! On a brighter note we have been receiving wedding presents, dropped off at the flat daily, from Steve's family and friends. An ironing board, pressure cooker, salad servers and sherry glasses."

29th July, 1977: The wedding cake did not travel well - the usual 86 miles.

"Last day at work as a single woman and I still hadn't told anyone! At 3.30 p.m. Val said I was wanted in the General Office. When I walked into the room there was a treasure trove of presents waiting for me! I couldn't believe it - a linen bin, fruit set, kitchen tool set, colander, breadboard, rolling pin and vegetable rack. I felt that I didn't deserve all that. The two bottles of sherry I had bought were opened and glasses filled. The next day - Wedding Eve, we packed and set off for Deeping St. James, Lincolnshire. Collected the beautiful cake from Val and put it in the new linen bin to keep it upright, but a piece broke off and we were distraught. When we arrived at Mum and Dad's, with jangled nerves, a lot of wedding guests descended on the house. It was all too much at first, but then Aunty Doris fixed the wedding cake. So to celebrate, we all went off to the pub and had a jolly old time!"

30th July, 1977: Wedding Day!

"Woke up with a bit of a hangover but the day was beautifully sunny and warm. I was sunbathing in the back garden to 'top up' my tan but I felt as if my Mum disapproved. Flowers, presents and bridesmaids arrived, then loads of guests. My mother-in-law was rather shocked that I wasn't ready yet. I remember Vicky my friend saying that half the excitement on your wedding day was rushing to dress yourself in all the finery and then in a totally composed manner to glide down the stairs. Suitably 'told off' I managed to wade through the crowds, dash upstairs, to put my wedding dress on and attach my veil with flowers in my hair and I was ready, in about 10 minutes. I felt I should have taken longer or perhaps I'd forgotten something. Anyway it was 1.45 p.m. when all the guests had departed for the church and the house was calm again. Dad poured us both a whisky to calm our nerves.

Wedding cake made by work colleague Val. Traditional wedding group photo.

The church service was the best part of the day where I felt cool, calm and happy. Everything else just flew by - the wedding breakfast and evening party. Steve and I left at about 9.30 p.m. in our 'going away' clothes. I had no idea where we were staying until we arrived at the Talbot Inn at Oundle, Northamptonshire."
NB. The photo in the bright sunshine caused squinting eyes except for mother-in-law whose face is in shadow due to the hat!

31st July, 1977: From Haunted Hotel to Canal Barge.
"Walked down to breakfast on the staircase which comes from nearby Fotheringhay Castle. Mary Queen of Scots walked down these same stairs to her execution. How romantic! Arrived at Ellesmere at 1.15 p.m. for our canal barge honeymoon. After one hour of instructions we were off. It was great at first because there were no locks just bridges, so I sunbathed and read my book on top of the boat. Then a cold wind sprang from somewhere which wasn't much fun. I decided to take over at the controls and steer the boat as there seemed to be nothing to it. Well, I was wrong and managed to get the boat wedged horizontally across the canal. Even the cows in the fields stopped grazing to look at us in amazement! Steve had to take over and move the boat round the right way and I was banished to below stairs! We arrived at Grindley Brook, the first set of locks and these were staircase locks! There were lots of boats about too. Steve was worried but the lock keeper showed us what to do and it was fairly easy after that. We considered it good practice and moored for the night next to a pub."

Off to the reception/wedding breakfast at the Deeping Stage.

Canal barge honeymoon.

2nd August, 1977: We escape the boat for comparative luxury of the Inn in Chester.

"Yesterday started sunny and warm so I was on top of the boat whilst we travelled serenely at 4 miles per hour. Just a few locks and then a long straight bit. It became rather windy again, so I shut myself inside the boat but it was full of exhaust fumes. Also the bed is very small and uncomfortable and condensation drips down so you get rained on while you sleep. Everything seemed so far removed from the wedding on this canal boat. I started dreaming about luxury hotels. Today we motored on to Chester but had to get through 5 locks and they were just too heavy for me to operate. Eventually moored outside the city walls of Chester. Instead of a luxury hotel we booked in at a pub hotel for the night. Spent the afternoon exploring the quaint place with its double decker shops. Walked around the Walls and the Cathedral with all the other 'grockles', In the evening we dressed up and went to the Claverton, where a jazz band was playing and it appeared to be the 'in place'."

4th August, 1977: We find some child labour to operate the locks!

"The pub bed was so comfortable, compared to the boat that we didn't want to leave it. Wrote a few postcards and then back on the boat where we had 5 locks to get through, out of Chester. Luckily, there were some little boys who operated the locks for us, in return for a free ride and some bread as they were starving! More sunbathing, reading and then 2 more locks before arriving at Beeston. Moored in a beautiful spot. At night the canal was ever so spooky with the mist rising. Today we walked up the hill to Beeston Castle. Evening mooring was at Wrenbury and we explored the delightful village."

6th August, 1977: Honeymoon Part 2 and another boat!

"It had been raining and it was damp. We had breakfast and the place smelt of eggs and damp. I could not live on a boat permanently. I was feeling miserable, but as we made our way to Harleston Locks I became absorbed in my book. More rain until we were through Grindley Locks and then sunshine all the way to Ellesmere. Moored in the Quay, had dinner at the Boathouse and a drink in a lovely old hotel. Today it was just one hour to the boatyard at Maestermyn and I was so glad to get off the boat. Drove back to Birmingham to unpack, wash some clothes, and re-pack for our 2nd week away on yet another boat in Poole Harbour."

10th August, 1977: We swap a barge for a yacht but the word 'luxury' does not come into it!

"After just one night on the boat at Parkstone Bay, Poole Harbour, we decided to book into a B&B in Southbourne on the seafront. Having had enough of living on a small boat, as the yacht belonging to Steve's Dad, was even smaller. Once settled, we caught the ferry to Studland for an 8 mile walk. On the beach part of the walk, we came across a nudist colony. The women were wearing only necklaces and the men were playing beach volleyball. Continued on our way along the cliff top to Swanage. From there we caught the bus back. Hoped to see the new James Bond film 'The Spy Who Loved Me' but the queue was enormous. Had a drink at the Seagull instead and dinner back on the boat where I bumped my head and burst into tears. I am sick of boats! Back on dry land we went looking for the night life and ended up having a 'tiff' in Tiffany's - not one of our better days!"

14th August, 1977: The Tartan of the Stewarts, the McDonalds and the eternity ring.

"Bought Steve a sketchpad so that he wouldn't get bored while I sunbathed and read. As he wouldn't sketch, I decided to see if I had any skills and drew him. I think I need lessons. In the afternoon we went to see Steve's Grandfather, and when we arrived he was dressed up in tartan trousers and jacket! Something to do with my maiden name McDonald and the

George's connection with the Stewarts. He gave me an eternity ring which had belonged to Steve's Grandmother Alice. We stayed the night on the floor in sleeping bags. Today we drove to Lincolnshire to collect wedding presents and the wedding photos. No-one was in when we arrived so we had a great time opening all the presents and looking at the photos, re-living the wedding day. After tea we went for a drive around all the new housing estates that are springing up in the Peterborough area for the 'London overspill' people. Managed to get a 'wall tie' in one of the tyres which resulted in a puncture!"

23rd August, 1977: Making use of the wedding presents.
"I wasn't look forward to returning back to work and evening cleaning. We were busy, too, at work with non-stop enquiries in the office, but fortunately a temp called Anne was tackling all the typing. After work, we went to our other job, cleaning offices, then back home. Steve was keen to try out the mincer (one of our wedding presents). He got meat everywhere! We gradually settled into a routine and one evening I threw a bone to the dog next door from the balcony outside our kitchen door. It was a particularly still night and I could see the backyards of all the terraced houses. I do like being at home. This weekend we went out as a foursome with Anne, the temp from work and my brother-in-law Malcolm to the Bell cider house and the Barn disco, trying hard not to appear to be matchmaking. It wasn't a successful evening, so we took Anne home. The three of us were quite melancholy until I started reading out my old diaries and we started laughing again."

30th August, 1977: We find a little bit of green belt away from the metropolis, although it is still within sight.
"University officials want to raise the price of the flat we are trying to buy. It didn't stop us looking at it again on our way to Zohreh's for a meal, I just hope it is still within our reach. Soodi and Clemencia were with us too. In my lunch hour, I have been looking for a hairdresser to trim my hair, but they are all so expensive charging £3.50 - Vi in Cardiff would have charged 90p. On Saturday we left the dinner cooking in the oven and went up Handsworth Hill or Sandwell Park, a little bit of green belt. I could see the rows of terraced housing and the skyscrapers of the city behind. Yesterday was bank holiday Monday and my brother Ian's 22nd birthday. We went to see him in Bristol. In two day's time he is hitch hiking to France on his own for a holiday. I told

Looking down on Birmingham.

Clemencia, Zohreh and I at the Birmingham Show.

him not to tell Mum. Woke up today with the postman banging on the door to deliver our holiday photos. We had an extra day's holiday and I could hear the bank clerks working below. Went out to stock the freezer with food from Bejam."

4th September, 1977: We only had BBC 1, BBC 2 and ITV but somehow there was always something worth watching.

"Sent out all the course joining instructions, which was a job well done at work. I've been falling asleep in front of the gas fire each night which is not good, especially as I've missed some of my favourite programmes on t.v. Friday night I had invited Zohreh, Clemencia and Soodi to a wine and cheese evening at our flat. I carefully labelled every cheese with its name and country of origin. The next day we all went to the Birmingham Show together. We looked round in the warm sunshine and ended up watching the parachutists and police dogs. Today we went to Clent, stopping at Whittington and walked down by the canal and river where two barns were being renovated. The course of the river had been changed to accommodate the sewage works.".

18th September, 1977: Never a dull moment on campus - desperate to buy the flat.

" We had to go shopping for something evil and wicked to wear, for a fancy dress party. It was lunch time, I was meeting Steve so I just had to leave the office full of people wanting things and the phone was ringing! The theatrical shop were charging £5.40 to hire a costume. After a few phone calls I found out that no-one else was really dressing up anyway. The party was in Peterborough at a house where Jane was living. There were lots of 'frightfully, frightfully' people there. Back in the flat, disasters in the kitchen yet again as I forgot to defrost the chicken and the jelly for my trifle wouldn't set. Feeling a little jaded I went to see Zohreh and what a fun night it turned out to be. Two Mexican students Edgar and Victor were there. After wine and snacks we were belly dancing, which was hilarious but Victor's style of dance was more like that of a matador. Today we borrowed the new Ford Granada car belonging to Steve's Dad, and went to look at a show house in Hall Green."

25th September, 1977: Consuming alcohol in the workplace was quite normal!

"We had a weekend of nothing to do which I thought was bliss, but then everything started happening. Mum phoned to say she and Dad would be over on Sunday, Dick and Susie would be coming to see us for the day on Saturday, and Tony and Sharon wrote to say they are in the area all weekend and had bought us a belated wedding present - a wine making kit - so wanted to meet up. By this time it was after dinner and I was trying to think of menus to feed them all. I started to feel sick as my stew hadn't been up to much. Work has been horrendously busy and also we have workmen in taking out the blackboard and putting up partitions. It was getting so hectic and nerve wracking on one afternoon that Val and I got the sherry bottle out!"

2nd October, 1977: Good news from the University at last!

"In the middle of all the madness at work, Mr Shoaie-Nia, one of the students brought me a beautiful picture frame which I now have on the wall. I needed something a little different for my Grandparents wedding photograph taken in 1926. The phone was constantly ringing and one of the calls was from the University Estates Office to say that they will sell the flat to us on Hamstead Campus, the crucial part being that we can have a 100% mortgage! The chaos in the office didn't seem so bad after that piece of news! We also had enrolment day this week which I always enjoy. Quite a mixture of nationalities on the postgraduate courses - Chilean, Iranian, Greek and one French. The School of Hairdressing was a good place to have my hair trimmed. The price was only £1.20, but the downside was that it took 2 hours! We signed the papers for the new flat and have been to Adelphus in Yardley to buy some unit furniture upholstered in a Morris paisley design covering. I saw the city of Coventry for the first time yesterday and the old and new Cathedrals plus the shopping precinct. Too many small shop units which I found gave a limited choice of goods. Today we had a walk on the Lickey Hills."

9th October, 1977: 90% of our postgraduate students are from overseas and struggle with our language!

"At work I decided to lock the door at lunch time for some peace, but Val gave in and opened up. We feel sorry for her, as she has the biggest workload and even stayed at work until 8.30 p.m. to get on top of it. That was not enough apparently, as one of the Professors came chasing after her for a course list which she hadn't managed to do! The day after there was a phone call for Val to say that her father had died. She was in tears and Phyllis took her home. How much can a girl take - we are sending flowers. The work piles up, but she will be appreciated when she returns. A new experience this week when Steve's parents took us to Rowfreeze, where you buy half a lamb, pig or cow and it is chopped up, put in bags for the freezer. Much cheaper to buy meat this way, but I would rather not think about it!" NB. Maples Furniture Store which housed the University of Aston Management School is now Tescos on the ground floor with conference facilities above.

16th October, 1977: I now possess an Access credit card....will it replace the need for cash and cheques?

"Viv started today with her Brummie accent and cigarettes. She works well, we like her and so grateful for her help. We now have two part-time ladies helping out with the office work. There have been two celebrations at home. Only one office to clean after work now and Steve will do this on his way home. After a year of two jobs I can now relax a little. The 10th of October is the anniversary of when we first met at that party in Cardiff. We celebrated with a meal out at the Great American Disaster and a drink at the Midland Hotel across the road from the restaurant. Our mortgage for £9,000 came through which is the exact price of the two bedroomed flat, so no deposit needed. I now possess an Access Credit Card. I need to practice with this new way of spending, so I shall be hitting the shops next week!"

30th October, 1977: The history on our doorstep.
"Went out at lunch time to buy a brown cardigan and came back with a white angora jumper. Whilst in the street I was grabbed for a questionnaire on sun tan lotions. After work on Monday Steve whisked me to Progressive Cleaning Company to type an urgent specification for his Dad - the secretary hadn't turned up! After 2 hours work I came away with £3 which I was delighted with. I bought a new blouse and polo neck jumper (to be worn underneath) and wore it for work. Everyone remarked on how smart I looked (I must look pretty scruffy normally!). Today we took a walk to the canal behind the site of James Watt's factory - the Soho foundry famous for making steam engines and now owned by Avery weighing machines. We ambled along the towpath into town. It was as if we had stepped back into a Victorian era."

3rd November, 1977: The power cuts that were the forerunner of the winter of discontent.
"First week of November and after the rain and gales in the night I got up early, put on a lot of clothes and my boots for work, and I was still cold. On the way home there was a power cut lasting 20 minutes, and it was not good as I had to walk down Rookery Road in the dark, with no street lights. I made Shish Kebabs for dinner which was very adventurous, for me. On Wednesday night I stayed at work to finish the last 20 pages of Miss Poon's project, for which she is paying me. No heating in the office by then so I was really cold and bought fish and chips on the way home - just carrying them warmed me up. As we were eating, we had a 15 minute power cut so it was fish and chip supper by candle light. Staying late in the office to type more work for Miss Poon was a bit of a waste of time with all these power cuts. One evening in the dark, I was waiting for the power to come back on and decided to try and read my book by the office lights across the road which were on a different circuit. Another night some students kept me company, talking in the dark, until the power came back on. For the rest of the week I've been checking the local newspaper for the high risk areas."

13th November, 1977: To hitch-hike was quite a normal mode of travel!
"Miss Poon came in with more project work which has kept me busy in the office when everyone else has gone home. Iqbal

Ahmad has given me a lift home most nights which is quicker than the bus. Took a day off to make a long weekend with Mum and Dad who had rented a cottage near Weston-Super-Mare, at Goose Green, Kingswood. Very cosy with a log fire. We visited my brother Ian in Bristol who we joined for a Bonfire Night party. Mum was impressed with the city of Bath and was drinking gallons of the spa water for her health. Yesterday back at the flat there was a knock at the door and there was Ken, a friend of Steve's from Cardiff. He was in Birmingham for a 'Friends of the Earth' meeting. We all went to a Latin American folk evening at the Tea Warehouse and the next day took Ken to the M5 so that he could hitch a lift back to Cardiff."

17th November, 1977: It turns out that I will be having four Christmas lunches in one week!

"Our new 'L' shaped unit furniture arrived from Adelphus and we managed to take it up the two flights of steps ourselves after being given the key to the flat for decorating purposes only. I am developing muscles! While Steve has been at Villa Park watching football, I have been at the Library researching where we live. His interview for Team Architect went well, but lack of a few years of experience went against him - we shall see. Buckingham Palace announced that a baby son had been born to Princess Anne. Christmas lunches are being organised at work with all the different departments. It appears that I have four lunches in one week during December! On Wednesday lunchtime this week I went with Phyllis to the Public Sector Management wine and cheese lunch. We both had 2 large glasses of wine each and I became rather talkative. I thought the afternoon would be dire, but lots of people came in with queries which kept me awake in my tipsy state."

25th November, 1977: I will be working in a building that resembles a wedding cake.

"Bromsgrove Residents' Association dance this week, which was a good night out and back to Peppy's for coffee so we didn't get to bed until 3 a.m. The next day we had to start working on decorating the new flat without any heat or electricity. We kept on the move, and I ripped up the carpet tiles from the old flat and laid them in the new one. At work we had a tour around Nelson House, the new purpose built Management Centre building down the road, opposite the Pot 'O Beer pub in Gosta Green, where the main campus is. We will be moving in next year some time. The shape of the building has been compared to a wedding cake! Back in our office a clock was being assembled on the wall, so that will put an end to my being late for work! Surprisingly some good news - Steve actually got the Team Architects job. We went for a celebratory drink to the Parson and Clerk on the Queslett Road - not a particularly classy pub!"

2nd December, 1977: I wonder how many more times will I have to push the car to get it started.
"The car battery was flat yet again so I had to push it down Rookery Road to jump start it. In the office my workload has decreased dramatically but I have taken on more student typing for extra cash after work. Whilst I was waiting for something to do, out of the corner of my eye lurked an essay of many pages, in its folder waiting to be done in my own time! 30th November had

University Campus at Handsworth Wood.

Top floor flat, Cassowary Road, Handsworth Wood.

Our Morris print 'L' shaped seating with ladders for the plants.

Dining area with newsprint wallpaper and Kentia palm plus Swiss Cheese plant.

been a good day as we took possession of the flat and spent time on the phone organising electricity and gas to be connected. My only purchase at lunch times has been a cream photograph album for the wedding photos. We were on our way yesterday evening to the Postgraduate Suite to see the band 'Rockin' Robin' and the car stalled yet again. Steve pushed it this time while I was in the driver's seat. Although we have just bought a flat, what we could really do with is a new car!"

11th December, 1977: The cat was not impressed when Rex came for his holidays!
"Stayed the weekend with Mum and Dad who are looking after Uncle Angus's dog who is a sweet Jack Russell terrier called Rex. This did not go down well with Gem the dog and Fluffy the cat. We didn't have a good night's sleep as there seemed to be a commotion of cat and dog fighting downstairs! The next day I was sleepy in front of the open fire, so I took the dog for a long walk but as there isn't much daylight this time of year, the walk was cut short - no street lights outside the village. We have had a week's holiday from work to move into the flat. After the gas inspector left we couldn't get the central heating boiler to light - he had turned off the gas! That was sorted and then the pump wouldn't work. The man downstairs said it should work after 24 hours! Amazingly it did! We hired a van and by the time we had loaded, unloaded and climbed 2 flights of stairs with everything, I decided we were never moving again! We now live in Myrtle House, Cassowary Road, Handsworth Wood."

16th December, 1977: The Babycham didn't last very long.
"I am now typing Mr. Otache's essay after work and nearly got locked in the office, as I forgot that the building closes earlier in the vacation. Mr. Ameale, one of the pre-diploma students came in bearing Christmas gifts. For me a Christmas cake, 4 bottles of babycham and a bottle of whisky. He came in again with 5 bottles of whisky for the lecturers but they wouldn't accept them as it was considered a bribe. To make matters worse the poor student had failed anyway! One of the many Christmas cards I had from the students said 'To my sister and her husband'. We were at the Opposite Lock Club for Steve's office Christmas party last night. The organiser Sheila made it quite obvious that she hadn't wanted the staff to bring their partners. The bistro meal was all convenience food from the freezer, with a long wait between

courses. The cabaret and dancing saved the night."

18th December, 1977: They had to move their half wrapped presents to sit down, so no surprises!

"Christmas shopping and the crowds were at a standstill in the Bullring. We didn't manage to find the 'all wool' tartan socks for Steve's Grandfather - I think we will need to send to Scotland. Met Pete and Gail in the Cabin. That place makes me feel depressed, it has no windows and is all stuffy and smokey. Steve's boss held a Christmas party at his house in Stourport - it was all 'jolly super' and evidence of social climbing became apparent. Today I didn't feel all that bright and breezy after all that booze and polite conversation last night. I was just about to serve breakfast at midday when my in-laws and Steve's brothers turned up as a surprise!. I was quite flustered as all their half wrapped Christmas presents were around the place, next to the sellotape, name tags, Christmas wrapping paper and cards, all in full view! They had to move everything to sit down! Well, now they know what they are getting, so in the evening I finished wrapping and made some mince pies. The dinner wasn't up to much as I couldn't tell whether the meat was beef or lamb but we had mint sauce with it anyway!"

23rd December, 1977: There were Christmas parties being held in all Council departments throughout the city.

"Instead of going cleaning straight after work, Steve collected me to go home and fix the gear box which appeared to be falling out of the car! The new part didn't fit so now all the oily bits of car are in the study. We walked over to see Sue and I put plenty of warm layers on. When we got there she was out but her parents were pleased to see us. We sat in front of their fire which was so hot and I was sweltering. The next day we had to catch buses to work, but by evening the car's gear box was fixed. We still had to push start it though. Last day at work today before Christmas. At lunch time we were called into the General Office for a sherry and mince pie. When Steve came to collect me he said that there were parties going on all over the city in all the Council offices."

26th December, 1977: We all had presents from the Jewellery Quarter this year - thanks to Malcolm.

"Christmas Eve carol service was wonderful in Peterborough Cathedral. We went on to the George and White Swan to meet everyone who is left in the area that I know. We had Christmas dinner at Mum and Dad's before travelling back to Solihull and having another Christmas dinner at tea time with the in-laws. I felt stuffed and could have done with playing real tennis instead of the game Richard had for Christmas on the t.v. which I think is called 'Pong'. Opened my presents and they had bought me a beautiful cameo ring. We all had jewellry this Christmas as brother-in-law Malcolm is working in Birmingham's Jewellry Quarter. On Boxing Day the whole family travelled to Southampton for Uncle Clive's engagement party. On the way Richard managed to lose his new gold signet ring in a layby!"

31st December, 1977: **Our old flat was broken into and wedding presents stolen.**
"It was good to have the rest of the week to settle ourselves into the new flat. We went to collect the last of our possessions from the old flat and found that it had been broken into! The stolen items were whisky and wine glasses, bottles of wine, 3 sets of fruit bowls, towels, sleeping bags and architects pens. The worst thing was, that the burglars had made a terrible mess of the walls and doors which we had spent hours painting. Also they had turned the emersion heater on. We took out all the fuses and gave them in at the bank downstairs. Went to the Police Station and reported it all. Today we went to a house for Steve to survey for Sue as she wants to buy it. He had to give her the news that it was falling down. Our end of the year treat was the Old Aston Edwardians New Year's Eve Ball. At midnight we went to another party nearer home, until 2 a.m. It is now 1978!"

1978

7th January 1978: **Our old flat will need boarding up and our new flat has been warmed up by a party**.
"No time to make New Year's Resolutions - last years will have to do. On New Year's Day woke up at midday when the doorbell

rang. Saw Steve's Dad driving off - he had called round to wish us a 'Happy New Year' - whoops! We discovered this when we walked to the telephone box and phoned the parents to wish them the same. The fresh air did us good. On our way back, we noticed the door to our old flat was wide open, so phoned the University Estates Department who are going to have it boarded up. I used the pressure cooker for the first time and so that it didn't blow up, I added too much water. It took ages to come up to pressure and all because I couldn't be bothered to read the instruction booklet properly. Back at work I have looked around the Sales at lunch time and sampled all the perfumes in Rackhams Department Store. This weekend we had a flat warming party and the first guests to turn up were Nicky, Tim and Graham followed by Sandra, Phil, Debbie, Pete and Gail. After 6 bottles of wine and a bottle of whisky, we got to bed around 4 a.m."

15th January, 1978: The Kenwood Chef was yesterday's Kitchenaid Artisan Mixer.

"Steve left the job at Sparkbrook and was presented with a cheque for £5 (weekly wage was about £60). My 25th birthday this week and I wasn't happy being a quarter of a century old. We went for a meal to La Reserve and there was music and dancing. I was most impressed with the present from Steve's parents - a Kenwood Chefette. Spent the weekend in Norwich at Marilyn and Tim's flat. On the car journey there, we had a scary moment when the accelerator pedal jammed - caught up in the car mat! The churches in Norwich were amazing and we finished our tour with a drink at a smart pub called The Gibraltar Arms. Called at my parents on the way home and Steve helped Dad putting roof tiles back on. I was asked to hold the ladder, but didn't put all my weight on it, so it collapsed and Steve fell off the roof! I fell under the collapsed ladder and had more scratches and bruises than Steve! Mum was annoyed with Dad and yanked me indoors!"

2nd February, 1978: The Kalle Infotec office machine and Annie Hall.

"It has snowed heavily this week - 4 inches everywhere. I was only 5 minutes late for work, but others had horrific tales of battling through. Had a night out at the cinema to see Woody Allen's film "Annie Hall". The car has broken down twice and the car battery is permanently on charge in the flat. I was sent on a training morning to learn how to use the Kalle Infotec machine -

it has a console and stores things and calculates and has quite a few coloured flashing lights! Lack of money has prevented evenings out so we stayed in and watched t.v. - Top of the Pops and The Good Life. On other evenings this week I have been staying at work to type student projects for extra cash and Steve is drawing up the plans for an extension for Sylvia my work colleague. Hopefully we should have some extra money soon as we badly need another car - preferably one that breaks down a little less often!"

9th February, 1978: Red lights kept flashing up on the console, when I was deleting, inserting, overloading - the lot!

"Spent one lunch time in the Gaiety Pub and met Steve's colleagues - drank 2 martinis in half an hour and was rather tiddley when I got back to the office. The staff had to be interviewed today by officers concerned with a salary upgrade application for Phyllis. I had more training on the Kalle Infotec machine and then was left to get on with it. I seemed to be deleting, inserting, overloading - the lot. Red lights kept flashing up on the console. By the end of the afternoon I'd put everything right, amazingly! We now have another car - a Ford Cortina, for the sum of £450. The car has been sold off from the company where Dad works."

19th February, 1978: The Ford Cortina is proving to be no more reliable than our old car.

"Lovely smooth drive to Deeping St. James in the Cortina, but the heater doesn't work and it was minus 6 outside! Luckily Mum had a welcoming coal fire roaring away. The next night we were meeting Jane at Peterborough Hospital Social Club and nearly didn't get there as the car's electrics were playing up. As we were about to drive back to Birmingham the near left hand lights were not working - I am fed up with cars! On Wednesday it was Valentine's Day and the postman brought a tax demand for £15 (when wages were £60 a week). I have been going back to the office most evenings this week between 7 and 9.30 p.m. to type Mr Humba's essay. I tried to drive the Cortina myself but it seems such a big wide car and I can hardly see over the steering wheel. Anyway the indicators have stopped working - electrics again! I went out and bought myself the latest fashion - a tweed hacking jacket as a consolation present."

21st February, 1978: After 3 glasses of wine I was making 20 typos per page.
"Flexi-time is being pushed at work but in the meantime, it doesn't help that the temperature is only 48°F. when we get there in the mornings and only warms up to a measly 50°F. all day. I agreed to go to the NALGO buffet lunch with Phyllis on Wednesday to warm up. I thought we might hear more about flexi-time but Phyllis wanted to know more about her chances of salary regrading. The weather turned milder mid week. After work there was a course party on Friday in the lecture theatre. I helped set out food and drink and most of the students and lecturers came in. I was becoming very merry with all the wine and Phyllis was worse. I was talking to the Indian students, mainly and the shrieks of laughter were getting louder with each glass of wine. At 7 p.m. the party broke up and I had to go back to the office to type some more of the student essay. I spent 15 minutes searching for it and once found, I was making 20 mistakes per page!"

3rd March, 1978: Lost on the Edgware Road and a Kentia Palm plant was a fashionable household ornament.
"Each night I have been home at 5.30 p.m. and then back to the office at 7 p.m. typing student essays, projects and theses, until the Porter has thrown me out. This weekend we set off for London at 8 p.m. on Friday night, stopping for a drink to calm our motorway nerves and got lost on the Edgware Road. Arrived in Putney at Dick and Susie's flat at 11.15 p.m. Woke refreshed in the morning but Steve's half of the bed had collapsed! Not sure what fish we had for dinner but every mouthful was full of bones. No-one else was bothered and thought it was delicious! Events at work - we all had a glass of wine at Maureen's 'leaving to have a baby' presentation. We have had a few wedding invitations arrive this week, so today went looking for suitable outfits to wear. I came back with a Kentia Palm plant for the flat!"

12th March, 1978: Selling the old Austin 1300 could be difficult when it refuses to start.
"Popped into the Cabin for a 'swift half' on Saturday before the Aston Villa match. Of course I prefer anything else to football so I went off to the Library to research some more on Handsworth but ended up with a book on Scotland for our holidays this year.

The first computer I ever used.   The Deeping Stage, Market Deeping 1978.

Stood for an hour at the bus stop in the freezing cold, waiting for a bus home. Went out for a quick drink on campus in the evening and ended up talking to Shahrooz and Kiran until 1 a.m. The next day was gloriously sunny and warm. Steve was outside washing our old Austin 1300 with a view to selling it, although it still wouldn't start! I do appreciate our new, modern and warm flat but wish we had a garden to sit out in on days like this. I did manage to fill the flat with smoke while cooking dinner last night. This weekend we were at Mum and Dad's and I drove my Dad's Ford Escort, as I feel I can drive anything now, after our big Ford Cortina. I even managed to park it in the Market Place opposite the Deeping Stage where we had our wedding reception."

21st March, 1978: I called the wrong Mr. Mousavi in for interview - is it such a common name?

"I am reading the book 'Read Better and Faster' but fell asleep and am not sure which page I'm on now, unless perhaps I finished it! At work I made rather a big mistake by calling the wrong 'Mr. Moosavi' for interview! Mr Otache came in with a small essay for me to type and a £1 note. Otherwise I've been battling with the Kalle Infotec machine. This weekend we were in Southampton for Steve's Uncle's wedding. Just outside Andover, we stopped at the Filly Inn and I had a schooner of sherry. Today is the first day of Spring and we had lots of weather - April showers, March winds, sunny intervals and a few flakes of snow. My pork chops in tomato and pepper sauce turned out well. Spent the evening working out our finances and depressingly it looks as if we will not be able to afford a holiday this year unless we get another evening

Uncle Clive's wedding to Dianne.   Sue and Dillon's wedding on a very windy day.

cleaning job."

25th March, 1978: Has Pomagne - cider champagne disappeared, along with Snowball - made with Advocaat?

"Overslept so it was a rush for work. I discussed my lack of finances with Val and then felt depressed for the rest of the morning. I offered to type Claire's questionnaire which was hard to decipher and with lots of tabulation to work out, but the concentration took my mind off everything else. It was Sylvia's birthday so we had a lunchtime drink at the Brown Derby. The next day we were at Sue's wedding presentation and the Pomagne was free flowing. I cooked a meal for Steve's parents and brothers on Good Friday - Coq Au Vin and Fruit Cobbler. Steve's Dad kept complimenting me on the food and gave us £1 each for an Easter present. Easter Saturday was Sue's wedding at Hall Green and the weather was atrocious, so wet and windy that photos had to be abandoned, before Sue's veil ended up on the church spire!"

3rd April, 1978: The last ever Noel Edmonds Breakfast Show on the Radio.

"We had the week off to go to Cardiff for Steve's Part 3 Architect's exams. As it was an early start, I had the radio playing on my lap to keep us awake (car radios were a luxury item). We stayed in the Romford Hotel. I spent my time catching up with old friends in the tea breaks and lunch times, especially Louise and Jackie. On the last morning we listened to Noel Edmonds Breakfast show on the radio, as it was his last one, a sad occasion. Studley Castle provided us with some extra cleaning work, when we got back.

We cleaned all of the walls and floors in the kitchen which took 2 hours. I felt shattered but still had the energy to appreciate the beautiful house and gardens. We had earned £7 but the car headlight bulb had just gone so that cost £6.10. Today we had a cheap and enjoyable afternoon walk to Handsworth Park, Perry Park and back along the River Tame. In the evening I had another Library book to read - 'Rapid Reading made Simple' which worked wonders for my concentration."

9th April, 1978: Dancing on the deck of a boat whilst cruising down the river.

"We were offered an evening cleaning job - all the toilets at Studley Castle College, every night for £35 a week between us. It is only temporary and if we want a holiday we will have to do it. Steve's Dad then told me that I should get our fridge freezer seen to as it is making a strange noise! On the plus side, we went to Worcester, invited by 3 of Steve's work colleagues who he hardly knew. It was a fantastic evening as we were partying on a boat cruising down the river into the night! Drinking in the bar below and dancing on the deck and no one fell over board! I stayed with Jean in Wiltshire this weekend while Steve was helping paint his Dad's boat and he was also surveying his Grandfather's house in Abbotts Ann, Hampshire. Jean and I took Ambrose the dog on some good walks across to Chiseldon Army Camp and along the old railway track. Dinner was nicely cooked in the Rayburn when we got back".

13th April, 1978: The rock-jazz group Funktion was our treat after cleaning 55 toilets this week.

"The sun shone brilliantly through the curtains first thing Monday morning, then mid-morning we had snow blizzards for 2 hours. It didn't stop me shopping for jeans in the lunch hour. I tried a few pairs on and the tighter they were, the sexier I looked! The problem was that I just couldn't move in them, let alone sit down! Also had my hair trimmed and flicked out at the School of Hairdressing. Everybody was so hostile in there except for the extremely pleasant Persian girl who cut my hair. I actually walked out liking my hair for once and gave a £1 tip, although my trainee hairdresser wasn't allowed to take it so I had to give it to the sulky receptionist who didn't even smile. I think they need training in Customer Care. We were cleaning 11 toilets every evening this week so at the weekend appreciated our evening out. We met Malcolm and Marian at the Mercat Cross. The rock-jazz group 'Funktion' were playing and Malcolm's mate Stuart was the guitarist. Marian seemed very young for 29, in her clothes and outlook."

23rd April, 1978: I don't want a washing machine any more, as on Campus the Launderette is next to the Bar.
"Ladders are being made into a wall unit by Steve in his spare time. While he was doing this I sat down with a biscuit and read the daily newspaper. I wish I hadn't as it depressed my whole evening. I read about the butchery and sadism in Rhodesia which made me feel sick and suicidal. I now have some more evening work - a thesis to type for Penny Warnes-Lilley and Steve has some plans to draw up for house alterations. We went for a cheap campus drink to celebrate, taking the Laundry with us as the launderette is next door to the Bar and there is always a collection of empty glasses on top of the washing machines. We met Kiran, Shahrooz and Shankar who always make us laugh. In fact I don't know why I should ever want a washing machine of my own in the flat, I would miss out on a social occasion! This weekend we had 2 cleaning jobs - Saturday at a Wire factory in Tyseley to scrub and seal floors in 3 offices. Quite an easy job and the caretaker made us tea while the floors dried. Today we cleaned offices at a Chrysler garage. It was really hard this time as the dirt was ground in. I had a headache and was too tired to eat or cook. The weather was beautiful and ideal for a walk but we were too tired although happy that we were earning money for a holiday."

1st May, 1978: Our evening meal consisted of a Mars Bar, crisps, cup of tea and a glass of whisky!
"I had to try 3 phone boxes before I found one that worked on Monday night. We needed to sort out arrangements for the weekend - we were cleaning Studley Castle kitchen for Malcolm who was spending the day in France. Also collecting an old van for Francis and Malcolm's disco equipment as it needed delivering to Andy's garage at The Star & Garter pub in West Bromwich! We were in Bristol this weekend but my poor brother Ian was in bed with flu so couldn't come out with us. We called in on Hilly and then John in Clevedon. He wanted to go to the amusements at Weston Super Mare, which I hate, and also it was pouring with rain. Having suffered that, we went back to John's for an evening meal which consisted of a Mars Bar, crisps, cup of tea and a glass of whisky!"

7th May, 1978: The next pressure after marriage - the patter of tiny feet. We did not need to look far to be put off!
"I have been staying at work typing most evenings, but by 9 p.m. I have had enough. Waiting outside for Steve and a lift home I meet the postgraduate students coming out of evening class and they are so friendly towards me and I get offers of a lift home - I am quite touched by this. At the weekend we went to see some friends who have a toddler and I was bracing myself for the 'when are you starting a family' pressure which has suddenly started. Anyway, we needn't have worried as they appeared quite tired and disillusioned. As fast as they clean and decorate the house, the little boy messes it up again. Everything felt sticky. When I left their house, unbeknown to me for quite sometime, I was walking around with a sweet wrapper stuck to my bottom! We are in no hurry to have a sticky house and furniture!"

14th May, 1978: Dreaming of a holiday keeps me motivated to scrub floors!
"Warm balmy evenings just lately and we have been for a few walks after work to take advantage of the light evenings too. Red House Park at Great Barr is a favourite. Even doing the laundry was a pleasure and sitting in the grounds at the campus with a box of washing powder in one hand and a drink from the Bar in the other. Shahrooz and Kiran brought their Palestinian friend along one night and there followed a great debate on religion. We went to the Pictures to see the film 'Close Encounters of the Third Kind'. Saturday we were up early to clean the floors and walls at Studley Castle kitchens. When we arrived at Steve's parents it had been their wedding anniversary the day before and we were supposed to have known that. Anyway we did the cleaning and went back to see the cards and flowers. Today we were up early again to do a 'scrub off' at Hall Green Greyhound Stadium. I used the scrubbing machine which was the easy option and I was day dreaming of our holiday in Scotland."

20th May, 1978: Our next goal has to be a house and garden surrounded by six foot fences!
"The Charter Ball at the University was great and I wore my wedding dress, as the theme was Mexican. We took Malcolm, Marian and Jim with us and danced to the jazz band, rock 'n roll

band and saw Slade, finally. I was deafened by them before we left at 2.30 a.m. Today the weather was beautiful so I decided to sunbathe and read my book in the grounds of the flat. First of all some kids came over asking questions and then when I encouraged them to go off and play, I nearly got hit by a football and run over by a scooter! To add to all that, their parents came over full of friendly apologies. I'm already dreaming of owning a house with a 'private' garden. For now, though I gave up hoping for peace and quiet and went shopping on College Road, buying suntan lotion and mushrooms. In the evening we went to the Dog and Doublet for a drink and walked along the towpath of the canal. We met a boat coming down so helped them through the locks but they got stuck as one of the paddles wouldn't close. It was really dark by then so we went back to the pub and phoned the Lock Keeper."

25th May, 1978: If some of your best friends are male do they go to your hen party? I was invited as a substitute!
"This week we have been to see the film 'Julia' which was good but a little miserable. Also I had been reading about the gross tortures to the Tasmanians by the British in the 1800's and the late night news was full of guerrilla warfare. This left me feeling pretty morbid. At work I have been typing and sending out all the rejection letters. I was sent to the Library by Steve's Granddad to find a book called 'Hunting Lions in the Grand Canyon'. The Librarians had never heard of it. I was out at Sue's hen party last night at Gino's in the shopping centre and then on to the Opposite Lock Club getting accosted twice in the streets on the way. Steve collected me at 12.45 a.m. It seemed strange that Sue was one of his friends and yet I was the one at the Hen Party - I just wondered if men were ever allowed to a Hen party?!"

29th May, 1978: Diving into the icy water of the landscaped gravel pits to cool off causes earache!
"Sue and Fred were married and it was one of the prettiest weddings I've been to. After the wedding party we went off to Julie's party in London held in the basement/crypt of a church. We were supposed to be staying in London but the weather was so hot that we followed Jean and Jane back to Wiltshire instead. The next day we drove behind Jean's friend Chris's sports car to The Tunnel in Cirencester by a canal which was being renovated and quite a beauty spot. After that we went on a rather long drive in the Cotswolds, mainly because Chris got lost. As it was a bank

Sue and Fred's wedding.

Sally, Jane and Jean - the bikini girls in Wiltshire.

holiday we spent Monday at the Cotswolds Water Park (landscaped gravel pits). Steve dived in and enjoyed swimming, but the water was so icy cold that he had earache all afternoon and had to take a couple of codeine and go and lie down. I had uncontrollable shivering so think I had a touch of sunstroke. We are not used to a heat wave on a bank holiday".

2nd June, 1978: Jean, Jane and myself as the Bikini Girls in Wiltshire.
"The scorching bikini weather continued and I daren't sunbathe anymore at lunch time as I was already sunburnt from the weekend. Instead I went out and bought some picnic things which I thought may change the weather, but hoped not. Sure enough there were rather scary thunderstorms when we were cleaning, out at Studley Castle. The lightning and immediate crashing thunder made me too hysterical to eat the delicious salad I had made. To make matters worse, we couldn't clean the place properly as no-one, not even the management staff or caretakers had the keys to the cleaners' cupboard! The storm hasn't made the slightest bit of difference to the temperature at work in the office - today it was 35°F!"

16th June, 1978: It was so hot that I drove the car wearing only my bikini.
"Steve broke the car aerial whilst trying to fix the car radio. We stayed at my parents last weekend and I was so hot that I offered to take Gem the dog to Nine Bridges to give her a shampoo and set in the shallow river there. Drove in my bikini with all the

windows open and both Gem and I got in the stream. I threw a few sticks so that she wasn't aware that she was being cleaned. I checked the grassy banks around as I know she likes to go and rub herself into anything dead or rotting, to disguise her smell apparently! It wasn't long before dark clouds came over and the wind started howling so we left before the storm. This weekend we were cleaning Burco's, a Black Country factory - uncontrollably dirty and old. It didn't take long to clean really, as there was no way of getting it spotless. We only have this job for five nights, thankfully."

28th June, 1978: Canal aqueduct over the River Tame and pub skittles.
"We went to Minworth and walked along the canal to Curdworth. In the evening a coach was laid on for the Public Sector Management staff and students for a night out at the Queen's Arms in Redditch to play skittles which was great fun. I bought 2 singles - Carly Simon 'You Belong to Me' and Blue Oyster Cult 'Don't Fear the Reaper'. Another towpath walk from Tamworth to Fazeley junction which took us along an aqueduct over the River Tame. When we got back from this walk the World Cup Final was on TV between Argentina and Holland. Today I went to a NALGO recruitment lunch and I wish I hadn't bothered as they seemed determined to want to recruit me because I mentioned the word 'flexitime'!"

7th July, 1978: The new manager gave us a talk and then we were told to ignore everything he said!
"Well, I managed to lock the car keys in the car this week while we were at the Queen's home in Sandringham. I don't think she was in residence. We had to call the AA. At work it has been a week of 'Viva Voce' (oral exams) and Board of Examiners Day so the office has been busy. There was time left over on Friday for the staff to go and see Nelson House, the new Management Centre building, but we were there longer than was interesting and getting cold. We had a talk by Barry Lewis who is the new Manager and that made me fed up. When he had gone Mr. Nicholls came marching into our office and told us to ignore everything Barry Lewis said and that we should only take notice of Phyllis otherwise he would come down with a heavy hand! He turned to me and said that I was too weak and willing taking on anyone's work! The next day he had calmed down and called the others into the office but not me! It all gave me a headache and to

alleviate the stress I started 'disco fever' dance classes this week - Saturday Night Fever - John Travolta style. When I went to the phone box for my weekly chat with my parents, my poor Mum was in bed with a migraine attack, brought on by Dad going for an interview for a job in Saudi Arabia!"

27th July, 1978: French erotic cinema at its best but I only appreciated the artwork!

"The Roman town of Wall is just a tiny village now but we enjoyed looking at the excavations of the camp and continued our walk to a disused canal. It was 'moving week' at work and the 18th July was the day we would have to start remembering to go to a new building every morning! Our desks, furniture and office equipment went on the van and the staff walked down Corporation Street to Gosta Green and waited. We had to eat our lunch standing up in the new kitchen area, nothing to sit on. Our furniture arrived at 3 pm. and has been put in a lecture room. In the evening we saw the film 'Bilitis' - rubbish story but a well presented film - like one whole David Hamilton poster. At my dance class tonight we were taught the 'tango hustle'. My brother Ian had been in Birmingham for a job interview and was disappointed when it wasn't offered to him".

30th July, 1978: Gretna Green and the mock wedding ceremony.

"We were on our way to Scotland for 2 weeks holiday - a reward for all the evening and weekend cleaning work we had done. Our first night's stop was at Gretna Green - perfect for a 1st wedding anniversary celebration. We went to Gretna Hall and got involved in a mock marriage at the Blacksmith's Shop. I was bridesmaid and Steve the best man. An official photo was taken as a souvenir for us all to buy. Back on the road we got stuck behind loads of caravans but reached Ardrossan in time to squeeze on to the ferry to the Isle of Arran. Our hotel bedroom in Brodick overlooked the sea. Spent the evening in the Hotel Bar - very cosy too with a fire in the grate which was needed, despite being the height of summer - this is Scotland after all! Steve was working his way through the fine selection of malt whiskies behind the Bar. The Landlord was giving him the history and description of each one. Approximately half way through I had to help him up the stairs to bed where he fell into a deep sleep or rather passed out!"

2nd August, 1978: Mull of Kintyre, oh mist rolling in from the sea, my desire is always to be here…..
"Lamlash Bay, Whiting Bay and Blackwaterfoot were places we stopped at on our tour around the island. I was quite surprised that the pubs are open all day. I needed a cup of tea by the time we got to Lochranza. This was the place we caught the ferry from to Kintyre and we gave two girls a lift to Campbelltown. They had heavy rucksacks with them. We booked ourselves into a hotel and the car into a garage, as the car needed attention. Later we drove around the Mull of Kintyre listening to Paul McCartney's song. We had a look for his cottage the next day, but the locals are very loyal and guarded as to where he lives! Next stop was Oban and we were booked into a very pretty terraced guest house. The town itself seemed to be choked with traffic. We booked tickets to see 'Step Ye Gaily' at Curran Halls. The best part of the day was climbing up to McCaig's tower in the evening sun which was beautiful."

4th August, 1978: Our McDonalds escaped the massacre as they were out sheep stealing at the time!
"It poured with rain as we set off for Glencoe - very apt, as it is known as the 'Valley of Weeping'. The McDonald clan were massacred here by the Campbells in 1692. Most hotels with their beautiful tartan carpets have notices up at Reception 'No hawkers and no Campbells'! I am sure they would not turn paying guests away, as this is Scotland! Anyway it is lucky that I have McDonald blood in my veins! We walked along the valley in the rain, but it stopped conveniently at tea time and being on a tight budget, we bought fish and chips at Kinlochleven and washed our hands in a stream. Had coffee back at the hotel and played with the hotel cat. Today we had haggis for breakfast and set off for Fort William in the rain and mist. We are using the Tourist Information Service 'Book a Bed Ahead' scheme. We do not get to choose our accommodation but it is always guaranteed and waiting for us. Today's B & B was someone's spare bedroom in a modern house on a housing estate!"

6th August, 1978: The white sands of Morar and the ferry strike.
"After a very large breakfast we set off for Loch Morar and the white sands. The clouds began to clear so we saw the gorgeous scenery in the sunshine. Booked a bed ahead at a remote place

called Elgol on the Isle of Skye, the south west coast. The guest house had very reasonable rates, tremendous value until you took the petrol costs into account, as it was a long way. Beautiful sunset on our evening walk along the rocky coastline. We had breakfast with some very pleasant German guests the next day. Set off to tour Skye but I wasn't that impressed - the scenery was just mountains and green hills. The lochs broke the monotony but the foreshore was all mud and that awful bladderwrack weed. Looked around Dunvegan Castle and then arrived at Kyleakin. It was cold, wet and windy by then, but we got a good hotel at extremely low rates due to the ferry strike. Saw some beautiful views around Kylerhea but forgot to take my camera!"

9th August, 1978: Beautiful sandy bays but cold - is Thurso gaelic for hypothermia?
"After 135 miles of travelling along a lot of single track roads and seeing the spectacular Eilean Donan castle, we arrived at Poolewe. The weather was awful so we motored on to Ullapool - a very picturesque fishing village. The car wouldn't start in the morning and the AA found the trouble which was 'closed points' so we were soon on our way again. Reached the north coast of Scotland with its beautiful sandy bays - too cold to enjoy them. Had a meal in Thurso and then reached John O'Groats - it was bleak! Oil rigs could be seen rising out of the murkiness. We stayed at a B&B in Wick, a pleasant but drab town. Today we were up early and the weather hadn't improved, so dull and cold, remaining at 12°C all day. Drove to Glen Glas where my branch of the McDonald family are supposed or originate from, but found nothing to resemble a village, just wooded glades. Perhaps the 'clearances' took care of that!"

10th August, 1978: Princess Anne calls at my Granddad's shop!
"Inverness is a lovely place, some fine buildings. Saw the film 'The Massacre of Glencoe' which explained a lot. Drove on to the Culloden Moor battlefield. Scotland seemed to attract battles, massacres and clearances! Braemar had a different feel being one of Scotland's highest villages. We eventually arrived in Blairgowrie to see my Granddad. He runs the Post Office and Swiss Cheese shop with my step Grandma Hanny who is from Switzerland. Princess Anne has called at the shop to buy their Swiss cheese on her way back from Balmoral. We met up with Mum, Dad, Ian and the dog Gem. Dad looked thinner after his

Gretna Green.   White Sands of Morar.   Blairgowrie Post Office.

bout of pleurisy. Called in on a few more Aunts and Uncles, ate haggis and neeps for dinner and spent an evening at a hotel where Uncle Tommy was playing the drums in his band. We slept in the caravan that my parents were staying in. There were not enough bed clothes and we were cold in the night. Steve had an idea - a tip from his camping nights with the Scouts. We put newspaper between the thin blankets. It was slightly warmer but noisy when you turned over!"

14th August, 1978: We must have travelled about 2000 miles so the car coped quite well!

"Took the chair lift to Glenshee today and had to leave Mum at the caravan with Gem as she gets car sick on the winding roads. Rather cold on top of the mountains. A visit to Pitlochry in the evening to see the salmon jumping and a beautiful sunset. This morning we woke up to the sound of rain pounding on the caravan roof. We were driving to Redding near Falkirk to see Uncle Ken. The car overheated and the AA put a new hose on, but said we may need the 'Relay Service' to get us home. Anyway, the car did not let us down and we were home at midnight which was a relief. I was disappointed that the first ten of our photos hadn't turned out. We had a day to recover and unpack and then back to work and evening cleaning. I had to remember to go to the new Management Centre building. Everything had been unpacked from the move and I had a desk by one of the sloping windows. There wasn't much light and the room felt cold and damp. At lunch time I had lunch with Steve in the Cross Guns which warmed me up."

21st August, 1978: I was having a good week until my Dad was rushed to hospital!
"On Monday I was invited to Egbert Bhatty's student flat with Shep from Zimbabwe, for lunch. Egbert cooked us a traditional curry. I was slightly late as I'd waited for 40 minutes outside the wrong flat! Anyway the food was delicious and the conversation fascinating. Tuesday I had lunch with Yvonne and John Churchill and we sat outside at the Pot 'O Beer overlooking the demolition of the Brewery. In the evening we were just about to have dinner when Steve's parents came round to say my Dad was in hospital hemorrhaging blood from his lungs. I was really worried so we set off for Peterborough Hospital. We couldn't see him until Saturday and he looked so ill and was breathless. Apparently he has small clusters of clots in his lungs and is now on blood thinning medication. He vows he will give up smoking! Today he seemed so much better and nearly back to his normal self."

31st August, 1978: More hospital drama - brother-in-law Richard this time to have his appendix out!
"I had to kill all the spiders around my desk before I could start work which made me slightly hysterical. I stayed late to type Mr. Otache's project. Cooked dinner, watched Top of the Pops and cleaned up the flat a bit. Just as well that I did as we had a visit from Steve's Mum, Aunty Marj and Malcolm. August Bank Holiday week started with my Uncle Colin and Aunty Sheila's 25th wedding anniversary party. Dad is still in hospital, bored and wants to escape which is a good sign. We had to go to Poole for the launching of Steve's Dad's new boat 'Alanjo' but the mast needed putting together. To make matters worse Steve's younger brother Richard was taken to hospital and had his appendix out. We travelled home to feed my in-laws cats. Back to work this week and today we had a free lunch and drink in the Centre's Dining Room - a practice run for the first of the residential courses."

12th September, 1978: Great Aunty Violet - 1895 - 1978.
"Still looking after the cats at Steve's parents house. I had several flea bites, and when I was closing the curtains, a huge spider was climbing up! I made a delicious salad while we were there, using the tomatoes from the plants in Steve's office. I have worked

My office behind one the slanting windows of the Management Centre

Great Aunty Violet, Uncle Jack and Freddie Day.

hard in typing the body of Mr. Otache's project and now have the diagrams, tables and bibliography to finish. Two presents have come my way this week, a tablecloth from Soodi and a Mexican charm, from a student who wanted to be accepted on the course! I heard that my Great Aunty Violet had died. It still brings tears to my eyes when I think of her only child, son Freddie being accidentally killed aged 7, in 1926. He was knocked off his bicycle by the Baker's van reversing. Whenever she saw a little boy around the same age she would cry, even into her 80's."

23rd September, 1978: Val's days are numbered at work as she is at loggerheads with the boss!

"Feeling quite important at work with people sitting around my desk wanting information and a personal and private letter was handed to me from Mr. Tan. It took a lot of detailed explaining, but I now think I have Carlos Olivera sorted out. Val and Mr. Nicholls were at each other's throats about the partition in our office, a large space which has been converted from a lecture room. Whilst all this was going on, Phyllis was trying to show me her holiday brochure, enthusing and recommending Majorca. In the evening, at my 'Saturday Night Fever' dance class, brother-in-law Malcolm came along and was the comedian for the night, making us all laugh. Poor Steve had been to a meeting after work and was shouted at which was very upsetting after he does his best for the residents."

30th September, 1978: 'McDonald of Glencoe' malt whisky loosens the tongue somewhat!

"The dentist was using gas to knock Steve out while an abscess in his mouth was drained, so I needed to leave work to go with him. After pain and sleepless nights it was a relief for him to get it treated and he is now back to his normal self. In the evening at my in-laws I think I drank a little too much of the malt whisky, 'McDonald of Glencoe', which we brought back as a present from Scotland. I was arguing that the RIBA (Royal Institute of British Architects) membership fee of £44 per year (now £393) was a rip off, when after all, it was just a glorified knitting club. By the look on everyone's face I was not making a good impression and perhaps I can justify my comments as 'the drink talking'! Yesterday, I went to the Typewriter Centre at lunch time, the other end of town, to buy a portable electric typewriter which was so heavy to carry back to the office. It is to use at home to type student projects and when I switched it on, it sounded rather noisy. Overslept today and was not on top of my work but Mark Oakley cheered me up when he brought me some runner beans. Tonight we went to the Halfway House in Sutton Coldfield and on to Steve boss's party. A very friendly crowd but I needed rescuing from a woman who was talking to me in great detail about pregnancy!"

5th October, 1978: I thought the pistachio nut had tasted strange - it seems I've eaten half a maggot!

"Deeping St. James is such a pretty village in the Lincolnshire Fens, so spending a weekend there at my parents, once a month is such a pleasure. At work I was eating pistachio nuts - a present from Mr. Seyed-Hassani until I found half a maggot in one of them. I must have eaten the other half so spent the rest of the afternoon waiting for symptoms of poisoning! The day started to get very hectic. My mother-in-law phoned to ask us to clean Studley kitchens on Saturday morning, a student called Secundus came in with a very thick project for me to type up and Marilyn and Tim were supposed to be staying the weekend. At that point, I took the phone off the hook, and decided to open the bottle of Grappa - another student present. Val and I forgot our problems after a glass or two!"

12th October, 1978: A VIP lunch and then typing student projects until 2 a.m.
"Enrolment and twelve students failed to turn up. Had lunch with Steve at Baskerville House - the Architects Department of Birmingham City Council. Felt like a VIP, waitress service, subsidised meals in a beautiful 1940's Dining Hall - and this was just the staff canteen! Poor Steve couldn't enjoy it as he was miles away and harassed by meetings. Dance class in the evening was even merrier as Malcolm brought along his friends Francis and David. Saturday consisted of cleaning Studley kitchens, afternoon tea at the in-laws and tackling Mr. Otache's project on my new portable electric typewriter all evening until midnight. Yesterday brought a lovely fat cheque from Henry Otache but I needed to take a day's leave to meet the deadline. Today I started typing at 8.30 a.m. and by 11.30 a.m. I was tired, making mistakes and finally finished at 2 a.m. I never want to see another project!"

14th October, 1978: A nostalgic weekend in Cardiff.
"A weekend in Cardiff for Steve's final exam - we hope. He was nervous but I was rather looking forward to enjoying myself, and I did. Walking through crisp Autumn leaves, I started at the YWCA hostel and then visited other old haunts. Called in to see Vi the hairdresser and Bobby who hadn't seen me for 2 years. At the Students Union I was talking to a 2nd year student who had heard about me! By now I expected my reputation to have died down! Had afternoon tea in Circles (Howell's Department Store) as Marilyn and I had done many a time. I bumped into Wenda and her husband in there, who were newly married. Met Steve and Dick after their exam and they were both happy so we celebrated eating and drinking at the Wimpy Bar, the Students Union, the Buccaneer and the Traveller's Rest."

18th October, 1978: My portable typewriter has burnout problems due to excessive use!
"We had a violent rainstorms which left a misty Autumn day and wondered what to do. Drove to Llanbradach to see Louise and David but they were out. Carried on to Monmouth stopping for lunch at the new Raglan services. Richard and Jackie have moved to a remote place near Monmouth so we drove on to see them. They were having an afternoon nap when we arrived, but I think they were pleased to see us. We were shown their beautiful stone house surrounded by 5 acres of land. It was a great

weekend, but back to work yesterday and at lunch time I had to take my portable typewriter back to the shop to be fixed. I was told that it wasn't to be used 4 to 5 hours a day as an office machine, which is how I had been using it! Today was not a healthy diet day. The Catering Manager took us to her flat at lunch time for wine and cheese to celebrate her birthday. After work I had the same - cheese and wine reception for the students. Must have a healthier diet tomorrow."

28th October, 1978: Another hen night......another wedding!

"We went to see the long awaited film 'Grease' and the queue outside the cinema went on forever. We waited nearly an hour. It was worth it though. I expected the film to be overrated but no - the music, fashions and comedy were great. I had more typing to do before I could go to bed. On Sunday a family party at the in-laws for Richard's birthday turned into Saturday Night Fever Dance lessons as everyone liked the demonstration Malcolm and I were persuaded (forced) into doing. I still had to type when I got home and fell into bed at 2.30 a.m. I was at Gail's hen party this week starting at the Night & Day pub and finishing at Mr. Moon's nightclub. Steve was with Fred at Pete's stag night. The wedding took place today between Pete and Gail, glorious day and beautiful church service. We were not expecting a six course meal at the reception and because of this I couldn't move from the table. This was a shame, as I couldn't get away from the conversations all about football!"

15th November, 1978: The start of the severe winter of 1978-79.

"House hunting in Handsworth Wood and a sherry reception in the Private Residential Lounge for the Public Sector Management. Evening entertainment: Steve brought the slide projector home from work and I had a slide show of Aston and some of my own slides from Cardiff. Lunch times seemed to be spent queuing in banks. A nervous Steve for an oral exam which I think is the last exam for Part 3 Architecture, but that is what I thought last time. It was in Cardiff and he couldn't eat breakfast before he left. The course is 7 years and you have to be determined and dedicated to qualify as an Architect. Yesterday the results came through the post and he had passed. We celebrated at the Duck and the Plough and Harrow on the Hagley Road before going on to look at some houses for sale in Great

Barr. The temperature has plummeted to minus 10 and it is rather windy with things banging about."

18th November, 1978: My shortcomings in the workplace have yet to be recognised by the boss!
"All the advertisements in the newspaper for management courses is paying off - lots of interest and work generated - the Management Centre is expanding and more staff needed. We went for a test drive in a Volvo 343 which was very impressive and expensive. Heated seats on some models which is appealing although my brother didn't know about this whilst accepting a lift in a Volvo - he thought his trousers were on fire! We looked at a house for sale in Shirley, but the doors were warped and it had a monstrously tatty extension/lean to on the side. More house hunting in Kings Norton and Solihull. I am a glutton for punishment as I took on more project typing. Unrest at work as Mr. Nicholls has called everyone into his office one by one to give them a list of their faults - apart from me! In fact he came to me and I was ready for him, but with a very humble manner he apologised for giving me a small amount of work! I wasn't aware that I was a 'favourite'!"

24th November, 1978: We took the bread rolls home and drank the wine.
" We are having to work through drilling and sawing noises at work as a partition is being put together. On our way back from the dance class Malcolm and I had to go to my in-laws dinner party and give a 'Saturday Night Fever' dance demonstration. It was most embarrassing being the 'party piece'. More Estate Agents and house hunting with a promising 1960's semi-detached in Olton. It was empty having been repossessed by the Building Society. Today in the office I was being told by one boss to type the exam results and told NOT to by another boss. I do wish they would talk to each other. I had a can of cider at lunch time with my sandwiches, so that I didn't care. Today there was more unrest and Sylvia is talking about leaving. Val and I found some food left over from a meeting, so we took the bread rolls home and drank the wine!"

1st December, 1978: It was news to Jane and I that cars needed antifreeze!
"Jane stayed for the weekend and Steve kindly put antifreeze in her car and discovered the radiator was broken! She then had to

go back to Peterborough on the train. A new radiator would cost £40, but she didn't seem alarmed. The good news was that the house in Langley Hall Road, Olton, was ours, subject to contract. At last we will have our own garden. The office saga continues and Val has had enough and handed her notice in! She spent the rest of the day feeling miserable as she doesn't really want to leave but feels she is being treated as 'deadwood' to be cut from the staff. I was called in to see Mr. Nicholls and thought 'here we go - my turn to face my faults', but no, he just wanted to tell me about the re-arrangement of the office. I must admit, I didn't take a lot of notice as the atmosphere is not pleasant at the moment. Whilst out at lunch time, to cheer myself up, I bought the record 'Lydia' by Dean Friedman."

12th December, 1978: 'Forditis' was the diagnosis from the AA man.

"It has been so cold that the engine doesn't warm up enough to make the heater work in the car, so the two hour drive to my parents wasn't the best journey. On Sunday night the car wouldn't start at all and the AA man said it was due to 'Forditis' - damp and cold engine! I am typing a thesis and a project in the flat and my fingers are too cold to work properly. I need some of those fingerless gloves that the market traders use. We had a day in Cardiff for Steve to survey a site in Butetown for an architectural competition. I should have stayed at the flat typing really but at least I got Christmas cards and letters written on the car journey. Typed when I got home and today I was paid £56, but still more to do."

18th December, 1978: I was ill in bed when prospective buyers were being given a tour of our flat!

"On the way to work the car overheated and we had to stop at Newtown. This time a hose was broken. I had to walk the rest of the way to work and was late. Marilyn phoned to say her brother Edward had got engaged to Sheila. Helped out at the degree congregation, pouring out sherry, but then had to wash up 300 glasses! Came down with a bad cold so was swigging Benylin from the bottle and felt too shivery and achey to go to work so took to my bed. I was fast asleep when Steve had to show some prospective buyers around our flat and into the bedroom! I felt too ill to care though! This morning I changed my medication to 'Lemsips' and by this evening I was on 'hot toddies'. I need to get better for tomorrow as it is Val's leaving presentation. She is already upset to learn that she is being replaced by 2 juniors!"

23rd December 1978: I recovered just in time for the Christmas partying!

"Steve brought me some Lucozade and Complan for breakfast in the hope I'd have the energy to get to work. I made it, and Val's presentation was ironically given by the man who wanted her to leave. We had bought her a set of cut-glass drinks glasses. All very sad really. I managed to make it to Steve's office Christmas party as they had hired Malcolm to be the deejay. Yesterday there was a bus strike and it was snowing, so the streets were deserted when they should have been packed with Christmas shoppers! It was our office disco and Christmas party too this week in the evening over at the Main Building. Mr. Nicholls insisted on dancing 'disco fever' dances with me, which was most embarrassing! As usual we had to divide the Christmas holiday between the two families. The first half with my Mum and Dad and after a big meal, getting warm in front of their fire we set off for the Greenkeeper, collecting Diane and Julie on the way. We met up with Jean, Jane, Fran, David Dave, Weasel, Corrinne and Moira to go to a party in Park Road."

30th December, 1978: Mum fell asleep between courses!

"We had our Christmas dinner on Christmas Eve with Mum and Dad which sobered me up after drinking sherry at Grandma's and apple wine and Chivas Regal whisky at Uncle Angus's. Mum fell asleep between courses! We went to midnight mass at Deeping St. James church which was beautiful by candlelight. Christmas Day on the roads was a delight, we only saw a handful of people about, usually dog walkers, wearing Christmas cracker paper hats and after all the sherry and wine hoping the the dog knew the way home! Christmas dinner again at Steve's parents, and the car which had behaved itself gave up outside their house! The next day we walked to Sue and Fred's and noticed 2 sports cars outside and 3 young men inside the house. I felt a mess, as I thought we were only going to see Sue and Fred! I cooked Steve's parents and brothers a meal which was a success apart from the croquette potatoes. I nearly didn't go to dance class with Malcolm because of the threat of terrorist bombs and central Birmingham is a good target. We went and survived. Tonight we watched the remake of 'Brief Encounter' 1974 with Richard Burton and Sophia Loren. Somehow the diesel trains, instead of steam trains and streetwise actors ruined the innocence from that very different era."

11th January, 1979: A new year, a new house (hopefully).
"We were out at Allied Carpets when the car radiator sprung a leak! The snow was thick on the ground but the car got us home. At work a new junior started and Val came in to collect the rest of her belongings. Sad state of affairs. My workload has increased so much that I've only been able to take a 10 minute lunch break. I have three course organisers who dictate letters, memos, timetables, course programmes etc. I don't know which to do first. Sometimes I get nothing done with all the student enquiries either in person or on the phone. A year ago I would have been given help but mentioning this to Phyllis brings flippant remarks and sarcasm. Perhaps they want me to leave too!"

21st January, 1979: The second oil crisis which means no petrol again!
"My 26th birthday was one of the best I'd say. Everything was perfect apart from my problems at work. I had the day off so we ordered carpets and went to the Duck for a drink. Apart from that we couldn't go far as there was no petrol to be had. Instead we kept warm in the flat and drew up a floor plan for furniture in the new house. I had the week off to move which happened to be the coldest of the year. Of course, the heating in the house didn't work and after several days of waiting in for gas, water and electricity engineer, we are at last warm. Steve started smashing up the kitchen and whilst putting up new wall cabinets he drilled through a live electric wire. We then had no lights downstairs! The good news is that we have a garden with a tumbledown shack at the end. This was described in the Estate Agent's brochure as a fashionable gazebo!"

14th February, 1979: All work and no play drives me to booking a holiday!
"I went back to work and I couldn't see my desk for the files piled high! Steve had an enjoyable day tobogganing in the snow outside his Aston office! In my precious spare time, I've been cleaning at Studley, typing for Mr Otache and pulling and scraping wallpaper off the living room walls. We went to the Ring 'O Bells garage in Hampton in Arden to talk about the Volvo 343. Birmingham City Council are offering cheap car loans for essential car users. I have managed to collect a whole load of

71 Langley Hall Road, our new house and Christiane.  | Back garden and plum tree from the 'fashionable gazebo'.  | Our brand new Volvo car - no more push starting cars.

holiday brochures and quite fancied Jesolo in Italy. Viv put me off as she has been there and says it is like Blackpool only better weather! Instead I am thinking of Yugoslavia and we would be flying for the first time ever! Yesterday, I finally got on top of my work and even managed to tidy my drawer. Snow has kept the course organisers away so they will have a mountain of work for me, come the thaw!"

18th February, 1979: Our parents' generation fail to appreciate contemporary interior house decor.

"The snow has been so bad that I slipped over twice this week on my way to the bus stop. A man came to help me up and slipped over next to me, and it made me giggle, but the poor man didn't share my amusement. When I got home the washing machine and tumble dryer had arrived and I feel we are so lucky! Mum and Dad had been cut off for 2 days, as all the roads out of their village were blocked with snow, at least they can keep in touch by phone. The roads have been cleared here and I know that, because, we were in the middle of our dinner when the in-laws came round. We live much nearer to them now and I wonder if it is a good thing! Acocks Green, up the road, is a good place for building societies and ironmongers, so we didn't have to go far on Saturday which gave us more time for putting hessian up on one wall. My mother-in-law is quite shocked that we are decorating our lounge with sacking cloth. The other wall has the newsprint wallpaper as we still had a spare roll left. It all looks good with our Dewar's Whisky pub mirror."

5th March, 1979: We have the luxury of a garden, so need a lawn mower.
"The fashionable tumbledown gazebo at the bottom of the garden has got to go. After buying a lawn mower we cut the lawns and then I bought a deckchair in anticipation of spring and the weather promptly turned to snow - again! Nearly didn't get home as the car wouldn't start for ages. I have had to call in sick at work with a really bad cold and Sylvia phoned back to say that the pressure of my workload is being discussed and something must be done about it! After that, I was quite pleased that I had a rotten cold! Every cloud has a silver lining! I took my bottle of Night Nurse with me to Mum and Dad's for the weekend. We ventured out to see all the new housing, shops and schools around Orton Goldhay as part of Peterborough new town, and all the new buildings at Perkins Engines where my Dad has worked for years. My Mum also worked in the offices there and me too during the college holidays. Change is happening really quickly and with the London overspill people moving in, I wonder if the local accents will be replaced by cockney rhyming slang!"

28th March, 1979: Situations Vacant!
"We went to the Architect's dinner dance and we were the youngest ones there. I made Moussaka and Ratatouille this week as I am becoming quite adventurous in the kitchen. On the way to work I decided to apply for jobs at Birmingham University as the atmosphere in the office is not good and everyone is fed up. I was amused when I got to my desk as on my name plate the letters had been rearranged to spell 'Sal's Orgy'! We cooked a meal for Steve's parents and brothers this weekend. When they had gone I got the job application forms out and filled one in for a job at the Information Office of Birmingham University. Today, while no-one was around I rang Birmingham University to get an application form for the Dental School's Admission Secretary's post. It is a higher grade so a better salary. Now I wonder where I will be working this time next year!"

9th April, 1979: I stood looking at the Dental School and wondering if I would be working there.
"I went for my interview at Birmingham University but was not impressed. I would not be gaining anything. Saturday morning we spent on an office clean in the city centre and rewarded ourselves in the evening at the pictures to see 'An Unmarried

Woman'. The film was showing at the Metropole Hotel which is very posh. Steve has been working very hard on 'foreigners' - drawing up building plans mainly for house extensions. Midweek I was given a date for an interview at Birmingham University's Dental School, the Admissions Secretary post. I don't feel all that hopeful, but still went to look at the the Dental Hospital, behind the General Hospital in my lunch hour. Today I was there and interviewed well - I feel I gave a good impression and may be in with a chance. When I got home I began to think about it and got a headache!"

21st April, 1979: The job is mine - Admissions Secretary at Birmingham Dental School!

"At the beginning of the week I had a phone call at work to say I'd got the job at the Dental School! The salary is £3,333 p.a., more than I'm getting now, so I would have to take it. Gave in my notice the next day and it didn't even cause a stir! The new junior was giving Phyllis a lot of aggravation and no doubt I will be replaced by a junior and I think Phyllis will be the next one to leave! Anyway, I forgot about work as it was Easter weekend and I enjoyed myself at Mum and Dad's . Steve and I did the tourist trail around Stamford and we went to see an old college friend who I was bridesmaid for. She had a lovely little family - baby and toddler and yet her husband has run off with the barmaid from the Tally-Ho Inn! We saw Jean in the evening and she told us all about her sensational adventures in Australia and brought us back a boomerang!"

9th May, 1979: One door closes and another opens - exciting times!

"I went to see my new boss at the Dental School who gave me the Admissions Secretary's notes to read and asked me to go to lunch next week to meet the Course Organisers! In the evening I read the notes and felt quite appalled at everything that is expected of me. Back in my old job, I have had work taken off me now that I am leaving! Midweek I came down with a rotten cold, my nose wouldn't stop running and I had to meet a lot of new people for my new job. I dosed myself up with Contac 400 and felt quite spaced out! I think the lunch meeting went well! I am writing this on the 4th May, and Margaret Thatcher has become the first woman Prime Minister for Britain. Yesterday was my penultimate day at Aston University and the work was still piling up only now I couldn't care less! My last day today started badly with a 3 page letter dictated by one course organiser plus a mountain of other stuff, all needed by the end of the day! I opened and started one of the bottles of wine I had bought for my leaving presentation. I did like the Purbeck Pottery dinner service that was given to me. In the end I just had to leave the work for someone else!"

12th May, 1979: I need to be more 'well travelled' apparently!

"Five days leave before starting my new job and I was bogged down with typing at home - a project and a Ph.d thesis. I had a break to go to the Library to try and find out about Langley Hall Farm which our street was named after. One of the buildings is still there as part of the Working Mens Club at the end of the road. At the weekend we went shopping for a cheap bed but only found an expensive one we liked. On Saturday evening we were invited to Martin's party which was full of social workers. It became clear at this social event that if you hadn't been to America, then you were a nobody! I have only ever been on a day trip to Calais, a week in Knokke, Belgium with my friend Helen and Jersey, if you can count the Channel Holidays as 'abroad'. I obviously need to catch up with the travelling experience and we will be starting this summer by 'flying for the first time' to Yugoslavia. I don't think anyone was particularly impressed!"

24th May, 1979: Walking the canal towpaths is so relaxing.

"Such a hot sunny day when I started my new job in School Office at the Dental Hospital and it all went well - perhaps I've got the horrors to come. At lunch time I walked to the Management Centre to collect some more Ph.d typing. The rest of the week seemed very uncomplicated too so I am just waiting for the difficult times. I am sure there is a lot to learn. I did the 'juniors' job today as there was nothing much to do and Deirdre, the junior, had fallen down the stairs and hurt her leg. It took me nearly all day to take the post round as I kept getting lost and I am still trying to learn who everyone is. I suppose this is the best way to find out. The stress reliever day of the week is Sundays and our walks along the towpath of the Grand Union Canal. We will soon be reaching Warwick."

11th June, 1979: We have a brand new car!

"My French penfriend Christiane, who I started writing to aged

14, turned up with her husband Alain this weekend. They are lovely but talking in broken English and French is quite exhausting. They have had to amuse themselves while we have been at work. Our new Volvo car arrived so Steve was extremely happy especially as we have never had a brand new car before. It has an automatic gearbox for city driving which should make life easier along with the fact that it shouldn't break down. We tried it out by taking Alain and Christiane to Warwick Castle in the rain then on to Stratford. Back at work today and we were unable to send any letters out because of the bombs at the Royal Mail sorting office!"

24th June, 1979: The Crooked House and it took a lot of convincing Mum that it was safe to go inside!

"It is five years ago since I left home to live in Cardiff. I was pondering over this at the Dentists and was told I have a good set of teeth and no fillings at all! Sylvia left the Management Centre today so I went over at lunch time for her 'leaving do'. I heard mutterings that the place was going to be renamed 'The Mis-Management Centre'. Sue and I have been sunbathing at lunch times in the churchyard of St. Phillips' Cathedral in the centre of town. This weekend we took Mum and Dad to the Crooked House pub in the Black Country at Himley near Dudley. I assured Mum that the pub has been made safe from the mining subsidence. There are many optical illusions inside including glasses slowly sliding across 'level' tables and a marble appearing to roll uphill."

1st July, 1979: The wedding ring test prompted by a another announcement!

"Open Day for the Dental School on Monday and the next day we had to go to a fire film and lecture to do with Health and Safety training. The train home to Olton station was delayed as there was a rail dispute. The whole George family went out to the Tom 'O the Wood pub on Malcolm's 21st birthday, the bigger party being held at the Greswolde in Knowle on Saturday night for the extended family. Jane, in the office, announced she was pregnant so that prompted the 'wedding ring' test. This test involves threading a wedding ring onto a thread or piece of hair. Hold the dangling ring over the pregnant belly of mum-to-be while she is lying down. If the ring swings back and forth like a pendulum, she is carrying a boy. If the ring swings in a strong circular motion, she is carrying a girl. No hard science supports this test beyond wishful thinking! They tried it on me and apparently I will give birth to a girl in 12 months time! Met my friend Barbara at lunch time and as usual her conversation was detailed trivia and no interest in any other topics. This weekend we went on a canal boat trip to Spon Lane. It was cold though and the other passengers were rowdy. Our canal towpath walk around Lapworth was the prettiest one yet."

9th July, 1979: A weekend in Llanystumdwy.

"We had the news today that my boss's marriage had broken up, which is the second time this has happened when I have started a new job! Fortunately, this time I wasn't involved in passing telephone messages in an emotional triangle. Not much work, being the summer holidays. A long weekend in Wales thanks to Mum and Dad hiring a cottage in Llanystumdwy. Some good walks along the beach and down a steep path to a ghost mining village. Abersoch was a quaint place. We collected the keys and waited in the cottage but Mum and Dad didn't arrive. Found a phone box and Mum answered the phone to say Dad was ill with a stomach bug but they hoped to travel the next day. We explored Portmeirion the next day and my Dad looked awful when he did arrive. We had to go home Monday but spent the day in Barmouth. Dad stayed in the car as he really wasn't well, but when I phoned yesterday he had recovered. I can relax now."

15th July, 1979: The new boat is shipwrecked off the Isle of Wight.

"Back to work and nothing much to do until the Course Organiser called me in for dictation at 5.10 pm. Trains were running late so I didn't get home until 6.45pm. The highlight of the week was being an usher at the degree ceremony. Unlike Cardiff we didn't have a cap and gown to wear, so I didn't feel quite so important. I had lunch at Aston Management Centre to see everyone, and literally did. Back in the Dental School Office we were quite disturbed by a mentally ill woman who came in. On Sunday we had a phone call from Steve's Dad to say he was virtually shipwrecked on the Isle of Wight, in the new boat. He was calling from a phone box on the Island. I am intrigued to know the details, but will have to wait."

27th July, 1979: Train and Hovercraft to Paris.

"I was filling in 'A' Level forms at work. We met Malcolm at the Airport Social Club and he told us the details about the shipwreck. Apparently the mast fell down and hit him and after that they were drifting aimlessly at sea until another boat came to the rescue. They were towed to the Isle of Wight but their mooring, car and belongings were in Poole. Last weekend we went to Deeping for Dad's 51st birthday and went to Peterborough's new big leisure park - Ferry Meadows - very rural and the Nene Valley Railway goes through the middle. This weekend we set off for Paris to stay with Alain and Christiane. Train to Dover and then hovercraft and train to Paris. Alain collected us at the railway station and I was appalled at how the French drive and it seems that traffic lights appear to be optional!"

28th July, 1979: I must not buy yellow clothes!

The Crooked House at Himley.

"Croissants for breakfast, fondue for dinner and I still don't know what 'couscous' is. Alain and Christiane act as concierges for these ultra modern flats in the centre of Paris. As they had to wait for a relief caretaker we had to stay in until 3 p.m. and I was dying to get out there and see Paris. Eventually we saw Notre Dame, Ile de St. Louis, Pompidou Centre, Montmartre, Sacre Coeur and the Eiffel Tower. The one thing I learnt was that yellow attracts greenfly as my top was covered in them! We ended up at a wine bar - Chez Felix - where Alain plays the drums and the extremely hot streets were crowded with evening revellers."

30th July, 1979: Beaubourg or Pompidou Centre - an architectural gem according to Steve!
"Travelled on the Metro and went to the Latin Quartier after a boat ride on the River Seine. In the evening we went by car to have a meal with people

Beaubourg or Pompidou Centre.

155

in Massy. I was annoyed with Alain's driving at 90 mph on the peripherique - ring road around Paris where overtaking is allowed in any lane! He was doing it on purpose as he knew I was scared. Today was our 2nd wedding anniversary and I was amazed that I was still alive after the race track roads in France. I was even shocked to see cars bump other vehicles out of the way to park in a space! After shopping in the Champs Elysees we caught the train and boat. Our evening dinner was on the train between London and Birmingham, which with just a little imagination was similar to the 'Orient Express'."

6th August, 1979: Compton Wynyates as our French friends are back!

"In the post I received a poem from Steve's Grandfather about a woman's place being in the home with babies. I was annoyed by this, but realise that he was born in 1897 when the world was a different place. I wrote a poem back to him about modern times and the fact that two wages are needed to pay the mortgage! Saw my friend Barbara at lunch time, but she wasn't remotely interested in Paris. A very slack afternoon workwise and I was nearly falling asleep on my typewriter. At the weekend Alain and Christiane stayed on their way to a holiday in Scotland and brought me an ironware fondue set, as I was so impressed with theirs. We went out to Compton Wynyates and enjoyed the sunshine and the tour. Yesterday they left for the Highlands of Scotland. Steve was busy trying to fit a car stereo into the new car but it failed to work properly."

14th August, 1979: The rain and the midges put them off Scotland!

"Collecting information for 'A' Level results most of the week. After work on Friday rushed around like a madman cleaning the house and preparing a fondue for dinner. Then waited and waited - Jean and Jane eventually turned up at 10pm! On Sunday we went to the Regatta and cricket at Stourport. Alain and Christiane called in on their way back from Scotland. They had travelled 2000 miles and came back because of the rain. At the dinner table we remarked at the difference in table manners - the french are allowed elbows on the table and we are taught not to!"

21st August, 1979: My Mum appears to collect news cuttings on plane crashes!

"Had to go to the Main University to collect 'A' Level results and my two bosses wanted me to have lunch with them which I dreaded, but actually enjoyed myself. Steve's friend Sandra is getting married soon so we had a drink with her in the Towers at Great Barr and whilst out shopping I saw a pink sundress, grey velvet jacket which I bought for the wedding complete with a pink flower for my hair. Phoned my Mum, and as she is scared of flying, is not expecting us to survive the flight to Yugoslavia and told me loads of scary stories about being up in a plane. I wish I had not phoned! Met my friend Barbara today at lunch time and I don't know why I see her as there was nothing interesting to talk about. The one good thing is that I really feel settled at the Dental School now."

26th August, 1979: When the sun comes out I just have to down tools!

"A surprise family birthday party at Steve's parents for his Dad and Sandra's hen night at Plum's Wine Bar this week. Hampstead church was the venue for Sandra and Phil's wedding with a reception at the Post House - I really enjoyed myself. The next day was bright and sunny so I abandoned the washing up piled high in the sink, the mess on every surface and the tip in the living room, to go out into the garden with my book, in case the weather turned. I was totally relaxed and emmersed in reading, also took my t-shirt off to get a pre-tan for the holidays, as the neighbours were out. There was a knock at the door, so I quickly put on my top and rushed to the front hallway. It was Steve's Mum and brother with some visitors from the Isle of Wight. They were looking at me strangely and I realised I was wearing my top inside out! I felt and looked guilty then had to wash up cups to make them a drink and clear a space in the living room for them to sit. I remembered the tip of a friend's mother, who always went to the door with a duster in her hand (and a cigarette), which does give the impression that you are in the middle of tackling the housework."

3rd September, 1979: Fenland Air Show and then off to Heathrow.

Steve had the day off work to try and put the kitchen back

Porec, Yugoslavia   Venice

together properly after fitting new units. After dinner I was reading a guide book on Yugoslavia but fell asleep. Work is starting to get busy and after typing 18 letters in the morning I had lunch in Hawkins Wine Bar and saw a student from the Management Centre in there. He persuaded me to type his project and I agreed but felt depressed afterwards. This weekend we went to the Fenland Air Show and took Jane's friend Linda from the USA. It didn't compare with the air shows they have in America whilst lying on the beach drenched in sun and fantastic weather apparently! Back at home, we were packing for our trip abroad, flying off to better weather than we had in Scotland last year. After a few irritable arguments about plums and caterpillars due to the plum tree heavy laden with plums, and whether to make plum wine, plum pies or jam, we agreed to disagree and got on the coach for London Heathrow."

5th September, 1979: Our first ever flight and the plane was cancelled!

"Not a good start to our first ever flight. The plane was delayed indefinitely due to engine failure, so we were taken to a hotel but our luggage had already left. We then had to get up at 5.15 a.m. for breakfast even though our plane didn't leave until 11 a.m.! The good thing was that we arrived safely at Pula Airport - a wooden shack of an airport and a coach was waiting to take us to the hotel which was rather basic, but then it was a cheap holiday. I was convinced there would be lots of creepy crawlies and I was trying to kill this spider type creature on the wall when I realised it was just a mark. On our first full day we walked to Porec. We found a nudist beach where the only clothed people were 2 policemen walking round with guard dogs and making sure that everyone was naked in this area!"

7th September, 1979: The hydrofoil to Venice.
"Yesterday we took the boat to Porec and managed to buy some presents before the bell for the siesta rang. I noticed how quickly the sun goes down in the evening. We were on the terrace with a drink at 6 p.m. to watch the sunset which lasted all of 5 minutes! There was dancing by the pool later on. Steve has developed an allergy to this place - stinging eyes and streaming nose. We caught the hydrofoil to Venice today which took just over 3 hours. I enjoyed the tour around St. Mark's Square and a glass factory. The trip on the gondola was great too. The downside - the public loos - just a hole in the floor, the queue was long and it was disgusting when you got there. Some tourists just turned round and walked away. The beer was expensive at £1.50 a pint. On the boat back we booked for the delicious dinner at the Captain's table."

10th September, 1979: We nearly capsized when everyone ran to one side of the boat!
"A trip down the Lim Fjord for lunch on Katrina Island was a treat, but Steve is still suffering badly with his allergy to something. On the boat back from a tour around Rovinj we passed the nudist beaches at Vrsar. Everyone rushed to that side of the boat to get a good look and we nearly capsized! Yesterday was our last day and we relaxed on the nudist beach - no one knew us! Not good as parts that have never seen the sun reacted badly! I felt shivery and had an early night. Today, we bought our 'duty frees' from the shack that is Pula Airport and amazingly our plane was on time. I was relieved when we landed in England. I expect my Mum will be surprised that I am still alive!"

19th September, 1979: There is a pregnancy epidemic at work!
"Went back to work and found out that three office staff are pregnant - there seems to be an epidemic! I now have lots of work as term is starting soon. In our garden we have an abundance of plums on the tree so I made plum crumble and started preparing the rest for plum wine. Jane's friends Linda and Rochelle from New York stayed the night on their way to Wales and made us laugh with their observations on England.

My cousin Graham's wedding to Carol.

They were not keen on Guest Houses in the UK - no ensuite, not many with showers, just the horror of a shared bathroom along the corridor! USA of course is bigger and better! I doubt if the facilities in Wales will meet their standards, but I hope we get to hear of their adventures!"

23rd September, 1979: I bought a book 'Beginners Guide to Family History.
"There is a shortage of student accommodation and an urgent appeal was sent out to all staff for any spare rooms at home, on a temporary basis. I put my name down. Work has been hectic and we have missed out on lunch hours and stayed on after work. At the Management Centre I was overloaded with work, but it is different here, we all muck in together. I felt guilty on Friday as I had to leave them all to it as Steve was waiting for me in the car park and we were all packed up to go to London for the weekend. We stayed at Dick's parents house as they were away. After a delicious meal we had to sit and listen to weird music. I was reading the book I had bought when I nipped out to buy a sandwich as lunch time - 'Beginners Guide to Tracing Your Family History'. Yesterday being Saturday I hoped the London Records Office might be open, but no it was closed so instead we tried to find 'Three Dagger Court' in the parish of St. Giles Cripplegate in search of the ancestral homes of my Great Grandparents. My Mum seems to think that their homes went in the Slum Clearances and the site is now underneath the Barbican

Centre."

1st October 1979: I went to London to join the rally of strikers but found the Record Office instead.

"Made a serious 'faux pas' at work when I mistakenly sent a reject note to Halls of Residence of a student who had actually been accepted. As a result Halls were now full and I had a very irate mother to deal with. Jean Jobes the Admin Officer had to sort it out for me. I went out at lunch time feeling quite incompetent. I then bumped into the Business Management student who I am typing a project for and he asked me out to dinner! Well I must be doing something right. At home we have been decorating, a visit to the Ideal Home Exhibition at the NEC for ideas and an outing to the pictures to see 'Dracula'. Today we were on strike at work, so as I am a Nalgo Union member I took advantage of a cheap day return on the train to London to 'join the rally'. Shame I couldn't find out where it was although I didn't search too hard as I came across the Records Office who were open for business. I had great fun in there on a treasure hunt for my ancestors!"

6th October 1979: We got lost and nearly missed the wedding reception!

"I was trying to work out an awful timetable when I had a phone call from the Student Accommodation Office asking if I could take a 'fresher' for our spare room. Wondered if I had done the right thing, but when we met Vincent, he seemed like a pleasant young man and we will collect him and his belongings on Sunday. I had a meeting with the Course Organisers in the afternoon and we discussed the admissions procedure over a bottle of sherry! This weekend we were in Deeping St. James for my cousin Graham's wedding. A lovely mild sunny day but between the church and reception we managed to get lost and turned up late, when everyone had sat down for the wedding breakfast! On the way back to Birmingham, we collected our student lodger - Vincent."

20th October 1979: My mother-in-law was a publican's daughter and loves family parties.

"At a Union meeting at work, we were persuaded to take more action. It must be the fashion as the buses were on strike this week so the traffic on the roads was chaotic. I hardly notice Vincent, our student in the house as he is so quiet. The rules are that we provide breakfast in the week and full board on Sundays. Friday evening we went to Nottingham to see Jane in her room at the Nurses Home. Not only did she have her boyfriend Neil in the room, but a dog as well - both of which are strictly forbidden! Back at home, in the garden, we pruned the plum tree, racked the wine and went to a family party at Steve's parents' house."

25th October 1979: A neat and tidy desk gives the illusion of being up to date with your work!

"More house decorating, a walk around Wythall and a drink at a new pub in Shirley called The Drawbridge. I felt panicky at work until I tidied my desk at lunch time, and then it didn't look as if I had too much work to do. I still took minutes home with me to write up though. Yesterday I went to the General Hospital canteen next door for lunch and came out feeling full and fat, but the huge meal lasted me for the RIBA Midland Institute lecture on the Restoration of Venice. Today I met Viv at Hawkins Wine Bar for lunch and at the end of the afternoon we had the Student Guide Party. I spent most of my time drinking and laughing with the hygienists, orthodontists and technicians. I was good for nothing when I got home."

5th November, 1979: I am a Brummie after all!

"Today the Director of the Dental School treated us to a sherry just before lunch as an appreciation of us struggling to get to work during the bus strike! At the weekend we did a six mile walk along the canal towpath from Kings Norton to Selly Oak and back through Bournville. Took a day off yesterday for a trip to London Records Office for the birth marriage and death indexes at St. Catherine's House. The indexes are in huge ledgers requiring strong arm muscles and they are dirty and dusty. I was working up quite a sweat in there but made a startling discovery. The ancestors on my mother's side came from London which is what we knew, but before that they came from Birmingham! I later found out that some were buried in St. Mary's churchyard and the Dental School is built on top of that very site!"
Reader: the photo (page 172) shows my cousin Sally and I outside the dental hospital next to the church railings which are the only evidence left of the church."

13th November, 1979: At work, I can't always 'swim with the tide'!
"I had to bring more work home to keep on top of things. I didn't feel so inadequate when Lyn told me that previous Admissions Secretaries did the same thing. At lunch time, yesterday, we all went to the Filibuster for a drink as Jane was leaving and later on in the afternoon we had sherry at her leaving presentation - all baby related! Malcolm came round in the evening wanting sympathy as his Irish girlfriend has stopped writing and phoning. Watched 'To the Manor Born' on TV when he had gone. Today, not only was I late back from lunch but unfortunately my boss was waiting for me, to explain that I'd missed out part of the UCCA procedure! Oh dear, two black marks!"

29th November, 1979: Party time in Stourbridge for Dental School staff.
"I have been catching the bus home and reading my book so feeling sick by the time I get in. Jill, at work turned 21 so we went to her party at Stourbridge - first time we have had an evening event with all the staff. I'm still staying over at work until 6.30 p.m. and then taking work home! We were out in the evening looking at a large house in Henley-in-Arden which is for sale but it looked haunted to me. Today at work we had the dental course student interviews and I feel ahead of myself at last. Had my full lunch hour walking around the shops in town. Saw plenty of Christmas presents I would like to buy for myself, but nothing for anyone else! Steve has been for a job interview in Milton Keynes - it had gone well, but he would need to give 3 months notice in his present job which might jeopardise his chances."

13th December, 1979: Perhaps Christmas shopping by mail order would beat the crowds.
"Christmas shopping, and Birmingham City Centre was heaving with people. We will have to try looking for presents in Solihull instead. The evening was spent in the King Arthur pub with 3 other couples and I feel as if we are the outsiders of a clique. Caught the bus to Selly Oak on Sunday and walked back along the canal towpath into town. It was just about light enough when we got back to dig our Christmas tree up from the garden. This week we had our staff Christmas lunch in the canteen which was delicious. My boss (male) had to sit on a table full of 10 women

but he didn't seem to mind. On the bus home I was almost asleep and missed my stop at the Gospel Oak. That made me rather late arriving home and Steve was worried, but luckily I had walked past a fish and chip shop which was open, so dinner was taken care of! We have all had our free afternoon off work for Christmas shopping and at the General Hospital there was a choir concert of medieval carols, so it really felt Christmassy. Back at home Vincent had gone home for the Christmas holidays and had left Steve and I a present each under the Christmas tree. We are lucky to have such a kind and thoughtful student lodger."

26th December, 1979: On Christmas Day two turkey dinners is becoming the norm!

"Christmas shopping in Solihull and Acocks Green wasn't very productive apart from putting us in bad moods. We did buy some yellow paint for the living room radiators and they now look like a feature of the room! The highlight this week was the 'Dental Incidentals', a stage show featuring academic staff and students on the stage. It is an annual tradition and is quite hilarious. On Christmas Day we were at my parents' house opening presents in front of the cheery fire. At last Steve had bought me the correct perfume, Chanel No. 19 instead of Chanel No. 5 which I always have to exchange back at the shop each year. Had a turkey lunch, with all the trimmings, Christmas pud with brandy sauce, then hit the deserted road for another turkey dinner in the evening at Steve's parents' house! On Boxing Day it was my turn to cook for the in-laws so I made Boeuf Bourguignon with Strawberry Gateaux for pudding. Two evenings in row we have spent playing Scrabble which was brother-in-law Richard's Christmas present. Fresh air and exercise is on the cards for tomorrow."

3rd January, 1980: America - Route 66 - let this be the year!

"Off to London again and managed to sneak in some family history research - the GLC were so helpful and I discovered more ancestors, as gold chain makers living above the shop in Shoreditch. Now where does that area feature on the Monopoly Board? We met up with Julie and Nigel in Dulwich and went to Diane's flat in a converted warehouse. We were home to see the New Year in at the Old Boys Club (King Edward's Aston). The last day of the holiday we spent decorating the bathroom and Steve painted stripes on the walls - an idea from the House Book.

We didn't feel like getting back to the rat race after a lovely 7 day holiday. It never is as bad as we think though. I couldn't believe how busy the shops are - crowded with sales shoppers - just like Christmas. It is time to plan holidays so I just headed for the travel agents to pick up some brochures. Steve is talking about driving a car along Route 66 for an American holiday."

12th January, 1980: The Jaguars and Rolls Royce in the restaurant car park indicated the menu prices!

"It is that time of year for shopping in the Sales and Travel Agents. My 8 year old boots have started to let water in so I bought new ones at £30 from Miss Selfridge. We went to see 'Manhattan' at the pictures and Woody Allen was at his best. A serious picture with a subtle humour. It was my 27th birthday on Friday. I made some choux buns to take to work and there was a present on my desk from everyone - a plant and a new umbrella. We set off on a cold and frosty night for a weekend at Jean's in Wiltshire, stopping for my birthday meal in Burford at a place aptly called 'The Winter's Tale' (now known as Burford Lodge). 'The Good Restaurant Guide', which I looked at in the Library gave this place quite a high rating. So, I should not have been alarmed to see Jaguars, a Rolls Royce and expensive sports cars in the driveway. Anyway I had Steak Diane which was delicious and shockingly expensive. Needless to say, we only had the one course."

17th January, 1980: I am such a townie - I need central heating!

"We were bad tempered waking up in Jean's house as we are so used to central heating and I was frozen. Got up quickly and got warm by the Rayburn in the kitchen. Had a brisk walk over Barbury Castle, an old iron age hill fort, which got my circulation going. Home and back to work where I was in a good mood until my boss called me in to discuss a few dissatisfactions! I stayed on until 6.30 p.m., partly to create a good impression and also it was snowing and I was hoping Steve would pick me up. Our student lodger Vincent was back and I made his day by saying that his girlfriend could stay for the weekend. He is over 18 and away from home, but I felt a bit responsible and did wonder if I should give him a talk on acting responsibly, but then it is not my place! Today work was harassing. On the coldest day of the year our large office window was taken out for repair. I was freezing, there were constant drilling noises, the fire alarm kept going off and Tracy the new girl was talking non-stop. I had a sherry as soon as I got in from work."

25th January, 1980: Surprisingly, matchmaking pays off occasionally!

"Went into Solihull and bought a slinky little pink dress with a split up the back. I wore it for Jude's party at the Greswolde and we took Malcolm, Francis, Sharon and Elizabeth - in the hope of doing a little matchmaking. I woke the next day with a headache and read an article in the Sunday newspaper on 'stress' which made it worse! A walk along the canal blew the cobwebs away. This weekend we went out with two other couples - Steve's Team Leader and his wife Carrie who moaned a lot and the other couple who seemed to have no sense of humour. They say that some people are better for knowing but I doubt if we'll see them again."
Reader: The matchmaking worked as Sharon eventually married Francis.

9th February, 1980: My Great Grandfather left the family home and was never heard of again!

"We went to the pictures to see 'Yanks', an excellent film. The evenings spent in this week haven't been so good with our useless stereo jumping on every record and the pilot light on the central heating boiler constantly blowing out. It is a delicate operation trying to light it with tapers. Steve has taken on another evening cleaning job at Hall Green Greyhound Racing Stadium to earn some money for our summer holiday. At the weekend we set off for London on Saturday at 6.20 a.m. and arrived in Islington at 9.40 a.m. for the family history trail. I took photos of the site of my ancestors' homes on Carthusian Street, the parish church St. Botolphs and then we had lunch at the National Theatre overlooking the Thames. The GLC sent us to the Guildhall where we searched through more church records. None of my ancestors died as a result of fighting in the First World War, but 2 died of the Spanish flu in 1918 which proves that this epidemic killed more than the War. I also found out that my Great Grandfather who was 'a bad lot' and 'work shy' according to family, disappeared without a trace - probably no-one looked too hard! We drove to my parents after all that and Mum was quite excited on my discovery of her father's family. Yesterday we had an interesting evening out with Linda, Rick, Jane and Geoff in the Bluebell at Belmesthorpe."

2nd March, 1980: Our precious weekend was hijacked!
"Oxford and Milton Keynes were the two places Steve went for job interviews this week. At Oxford they wanted an older person and the Milton Keynes job wanted more design experience. Back to the 'Situations Vacant' in the back of the Architects' Journal then! This weekend started in a relaxing way on Saturday morning watching 'Swap Shop' on tv. The phone rang and it was Steve's Dad to tell us that Granddad George was coming over so could Steve take his Mum shopping. I felt that our weekend was no longer ours and had been taken over. We had to go round to the house and suffer lots of nasty criticism all the time, but I am told not to take it personally as a lot of old people become bad tempered and grumpy. Before the said Grandparent went back to Hampshire he wanted to come and see us in our 'cottage'. I braced myself for more verbal abuse and thought that one day I might look back and find it funny!"

12th March, 1980: A woman who was employed to clean a house every day was known as 'a daily'.
"Travelled home on the train with our student Vincent and when we got in he made me a cup of his coffee. Such a lovely lad and we hardly know he is in the house. His girlfriend Felicity has stayed the weekend and they never surfaced from the bedroom! We drove to Kenilworth to see Marilyn's sister Carol and husband in their huge house. I was most impressed that they have a 'daily' to do the housework. It was very interesting to see how the other half live, and I was wondering if a change of career would enable me to employ staff! Last night we went to a concert at the Odeon to see 'Squeeze' which I really enjoyed and we saw a few people we know including Vincent. We were discussing our stereo with him and he agreed that we should have the deck fixed or buy a new one. Today we walked along the canal to Leamington Spa. Vincent was having a disturbing time with his girlfriend constantly phoning him and I felt that there was something drastically wrong."

21st March, 1980: The Bailiffs were on their way to our house!
"A letter arrived at our address for a Mr Parks - the previous occupier of our house. Now I know you shouldn't open letters addressed to other people but I am glad I did. It was a letter from

the Bailiffs saying that they were coming on Friday to take all the furniture out of the house to reclaim debts! We phoned the police for advice! They said that a policeman would have to be present with the bailiffs for such a procedure, so I was not to worry as nothing would go ahead. I went to give a pint of blood in the lunch hour and Vincent was donating a pint too, so I had my tea and biscuits with him. Steve had been for a job interview in Berkhamsted. Today I met him in the lunch hour and we went to British Airways to make enquiries about flights to America, then sat in the sun on a bench by the Cathedral. I was quite productive in the evening cleaning windows, making croutons and drawing up a family tree."

28th March, 1980: We live too near to the in-laws!
"Steve's Dad has joined the Solihull Ratepayers Association and is standing as a candidate in the local elections. We were roped in to deliver cards for him. I also cooked dinner for my in-laws including the brothers. Boeuf en Croute from my cookery cards and Upside-Down Pudding from my school recipe book, from the days when 'Cookery' went on to change its name to 'Home Economics'. We then played Scrabble. Every evening this week we have had to deliver election cards in every street, even in the rain. Steve had a job interview in Hatfield and is really keen for promotion as all overtime at work has been stopped. A work colleague Margot and husband Keith invited us out with them to the Alexander Theatre to see 'Kismet'. To my surprise, I quite enjoyed the evening."

22nd April, 1980: We can now enjoy listening to our record collection.
"On Saturday we put £7 in the building society, the sum total of our savings this week. Spent another week delivering election cards through letter boxes. Just as we finished the last lot, the Ratepayers Association representative was on the phone wanting us to deliver leaflets. I was furious that Steve's Dad had involved us. Steve and Malcolm have enrolled on car maintenance classes at the college which will hopefully come in handy and save us money. They were both bright and cheerful when they came back from the course and Vincent joined us for a nightcap and we listened to our new record deck - one that works properly - at last! Steve's parents came back from a week in Tunisia and told us about the dreadful time they had. It was cold and they were both ill with sickness which resulted in losing weight. It is more

normal to come back heavier after indulging in fine food and relaxation!"

26th April, 1980: Our country residence in Wiltshire - party time at Jean's once again!

"The lecture on canals at the Birmingham Architectural Association was so interesting, especially as we walk the towpaths nearly every weekend. Just saw a fleeting glimpse of Vincent and Felicity when we arrived home. At the weekend we were partying at Jean's in Wiltshire and took Malcolm with us. During the afternoon on Saturday we were helping with the party food and collected a few more partygoers from the railway station. We started the evening off at the pub and at closing time everyone came back to Jean's cottage. The party was really swinging, so many familiar faces and even my brother Ian turned up. In the early hours we all got in our sleeping bags and slept in a big heap on the floor!"

28th April, 1980: Country versus City for parties - no contest!

"After 5 hours sleep I didn't feel too bad as I hadn't drank too much. There was much talk about the 'goings on' at the party. Malcolm had paired up with the very pretty Indian girl Barbara. We all went for a walk on the Downs after a limited breakfast. It was a beautiful day and extremely funny being with the crowd and listening to amusing snippets of conversation. After going to the pub and having dinner, we eventually set off for home. Vincent and Felicity had an excellent weekend too with our house to themselves. Back to work today and Glenda started work in our Dental School Office, another defector from the Management Centre, which makes a total of 3 from Aston University. I was pleased to hand over the keys to her, as 'holder of the keys' was never my job."

30th April, 1980: Life down south appears to be all work, commute and no free time.

"I was in St. Albans today with Steve for a day out, while he was at a job interview. The town centre brought back memories of working on the market stall here with friend Brian who was selling plants and flowers grown at his family's smallholding in the Fens. I used to meet him at 4.30 a.m. outside the Red Lion pub in the High Street Eye, and on arrival in St. Albans I would help set the stall out. He always gave me something for my Mum from the stall and her favourite present was a rubber plant. Eventually the early morning start was just too much for a non-morning person like me. I do like St. Albans and Steve's interview, at the beautiful Tyttenhanger House, took two hours and he came out of the building at 7 p.m. We were rather disturbed that the car park was still full and the office workers still working away. We began to wonder what time everyone got home and the actual total of hours worked in a day, as opposed to the official hours!"

12th May, 1980: Booked our holiday in America or we could go to New York and Boston in Lincolnshire!

"Election Day and Steve's Dad was standing as candidate for the Solihull Ratepayers Association. He lost by 150 votes. This weekend was the Tulip Parade in Spalding so were were at Mum and Dad's. Malcolm, came to meet up with Barbara. Very crowded but fantastic floats all made out of tulips. Yesterday Steve was working hard designing houses for his boss as overtime money for the holidays. I went to Nine Bridges with Dad and Gem the dog. It is a great natural paddling place and shallow swimming pool teeming with small fish under a series of several bridges. In the lunch hour today we went into the Travel Agents and booked our holiday to America - a fly/drive to California. Aviation fuel had increased in price so the flights and car hire costs £537 each. We were advised by one of the Dentists at work to use Motel 6 for accommodation as they were basic, comfortable and cheap. On the way home we called in to Steve's parents to wish them a happy wedding anniversary but his Dad had forgotten this time!"

25th May, 1980: We visit Britain's smallest county - Rutland.

"There should have been a General Strike this week but everyone ignored it! I was reading my book about California, our holiday destination, then saw a programme on t.v. about the violence there - I just hope Mum didn't see it! On Friday in the lunch hour the General Hospital Choir recital was so uplifting, it took away my worries. This weekend was Whitsun so a long weekend, and whilst at Mum and Dad's we visited Rutland Water near Oakham. In 1976 a reservoir was created at the expense of the demolition of the village Nether Hambleton, the remains of which are now under the water. The locals campaigned to save the church and

Solihull Ratepayers' Float at the Solihull Carnival.

Sally and Sally 2nd cousins from the Crockett family.

won. It has been waterproofed and half submerged containing a museum giving the history of the creation of Rutland Water."

6th June, 1980: The one advantage of the Solihull Ratepayers Association is Carnival fun!
"There was a bus strike this week, so not many people turned up at work. There are more exciting things as we are taking part in the Solihull Carnival so the whole George family went to Belbroughton Costume Hire to look for outfits to wear. We are all on theSolihull Ratepayers Association float together with a jazz band, New Orleans, cowboy theme. I chose a 'dancing girl' costume. My father-in-law pointed out that all the other women involved are making the costumes for themselves and their menfolk, so therefore saving money! I answered by saying that the other women are lucky to have such creative talents! We spent an evening helping to decorate the Mississippi Showboat which was put on the back of a lorry. I just hope it is moving slowly enough so that I don't fall off!"

13th June, 1980: Solihull High Street will never seem the same!
"We all assembled at the back of the Civic Hall in Solihull, all dressed up and ready for the procession through the town. What a good time we had and afterwards walked around the stalls, that is, until it started raining. We sheltered underneath the lorry. After that fun it was back to household jobs - we delivered our old newspapers to the Scouts for recycling, stocked up on freezer food from Bejam and enjoyed more planning of our California fly drive

holiday."

23rd June, 1980: I am told that a second opinion would be unethical!
"The dentist said I need a filling and at the age of 27 I have never had one! Mum sent me a newspaper cutting suggesting that I should have a second opinion! Working at the Dental Hospital I thought that would be easy but Dr Shaw said that it would be unethical! On Saturday I was hoping to have a lazy day but I had to catch the bus and train to Four Oaks to meet Steve and his boss. They were working hard on designing houses and needed to dictate letters and have them typed up. Afterwards we went to see Steve's parents and I felt sorry for them as redundancy is imminent at the age of 52, and they are at a loss of what they are going to do as both work for the same place - 'Progressive Cleaning Services'."

13th July, 1980: Trials and tribulations balanced by carefree walks in the Lincolnshire Fens.
"I had to organise the Wine Party for Open Day. Sharon came back from a holiday in Majorca, slightly tanned and with load of complaints. She had gone with the 18-30 group holidays and there were tales of food being thrown across the dining room and general disorder and drunkenness! She did make us laugh though. In the evening I had a full tape of typing from Ken and didn't finish until 1 a.m. I phoned Mum who said Dad was in hospital and his operation was a success, but they found not just one, but two ulcers! It was a gloomy atmosphere at Steve's parents house as neither of them have a job. At the weekend we were at Peterborough hospital to see Dad and he was fine, we took Mum to Sainsburys, visited Grandma, and met Scoop (SueCooper) at the Bull Hotel for a drink. Also lots of walks around the Deepings with Gem the dog."

24th July, 1980: My father is a 'creaking gate'.
"Bought Dad a book for his birthday 'The Henry Root Letters'. I did have a little read of this bestseller before I wrapped it up, such funny tongue in cheek correspondence. It is just the book he needs as after further tests he now has an irregular heartbeat and overactive thyroid gland - but treatable. His sense of humour gets him through as he was telling the medical staff that he has been in every ward of the hospital except for Maternity. When we

arrived home, Steve's Mum had been admitted to hospital with a kidney problem. When I haven't been hospital visiting I have been in work where the temperature was soaring up to 80°F. At lunch time the City Library was the coolest place, so I have been in there reading book on California for the holidays. Steve's 28th birthday today and we had a relaxing meal at the Tom O' the Wood - after hospital visiting."

1st August, 1980: Old American cars are ugly but no doubt extremely comfortable to travel in.
"Had to have my first ever filling at the Dentist but it was painless. Our relaxing weekend walk was at Coleshill where the sun was shining, the church bells were ringing and a cricket match was being played - absolutely divine. We saw Steve's Mum in hospital after her kidney was removed and she was still in recovery with tubes everywhere. We were off on holiday so said we would phone regularly. We flew from Heathrow to America on a Jumbo Jet which was so big that it was hard to realise that we were actually flying. Landing at San Francisco, it took ages to get through customs and to collect the hire car, which was a Toyota Corolla when Steve wanted an Edison or Cadillac. We arrived at the Motel and went straight to bed at 6.30 p.m. which was really 2.30 a.m. in our time."

2nd August, 1980: Off the beaten track where tourists are never seen.
"We were wide awake at 4.30 a.m. so waited around for breakfast and then went out on the 3 mile Golden Gate Bridge walk, with all the early morning joggers. We managed to swap our hire car Toyota Corolla for a Toyota Celica although Steve really wanted an American car but that wasn't an option. Went downtown and the temperature was quite cool at 60°F., I was told that in San Francisco you always need to wear a 'wrap'. We drove on the freeway and came across a small town called 'Crockett'. As this is a family surname we just had to stop and look around. It wasn't a tourist area so we were viewed with suspicion. Met an old cowboy who opened up the Post Office established in 1883 and the proudly showed us the oldest building - 1880 in Crocketville, as it used to be known. He gave us a printed sheet of the history showing that the settlement had grown up around a sugar factory. It was very hot so we drove on to Vallejo and found a Motel 6 with an outdoor pool to cool off."

5th August, 1980: San Francisco awaits the next big earthquake.

"We looked at the showhomes for the new houses on the cliff top, then discussed the fault line and the earthquakes and how they were expecting another big one. We set off for Lake Tahoe and stopped off in Sacramento. We couldn't walk around the Lake as most of it is private land. Booked into the Motel 6 at Carson City but the heat was getting to us at 93°F. Saw all the casinos and 'quickie marriage chapels'. Today we went to Mammoth Lakes and had to bypass Yosemite National Park as all the accommodation would have been fully booked ahead. Saw snow capped mountains, hills and desert. The area was very much a ski resort in Winter. With the high altitude and hot sun I was getting a bad headache which I put down to a touch of sunstroke."

7th August, 1980: Death Valley with warnings everywhere!

"Arrived at Lone Pine in 103°F heat. Loads of huge dragonflies everywhere, like mini helicopters! Went up Mount Whitney and tried to stay in the shade. Had to have the noisy air conditioning on in our room to keep comfortable. Today set off for Death Valley with our 'hot weather hints'. Stopped at Stovepipe Wells and stocked up with Budweiser Beer and water. Had another break at Furnace Creek Museum. The scenery was desolate and dramatic. Skull and cross bones notices everywhere as if your car broke down you could fry in no time! Stopped at Badwater and the only other 2 cars there were British tourists, in other words 'only mad dogs and Englishmen! The car engine and air conditioning didn't fail us. It was a 300 mile journey to Barstow where we stayed in the Mojave desert (at a Motel 6)."

9th August, 1980: Lots of cacti in the dried up river beds and tequila in the shops.

"Visited the ghost town of Calico - a former silver mining settlement. We met some students from Birmingham Alabama there. We drove the 195 miles to San Diego and went to the old town. We were so hot and sticky due to the humidity but couldn't resist dressing up for one of those Victorian photos. I was 'Miss Scarlett' and Steve was a General in the Army. In the evening we

American car, but not our hire car   Badwater in Death Valley.

crossed the border into Tijuana. Despite drinking several 'margaritas' I didn't feel comfortable there. Young barefooted dirty children were pestering us in the pubs for money. The place looked and felt like 'second hand', 'shanty town' America with corrugated iron shacks down the side streets."

10th August, 1980: Nobody walks anywhere and there is a likelihood of being arrested if you do!

"The giant redwood trees were amazing and Disneyland was next. It was 95°F when we arrived and in the heat we hadn't the energy to talk to each other. Disneyland was great apart from the queues. We met Norm and Joan, who Steve's mother is related to and they live in Los Angeles, so we were staying with them. Universal Studios was the treat today and equally as enjoyable and as hot as yesterday. From there we drove down Sunset Boulevard to Beverly Hills. Enjoyed a new eating experience at a Japanese Restaurant where the food was chopped, cooked in flames on the table in front of us, in a sort of juggling act, and eventually thrown on to our plates!"

13th August, 1980: Cold and misty by the coast so wine tasting here we come!

"Santa Barbara is one of my favourite places and walking along the beach at a comfortable 78°F was just right. The long and winding slow road to Monterey was not pleasing Steve, coupled with the fact that the weather was overcast with a sea mist and cold - rather like a British summer really. We had a walk to Fisherman's Wharf. At Santa Cruz the weather was even worse so we turned inland to the road which went along the Napa Valley. From there the weather started to become hot and sunny again. This is a wine growing area and we stopped for wine tasting at San Jose. We left there armed with a few bottles of Paul Masson Champagne and feeling quite merry, so the weather was of no consequence any more!"

18th August, 1980: After a pleasant evening meal, breakfast was being served 5 hours later!

"Our last day was spent back in San Francisco and we were shopping for presents to take home such as Tequila, T-shirts and a jigsaw puzzle. We had dinner on the plane home and watched the film. On reflection we didn't have to shoot our way into or out of California and everyone adored our English accents - at times we felt like Royalty. As darkness fell we went to sleep but the night only lasted 4 hours and it was time for breakfast! We watched the sunrise out of the plane's windows. After we landed at Heathrow, how Steve drove home to Birmingham, I'll never know as I must have slept all the way. Phoned both sets of parents when we got in and then slept for 12 hours! Today had to cut the lawns - needed a scythe, set the washing machine going and visited the supermarket for food. What a great holiday!"

2nd September, 1980: I need to learn how to use a computer to request a parchment document!

"Back to work and I was thrown in at the deep end. Glenda was ill and slept in a chair in the Director's Office (he was on holiday). Other School Office staff were on holiday too so I appeared to be on my own with all the phones ringing. As the weather was good we had an evening walk to Bickenhill but kept coming across 'dead end' public footpaths. This weekend we went to London and stayed with Dick and Susie. Took some time out at the Public Records Office to find Wills of my Mum's family. Ventured to Kew for more public records. It was a very modern building with a computer ordering system. Some young lads, all of 12 year olds were helping us as we hadn't got a clue!"

20th September, 1980: 'Whisky In The Jar Oh'

"Took a day's holiday this week to go to Lichfield Library to research some more family history there. I must have overtaxed my brain as on the train home I missed my stop and had to go back! Our social life this week has consisted of a soiree at Solihull Ratepayers Association and I nearly set up a blind date with

Helen at work and my brother-in-law, that is until she saw a photo of him and said 'No'! I succeeded at finding a better photo where she could see the resemblance to Phil Lynott, singer with Thin Lizzy and then she readily agreed! This weekend we arrived at Mum and Dad's in Deeping St. James on Friday night to the sound of church bells as it was bellringing practice night. Today, in Peterborough Town Centre, we bumped into Shady in Timothy Whites."

27th September, 1980: Dastardly Dentists and Delightful Dolwyddelan!
"Today at work, I was in the Dentist's chair for 90 minutes surrounded by students. Although I have no problems with my teeth, I was told that I would need my one and only filling done again properly, and all 4 wisdom teeth would need digging out of my gums before they become impacted! I went back to the office in a state of depression and with jaw ache after keeping my mouth open for so long. My mind was taken off this by Marilyn's wedding in North Wales at the weekend. We were so welcomed and felt involved with everything. I presented bouquets to Marilyn's Mum and Sister as it is both their wedding anniversaries on this day too!"

1st October, 1980: Wonderful weekend of wedding celebrations.
"It took 3 hours to drive home from North Wales and then we had to set to and clean the house and spare bedroom as our new student Darren was moving in. He had changed his name from Roy and seems very pleasant, polite and talkative. Admissions timetables at work kept me busy and all the new students were coming into School Office. I was spared the dentist's chair as Terry the dental technician, turned student, didn't come for my teeth! After work Steve and I ate out at the Great American Disaster and went on to the Midland Institute for a lecture on the Holtes of Aston Hall. It was very interesting and with a slide show but we were aware that we were the youngest people in the lecture theatre by many years! Back at home, our student was talking non-stop but I managed to watch 'Butterflies' on t.v. for some light entertainment."

8th October, 1980: We conquered bed bugs in Cardiff but overun by flour beetle here!
"Glenda, at work, wants to know all about my social life and then spends the rest of the time criticising it! At the weekend Steve became irritated by our student lodger Darren's constant chatter, but I think he was just in a bad mood. We escaped to the Tyseley Railway Museum earlier than planned. My Mum was also irritable on the phone. My father-in-law came round with a query on his winemaking but I couldn't help him. He did tell me that they have a student lodger called Julie at their house as the University are still desperate for accommodation. Another annoyance is that we have found an infestation of flour beetle in our food cupboard (we must have been eating them in cakes), and it has now got into everything! Steve consulted the Environmental Health people at work and they have given us a smoke pellet. It is in the cupboard now and hopefully works while I am watching 'Shoestring' on t.v."

15th October, 1980: To be able to record tv programmes to watch at your leisure would be wonderful.
"There seems to be more bitching and backstabbing in the office but I was tired so normally wouldn't notice. On the way home we bought a 5 gallon wine kit. Jilly Cooper, the author was at Hudson's bookshop, so I met her and had my book signed. I was surprised that she is quite a shy person. Steve met his Dad at the pub to talk over future employment and job prospects. Their one source of income, their student lodger has left and they were offered 3 Algerian young men who are desperate for accommodation. My mother-in-law has taken on a job as housekeeper to a man whose wife has left home but not with the children, so he needs help. Apart from cleaning the house, shopping and laundry, he wants home baking too. We are looking into buying the latest technology - a video recorder. To rent one would be £18 a month."

31st October, 1980: My ancestors would not recognise Birmingham and yet would I, in 200 years time?
"We signed a rental agreement for a video recorder and when it arrived I tested it by recording 'To the Manor Born'. At work the minutes for the Admissions Panel meeting have kept me busy and eating out with Steve at the Tennessee Pancake House before

going to our evening class on Aston Hall. Our walk at the weekend to Elmdon Church was so pretty with it being Autumn. The yellow leaves looked like sunlight. Today I took a day's holiday and caught the coach to Worcester and the Record Office in search of my Midland ancestors. The search room was in an old church and nicely converted. I still can't beat my earliest record of Thomas and Ann's marriage in 1782 at St. Martin in the Bullring."
Reader: What would they think of the church today in the shadow of that eye-catching monstrosity of Selfridges.

6th November, 1980: It may be car city but not a good idea to push people underground.
"Alain and Christiane came to stay, laden with presents - an electric knife, cognac confiture and Lancome perfume. We got the Fondue set out for a meal. They were left to amuse themselves as we had to go to work but we all met up afterwards at Pizzaland. Moved on to Hawkins Wine Bar for a meal as it was more upmarket. Today I woke up to hear on the radio that Ronald Reagan had been elected President of America. Walked into the office at work to find Sharon in tears, she had been attacked at 8.15 a.m. on her way to work in the pedestrian subway. She was shaken but not hurt and we persuaded her to notify the police." NB: The pedestrian subways are now gone.

20th November, 1980: You were considered odd if you ordered a soft drink in the pub.
"I was rushed off my feet at work and Glenda and Sharon just sat and watched me! By the afternoon they had offered to help, so I cheered up! I do feel as if I am getting 'UCCA hysteria'. To make matters worse I fell from the top to the bottom of the carpeted stairs at home, due to some comfortable but too well worn slippers, which are now in the bin. I just hurt the bottom of my back which is all bruised. Apart from my aching back I was happy that my boss, Dr. Corbett, asked me to re type something Glenda had done, as it wasn't up to my standard! I felt sorry for Barbara who was told by her boss that she will never be any good at secretarial work! We went to the pub as lunch time for a drink and had a much better afternoon!"

29th November, 1980: Variety is the spice of life!
"The highlight of the week was 'Aston Hall by candlelight' and we took Margot and Keith with us. At work, five of us decided to go

for a drink at lunch time to the Bull at Loveday Street. It doesn't look as if it has changed in centuries and it was just like stepping back in time! My ancestors must have been in here. Yesterday evening Steve and I went to the campus lecture on 'Happiness' by David Attenborough which was short, entertaining and left us in happy moods. Today we were at Steve's cousin Angela's wedding. Andy Gray the groom's brother was a footballer turned t.v. and radio sports commentator. Angela, the bride, is a model and did look rather stylish at St. Margaret's church in Olton. The reception was at the Imperial Hotel and we danced the night away."

30th November, 1980: I am keeping an eye on the cracks on the wall - we are sinking!

"I'm bitten by the family history bug now that I know my Birmingham ancestors were buried underneath where I am sitting at my office desk - St. Mary's churchyard. I noticed on the walls of the building there are 'crack monitor plates' to measure whether the cracks are getting bigger. It appears that the Dental Hospital may be sinking into the old graveyard! I've borrowed books from the Library on the history of Birmingham so this week we have been out and about on the family history trail of old buildings that may have been there in 1872. Not many really, mainly the churches - St. Phillips' Cathedral, some old pubs and St. Paul's church in the jewellery quarter where we had a wander around. I was rather distracted by the pretty sparkly items in the workshop windows - gold, diamonds, sapphires, rubies and emeralds!"

10th December, 1980: Our house is up for sale.

"After a meal at the new American restaurant 'Denny's' on Wednesday night we went to our evening class on Aston Hall but it was a bit boring this week as the tutor didn't know much about Heneage Legge, a resident at the Hall. I had a headache most of the week and Glenda says it is because I eat cheese - my favourite food and so many varieties - I like them all! Our 1960s semi-detached house is on the market for sale as we can now afford a newer 1970s link-detached house with a georgian bow window. A rather old-fashioned couple came to view our house and criticised our secondary double glazing. I woke up yesterday to a news flash on the radio to hear that John Lennon had been shot dead which is rather tragic and sad. Today we had a Christmas lunch in the staff canteen which was delicious. Top quality cooks in the kitchens of the Dental Hospital."

13th December, 1980: Our neighbours are rather sensitive to rattling pipes.
"The Lecturer seemed pleased that our evening class was finished! The last part involved a visit to Aston Hall outbuildings and church. When we arrived home our neighbour came round to complain about our noisy central heating! It was very windy and I had to light the boiler 3 times as the pilot light kept blowing out. I forgot about this yesterday when I enjoyed my usher duties at the degree ceremony in an atmosphere bustling with prize-giving and centenary arrangements. There were loads of mince pies left over to bring home. Today was spent racking the wine, decorating the Christmas tree and writing cards. An evening out by coach to the Architect's Department skittles night out at Hartlebury was good fun, but now what is to be done about the rattling pipes."

24th December, 1980: I assume he is not building the boat during office hours.
"A busy Christmas week at work - lunchtime drinks with the Director, a carol service in the lecture theatre, the General Hospital choir carol concert, my afternoon off for Christmas shopping and the staff meal out at the Centre Hotel in town. Everyone is on alert for IRA bombs as the City is packed with shoppers and evening Christmas celebrations. I had two days leave so took myself off to Warwick and Lichfield Record Offices on the family history trail, but only found 'William, base-born child of Mary' which means my mother's surname should be something different! Steve was enjoying lots of Birmingham City Council office parties mainly at their office in Aston - an old Victorian building which used to house a fire station, Council chambers and a library for the Borough of Aston, made redundant when Aston was absorbed into Birmingham in 1910. One member of staff is renting the area where the fire engines used to be, to build a boat! I have just finished decanting the demijohns into 23 bottles of fine white wine."

1981

1st January, 1981: No one will remember now why we were not invited to the party but I would love to know!
"Steak in mushroom sauce and I excelled in my cookery skills for Steve's parents and brothers on Christmas Eve. St. James Shirley was our Christmas morning outing for the service and as usual we had our 2 Christmas dinners - one in Solihull and one at Deeping St. James. The next few days we just relaxed in the Lincolnshire countryside, taking Gem for lots of walks and occasionally venturing into Peterborough, oh and visiting Grandma. Extended family said they would come and visit but no-one turned up as I think no one wanted to leave their hearth and fireside, and probably TV programmes. There was the Val Doonican Special Years of Christmas, Dallas, Blankety Blank and The Two Ronnies. Back at work on New Year's Eve, and Sandra phoned to say we were Not Invited to Sue and Fred's party and we have no idea as to why not! We did have a great time at King Edward's Aston Old Boys Club dance and Malcolm drove so we drank. Left at 2 a.m. after several toasts to the New Year!"

12th January, 1981: A quiet birthday with the girls in the Dental School office.
"Catching up with people we didn't see as we were not invited to the new year party. Had a drink with Sandra and Phil at the Barton Arms and with Pete and Gail at the Stables. We had lots to talk about, but on mentioning Sue and Fred's party, everyone clammed up! I wonder if we'll ever find out the reason. We have a new student lodger called Dawn and Steve's parent's have taken in David. Still no jobs on the horizon for my father-in-law and no-one is interested in buying our house. It is my 28th birthday today and the girls at work bought me some posh lingerie and a classy notebook for my family history research. No money for a slap-up meal out so I cooked a steak dinner and we met up with Malcolm at the George in Solihull for a drink. He had bought me the Jolly Super Jilly Cooper book."

21st January, 1981: My hobby involves me only being interested in dead people!
"I bought the latest Abba LP 'Super Trouper' and a book called 'Violets and Vinegar' with my birthday money. We were taken out for a surprise meal in the evening at the Bell in Tamworth-in-Arden by Steve's parents as his Dad has been offered a job and wanted to celebrate. Back at home our central heating pump packed up so it was kettles of hot water for a morning wash. Today a new pump was fitted for £35, it is much quieter and the neighbours will be pleased, as the noise of the old one rather bothered them. We are just happy to have heat and hot water. Steve's parents came round while we were in the middle of dinner tonight! Afterwards I relaxed with a gem of a book I had found on the Library shelves 'The Epitaphs of St. Philips' Church'!"

1st February, 1981: Birmingham's air pollution of car exhaust fumes bothers me at times.
"I had a very pleasant letter from South Africa with a family tree but unfortunately our branch was not on it and I couldn't see even a remote connection. After work I was in the Library to search for some more elusive ancestors and got distracted by a publication called 'Midland Antiquary'. Yesterday, not such a good day at work. Dr. Corbett called me in to say I had made a spelling mistake on the 500 letters I had sent out! Today we gave Steve's Dad a lift to work to start his new job. At lunch time I took a refreshing walk to the shops but it is a pity that the air is filled with car fumes. Birmingham is well known as 'car city' unfortunately. Just as well we topped up on fresh air at the weekend on a walk around Meriden and last week at Wythall on Sunday in the leafy Warwickshire and Worcestershire countryside. Today is February the 1st and I have been sunbathing outside in a deckchair!"

15th February, 1981: A weekend in London and a dilemma about church.
"James Herriot's books are hilarious for light relief when I've had enough of genealogy. Sharon in the office announced that she is getting married so there was much talk amongst everyone about wedding plans. I bought 2 paper lampshades at lunch time and a book on headaches. On Wednesday evening Steve's parents came

round and started talking about religion - I do hope they are not going to force us to go to church! I used to enjoy Evensong with my Mum in my home village where it was all peaceful and short relaxing stroll to the church. Here would be a car drive away and a frantic search for somewhere to park. I have already made my a excuses about not going to 'Young Wives'. This weekend we were staying with Dick and Susie in London and they were out at Crufts Dog Show when we arrived. We had an outing to Hampton Court Palace and on to a house in Upper Richmond Road where a friend Nick is gutting the place to renovate. I am sure it will take him years of hard work to sort out."

25th February, 1981: The end of the world mysteriously and sadly became true!

"Arranged to go to Paris in May and Malcolm and Helen want to come but Helen's parents refuse to let her, so I am to write a letter of persuasion to them. If Helen can't go my mother-in-law insists she will take her place. Prince Charles and Lady Diana Spencer announced their engagement today but I couldn't help feeling that Charles was pushed into it. In the evening we went to a meeting about the 1981 census and we are going to become Enumerators. There seemed to be lots of paperwork and instructions to read. Today Glenda spent the whole afternoon saying that the world would end in 20 years time. She wouldn't let it go and I was getting quite depressed!" Reader: It was very strange but Glenda died 20 years after saying that - her only symptoms being swollen ankles and a bit of a cough - and she just fell asleep in a chair. The cause of death at the post mortem was inconclusive.

7th March, 1981: I suppose a comfortable flat in a tower block is better than no home at all.

"Muriel's house was burgled in the night - apparently there is a burglary every 20 minutes in the West Midlands! Glenda's superior attitude took over in the office and she talked about security and insurance and how she had got the best. We were all quite fed up. Darren phoned to say Vincent and Felicity had got married and were having a baby, so I was pleased for them. Enjoyed the Architect's Easter Dinner Dance at the Guild Club with Malcolm and Helen. Today we went to our Census Area and noted down the flat numbers in the Tower Blocks at Bromford. Discovered that Birmingham Race Course had to be demolished to build these blocks of flats for the thousands of families on the housing waiting list. Standing looking at the monstrous buildings and listening to the sound of the two motorways nearby, I felt so grateful that we lived in a house with a garden. In the evening I started reading all the census information but fell asleep as it was so boring."

22nd March 1981: Church, Census and Beauty Without Cruelty.

"We went to Nottingham to see Jane and to discuss her coming to Paris with us. Helen's parents have forbidden her to come. We had a very windy walk around Wollaton Hall. I collected my dry cleaning from town this week and it had blue stains all over it but as I was in a rush to get back to the Headmasters Conference I am helping with; I shall have to sort it out another day. On Saturday we went to a shop in Harborne called 'Beauty Without Cruelty'. They sell mock fur jackets and make-up that hasn't been tested on animals. Today was a right mix. At church in the morning for my mother-in-law's Confirmation where we met Bishop Hugh. In the afternoon we were delivering census leaflets to the Bromford tower blocks of flats. My legs ached after walking down 100 flights of stairs! A family party at the in-laws in the evening."

3rd April, 1981: Ladies Night - To honour Masons' Ladies, Daughters, Mother, Sisters and the other fine women about the world......

"Another Census Enumerator training session and evenings spent writing addresses on the census forms. All the rest of the evenings this week have been spent delivering the forms but not many people were in, so we had to keep going back and Steve took a day's holiday from work to catch up. Tonight we left the census forms to go out to a Masonic Dinner Dance - Ladies Night - with Steve's parents and their friends. Everyone seemed so much older than us and those who were the same age just acted older. Steve definitely does not want to join however much it upsets his Dad! At the end of the evening known as 'Carriages' on the invitation, balloons were released from the ceiling nets. We had to gather these up to take home for Steve's younger brother Richard, that is, until Steve reminded his Dad that Richard is 15!"

12th April, 1981: Every room was a shrine to Elvis Presley.

"6th April this week was the start of the census forms collection. We did well, everyone was friendly but I was really cold and tired by 8.15pm when we finished. Spent every evening after work collecting and then at home sorting the forms. Today we counted up and have only 56 more to collect. One man invited us in to his flat and I noticed he had an empty living room apart from one small table and one dining chair. Another lady talked to us through her letter box! She was very pleasant and we managed to answer all her questions, so she posted her form to us back through the letterbox! Another lady invited us in to proudly show us around her whole flat which was a shrine to Elvis Presley! It hasn't all been hard slog, we have had some interesting and amusing moments!"

23rd April, 1981: Cold, wet and windy so not ideal weather for a canal barge holiday, nor to stand and stare.
"Worked in the garden last weekend and helped Steve to build a dry brick wall to hide the compost heap. Everyone has been in a happy mood at work with the Easter holidays looming. I cooked a three course meal for Steve's parents and brothers before we left to visit my parents on Easter Saturday. We broke the journey near Market Harborough at Foxton Locks on the Grand Union Canal, being the largest flight of staircase locks in England, 2 sets of five. The holiday weather was cold, windy and not up to much so at Mum and Dad's we didn't leave the fire and watched Flambards on t.v. The highlight of my Easter break was visiting St. Catherine's House for the death records! I boarded a coach for London at Digbeth early, and spent hours pouring over the death indexes. I ordered 4 certificates for £16. It sounds morbid, but I really enjoyed myself! Back at work today my boss was on 'Cloud 9' after the best holiday he has ever had! I met Viv and Val at the Management Centre for lunch."

26th April, 1981: I was interviewed at home by a man from the Commonwealth Office.
"I opened a 'strictly private and confidential letter' by mistake which annoyed my boss. If he had known I'd read it out to the staff as well, I think it would have been instant dismissal! I must pay more attention when opening the post in future. At lunch time we had a farewell party for Jill at Hawkins Wine Bar. She is leaving to work as an air hostess. We had a relaxing weekend planned until Steve's Dad phoned on Saturday morning asking him to go over and sort the kitchen out for him - something to do

An airfield near Paris.

with fitting a kitchen fan. Today at home, I was interviewed by a Mr. Birkenshaw from the Commonwealth Office. My friend Diane has applied for a job in Hong Kong and has put me down to supply a character reference. I was surprised at the strictness of the rules, as the job is only secretarial, although I think it is in the Police department."

4th May, 1981: 1000 BC Egyptian children played with large hoops of dried grape vines.

"Quite a few staff came back off holiday today from Scotland and Wales looking tanned! Glenda brought a hula hoop into the office so we all had a go. We were mainly hula dancing as if on an Hawaiian island and luckily no-one came in the office. It is supposed to be good exercise to help relieve sciatica but no-one has that. I have been to the local Swimming Pool trying to learn to swim with Steve as my teacher. I managed half a length but only if I could grab on to him otherwise I kept going under and choked a few times. I went to the swimming pool again today and couldn't swim at all! More phone calls from Steve's Dad wanting help with the kitchen fan. In between times we are painting and decorating the house to try and sell it. Also I am scrutinising the job section in the Architects Journal to look for jobs away from the West Midlands."

22nd May, 1981: Every cloud has a silver lining.

"We heard the news today that our friends Margot and Keith are splitting up, which was quite a shock, but on the plus side Margot wants to buy our house! We were invited to their house for dinner and it was all very amicable. Now we have to set to and look for a house ourselves and rather liked the look of one in Harnall Close. On the local plans it appears that there is a factory to be built at the back, so we are undecided. Mum phoned to say that Grandma is now living with them and her house is up for sale in Peterborough. She was becoming very confused and was not safe to be left. Today, though, I am writing this in Paris with Steve, Malcolm and Jane. Alain and Christiane met us off the hovercraft in Calais filming everything on their video camera. We all stayed at their friends' house in Bettune last night."

25th May, 1981: We hadn't been told of the light aircraft experience, only of the boating lake at Versailles!

"We were on our way to Versailles when Alan stopped at the Aero Club and he has a pilot's licence. Steve and I were first to go up in the plane and apart from feeling a tad scared, I was exhilarated by the experience and the views over Paris. Then it was Malcolm and Jane's turn and by this time Alain was in 'fun mode'. He was doing all sorts of aero acrobatics and something like a 'loop de loop'. When the plane finally landed the right way up, Jane got out of the plane looking quite 'ashen'. She recovered in time for the meal at Sarah's house. In true French style there was about 16 courses and the meal lasted 6 hours! Everything is eaten separately - the meat came on its own, and once consumed it was followed by petit pois etc. Course No. 9 was stewed fruit and Malcolm sat waiting patiently for some custard, but of course it never arrived, or it might have been after the cheese!"

11th June, 1981: I wouldn't want a moat around the house - I still can't swim

"Back home, and our offer of £31,500 (to include carpets) has been accepted on a house in Glascote Close Shirley in Solihull. It could be a while before we move as Margot has to sell her house and we appear to be in a chain. Our minds were taken off this by going to look at another house on the market - far beyond our wildest dreams as it had a moat! The nearly derelict 15th century Berry Hall Farm down Ravenshaw Lane - a wonderful project if you had plenty of cash. I have been swimming yet again and can almost swim a length but can't stop or start without drowning! Today in the lunch hour I went to see James Herriot (Alf White) who was signing books in W.H. Smiths. I bought his latest vet book and wished I lived in Yorkshire."

25th June, 1981: Sex Therapy - Sin or Salvation.
"We have been out a few times with Margot and Keith to Romeo & Juliet's which is bizarre when they are splitting up with Margot buying our house and yet they act like a normal couple. At lunch times I've been out at the shops buying birthday cards at the Athena poster shop and collected some holiday brochures but I'm not impressed with the package tours on offer. Today I dressed for the hot sun but the weathermen had got it wrong. Just as we left work there was an open lecture by a Sex Therapist Dr. Cole, who works at the University. It was called 'Sex Therapy: Sin or Salvation'. Jenny and I were there for the introduction, but had to miss the film as we had buses to catch. These talks are very popular with a full lecture theatre and standing room only!"

4th July, 1981: We impress visitors with our ancient relics.
"Jean has found herself a husband in Australia and they came to stay. Lovely to meet Des and wedding bells are to be ringing soon. They came along with us to the Urban Renewal party at Balsall Heath and we were entertained by a folk group! There was coffee afterwards at another house which was a 'right tip' and I was shocked to find out it belonged to a Public Health Inspector! In the daytime we went to Ragley Hall in Warwickshire....a beautiful stately home to impress visitors with - there is nothing like this in Australia! Relaxed at home watching the tennis finals on t.v. between Borg and McEnroe and the latter won. Another treat when my brother Ian came with his friends Nigel and Phillipa - we all went to the NEC to see Bob Dylan in concert which was very enjoyable."

12th July, 1981: We are becoming professional wedding guests.
"Pierre and Sarah from Paris phoned to say they wanted to come and stay then I just put the phone down and Louise and David

Jean and Des are married in Peterborough.

The pool at the half finished hotel.

phoned with the same request. No wonder I keep having bad dreams about lodgers taking over the house! This weekend we were in Peterborough for Jean and Des's wedding at the Methodist church in Westgate. A beautiful day and I danced and danced at the Saxon Hotel afterwards - one of the best wedding receptions I have been to. Today we were all a little quiet after much merrymaking last night. We went out in the fields to pick strawberries as a hangover cure."

18th July, 1981: Too many visitors and I need a holiday!
"On our way home on Monday night we had to drive past our old flat in Handsworth and there were riot police in helmets with shields. Three days of rioting caused by unemployment, boredom and copying other gangs had all taken its toll. I went out at lunch time and saw some of the damage in the city. I woke up feeling edgy about the day as I needed to rush home and cook a decent meal for a group of 4 friends from France. To make matters worse we had a student guide party with wine on finishing work which I was involved with. I had to disappear and don't think I was missed once the wine was free flowing. Despite a tight schedule, it all went well and the rest of the week was quiet. Now this weekend we had Louise, David and baby Rhodri to stay from Wales. The fondue set came out again but I couldn't produce enough food for the Welsh appetites! After all this entertaining I decided that we needed a holiday and I got into bed with a pile of holiday brochures. On flicking through them I found a reasonably priced option - Bulgarian resorts on the Black Sea. I shall be at the Travel Agents on Monday lunch time."

22nd July, 1981: A hotel that is half built has some advantages.
"I had to be up on Sunday at at 8 a.m. to cook breakfast. No sooner had I finished that it was time to put some lunch in the oven. I thought that this will be my piece de resistance before I hang up my chef's hat so it was Burgundy Lamb with a pudding of Apple Meringue. I had cooked plenty this time and everyone seemed to enjoy it. I really wanted an afternoon nap afterwards but I had all the washing up to do. Louise, David and Rhodri set off back to Wales and Steve was called round to his parents for something. I told him to tell them that I was not available next weekend to help with their dinner party as I wanted some time off! Desperate for a holiday I was in the travel agents on Monday lunch time. All the cheap holidays had gone but there was a half built hotel in Crete! I decided that half a hotel would mean the dining room and swimming pool would never be full and crowded, so I booked it. On the way back to the office I bought a guide book on Crete and a new bikini. In the evening our old student lodger Darren wanted us to go and see him. The Erdington-Brookvale Village where he lived was pleasant but the houses very close together. I drank 2 large Martinis and we listened to Judy Tzuke."

27th July, 1981: I must remember not to tell my Mum when I feel ill.
"Steve's 29th birthday at the weekend and he had just had a pay rise at work! We went to his parents for a barbeque in the garden and ended up wrapped in blankets it was so cold. I am really looking forward to some Mediterranean weather. I couldn't go to work on Wednesday as my stomach was upset. Feeling sorry for myself I phoned my Mum who told me that she knew of someone who had died from a bout of diarrhoea! I wish I hadn't bothered! Felt fine today and my brother-in-law kindly took us to Birmingham Airport for our 4 hour flight to Iraklion and we arrived at 11 pm our time - 1 pm local time. It was then an hour by minibus to Elounda. The hotel room was beautiful, brand new, but like an oven!"

30th July, 1981: Outdoor furniture is a feature in the hotel pool!
"We booked our tours with Linda the Cosmos rep and we were sat

with another couple our age - a Mr. and Mrs. Day. We had lunch by the pool before walking along the hot and dusty track to Elounda. So hot and bothered after that and jumped into the hotel pool to cool off. Our chairs, tables and umbrellas were blown in after us! This was due to the hot mistral wind apparently! After dinner in the hotel we sat on the balcony looking at the sea. The Royal Wedding of Charles and Diana was happening back home and we had to wait until the evening to see the highlights on Greek t.v. Yesterday, the boat trip to Spinalonga was beautiful and evening dinner in Elounda. I am sleeping better now but keep getting bitten by something. Our 4th wedding anniversary today and a trip to the Plateau of Lassithi, stopping at a monastery first. Another highlight was going down into a cave - the birthplace of Zeus."

31st July, 1981: The tranquility was ruined by the 18 to 30 club!

"We have become quite good friends with Geoff and Mary Day and arranged to go on a trip with them to a mountain village called Karzanos. First we spent the morning in Aghios Nikolaos. Enjoyed moussaka for lunch on the waterfront. Later, with Geoff and Mary we took the coach to the bottom of Ida mountain. From there we had to walk or go by donkey up a path to the mountain village. It was a bit rowdy at the top as the 18 to 30 Club had arrived there first for a Creton Night Out! The wine, as much as you could drink, and the food - salad, cheese and some sort of meat was o.k. or so I thought. Away from the noisy crowd it seemed like a good evening out, but.... Steve was the first one to be violently sick.......!"

3rd August, 1981: Waiting to feel normal again.

"These last 2 days have been a 'write off' - me, Steve and Mary have all taken to our beds with sickness. We had to cancel our trip to Knossos and after a lot of negotiating we fortunately got our money back. Yesterday, I spent the afternoon by the pool underneath a Carob tree and read a Neville Shute novel. I felt much better by evening and attempted dinner but didn't eat much. Today we took the bus to Anjious to do some shopping. We had our last meal of the holiday in Elounda on a sea front Taverna with Mary and Geoff. Our plane left from Iraklion at 11.30 p.m.. When we landed we took Mary and Jeff into Birmingham Railway Station."

Reader: A year later Mary and Geoff had a baby girl and called her Sally. It is a shame that their marriage didn't last much longer.

17th August, 1981: Our house was a hotel once again.
"Dad had bought a Spitfire sports car. We saw it at the weekend and also looked at a 4 bedroom house in Deeping St. James which we could afford but we live in a smaller house because of the West Midlands prices. Realised we could live in a mansion in Lincolnshire but there are no jobs. Back at work this week and 'A' Level results are coming in. The weather is still good and a walk in Cannon Hill Park for some fresh air was a treat after all the city car fumes. Arrived home from work on Friday and half an hour later our 5 visitors from France arrived. We had an easy salad tea and a busy weekend followed. Luckily the weather held and after the shops in Solihull we had drinks the yard of the Mason's Arms and a boat trip on the river at Stratford. We all went to my brother's in Bristol on Sunday for lunch and a walk along the Esplanade at Weston-super-Mare to the old pier. This morning I had to cook everyone's breakfast before going to work! The phone didn't stop ringing in the office as the exam results are out and everyone wants a place on the course. Arrived home tonight, visitors gone, lots of laundry and house to sort out but there was a knock at the door. Steve's Dad wanting some typing doing. I had to count to ten!"

23rd August, 1981: The latest fashion at the hair salon.
"This week I have tried to relax as work is hotting up with begging letters and phone calls for places on the Dental courses. After work I've been sitting in the garden reading the 'Birmingham Post' book. Some 'maternity' information came through for the attention of the staff. I noticed that the junior, Jenny, read it intensely. We then had a discussion on unmarried mothers! I had an appointment with the hairdressers to restyle my hair and Steve took a 'before and after' photo. The latest style is the 'flicked out' look. I was doing all the gardening as Steve doesn't seem to be interested. I also drove to Olton Library for an evening class prospectus. Apart from a walk around Earlswood lakes we went to my father-in-law's birthday party where all the men seemed to be 'Masons'."

30th August, 1981: From Robin Hood to the Fen Tigers.
"An abundance of plums on the tree in the garden so I've been

making plum wine, jam, crumble, frozen a fair few and given as many away as possible. My in-laws have been round to borrow our lawn mower, use of the washing machine, wanting taking places in the car, typing doing, help with dinner parties and to watch our t.v. Decided I wanted to live in Bromsgrove. After dinner we went there and walked around the Tardebigge Locks. This weekend we met Jane and Chris in Nottingham and looked around the town and Nottingham Castle. My cousin Shonagh and her boyfriend were at my parents house when we got there. We had a chat but then needed to go to Crowland and meet Diane at the pub by the River Welland. It is rather disturbing that the river is higher than the land in the Fens. Drainage has shrunk the fields but the land is so rich and fertile for crops to be grown. It does seem strange driving up to the river. Just as well there are pumping stations everywhere after the floods of 1953!"

13th September, 1981: A man overboard and his bad luck didn't end there!

"Watched 'Sergeant Bilko' in bed on the t.v. before going to sleep as laughter is the best medicine. Steve is busy with drawings for a bakery on Soho Road, Handsworth. Keith collected us today with our picnic for a trip on the River at Stratford in his boat. It was moored just past Luddington Locks. Great sunshine for the picnic but on the way back it rained, dramatic skies and a slippery boat resulting in Keith falling overboard!! Even worse, when we arrived back at the car it had been broken into and a bag stolen. He was standing there dripping wet wondering what else could go wrong. I felt so helpless."

20th September, 1981: I was lucky and escaped the pre wedding ritual!

"On Friday Sharon's wedding presentation took place in the office and we dressed her up in a veil and 'L' plates, plied her with wine finishing with an Irish coffee. She left in a zombie like state. The wedding was this weekend and I had a heavy cold but still enjoyed myself. We had a week's holiday so on Sunday set off at 11 a.m. for the Lake District - it was pouring with rain. Stormy dramatic skies over Lakes Windermere and Ullswater but there was a welcoming fire at the farmhouse B & B. Had an evening meal out in Keswick but I couldn't taste a thing so I was even eating food that I don't like! My cough is like a bark and I was convinced I'd get pneumonia!"

23rd September,1981: The humble abode of Alexander McDonald.
"It was a long drive to Inverness and we stopped at Carlisle for lunch. Arrived at West Moniak farm at 6 p.m. Yesterday we started the McDonald family trail - my Dad's family at Alves, Inchstelly and Elgin. We found a quarry cottage where Alexander would have been the quarryman - losing an arm in an accident there. The long cottage would have housed the animals at one end keeping the place warm! Beauly for dinner. Today we were invited to Hamish and Myra McDonald's house and I admired their tartan carpet. Also discovered that my ancestor Alexander McDonald the gardener lived in what is now their shed, with a tree growing through it. Easter Kirkhill which means East of Kirkhill."

25th September, 1981: The ferry wasn't running due to lack of interest.
"Yesterday we set off for Ullapool via the 'Heights of Docharty' where we talked to Donny McDonald an old man of 78 who was working in a field. After buying lunch and a book in Dingwall we were on the road to Ullapool. I felt sleepy after taking Mucron tablets. We found a phone box and got through to the Altnaharrie Inn on Loch Broom, but as it is only accessible by the ferry which was not sailing because of lack of interest, we couldn't go! The bad weather, it seems, we had brought with us! Liz from the Dental School has given up her job to go and manage the place so I was keen to check it out! Instead we had a walk to the Lighthouse and a pebbly beach with dinner at Beauly. Today it was the long journey to Yorkshire stopping at Dundee for lunch and to the Perth Road where my Grandfather Thomas Dickson McDonald was born, in a flat over the stable block, in 1896. Arrived in Richmond at 7 p.m. rather tired."

27th September, 1981: On our way to the new Humber Bridge.
"It was pouring with rain, yet again when we set off for the Yorkshire Dales. We stopped to buy sandwiches and I also bought a copy of the James Herriot 'vet' book. We were heading for the newly opened Humber Bridge and stopped off at a little market town called Beverley. We had a cup of tea and a toasted tea cake in a cafe overlooking the market cross and thought it would be a lovely place to live. Crossed the Humber and drove

Our new link-detached house in Shirley.

down the A15 to Deeping St. James. Mum and Dad were going out to the ISS Cleaning Services dance so we went too. Today I still couldn't stop coughing and now I have a pain in my side. Dad says I need to see a Doctor, so I worried about it all the way home."

3rd October, 1981: I must eat garlic for my health but it could be a lonely existence.
"Back to work and I didn't feel too bad until everyone said I looked worse for going on holiday! I booked an appointment at the Doctors. My boss gave me quite a bit of work and talked about it all going on computer. I wasn't quite sure whether that meant I would be out of a job or not. Saw the Doctor after work who examined me and said my cold was on the way out and the pain was a pulled muscle as I strained myself coughing! Felt better after that. The cough linctus has made me sleepy but I'm not coughing although have a very croaky voice and still can't taste or smell, but I'm not dying apparently. Today we had a talk about computers but I didn't take much in as I felt drowsy and

then workmen were taking plaster off the walls - dust everywhere and everyone is coughing! I ate two small cloves of garlic before I went to bed as I had read that it has great medicinal properties!"

11th October, 1981: Our super sensitive neighbours are now complaining about noisy coughing!

"The weekend and I was mowing the lawns when our neighbours came to talk to me about the noise of my coughing! They were quite concerned but then it rather shocked them when I told them we were moving house. Hopefully this will happen next Monday but the people selling the house we are buying have been phoning us demanding we pay the interest on their bridging loan as our solicitor has not acted quickly enough! On seeing our solicitor he told us not to panic! We started an evening class in the old manor house in Solihull High Street. A half timbered Tudor building and a most appropriate place to do research using old parish registers to find out how far in miles people moved to meet and marry. This has been a welcome diversion from dismantling and packing up our home as the more we did, the more we found to do!"

16th October, 1981: One of life's most stressful events - moving house.

"We were up early and well organised for the removal men. My in-laws phoned to say could we go and collect a wine press for them! I had to explain that we were rather busy moving house! They then called round at midday. The move went well and the previous occupiers were pleasant after all their threats. We met one of the neighbours who is a pilot with a 2nd family and a gorgeous white cat called Sam. I love the house and the little close it is in. Steve's father and brother Richard came round in the evening with a bottle of wine but I was so tired and it did show. Today we unpacked, cleaned and went out to buy curtain rails, poles and light fittings. We went back to see Margot in our old house with a bottle of champagne for her. It did seem strange."

25th October, 1981: We now live in Glascote Close, Shirley so I must find out the history.

"Steve was in Wales to survey a building and I spent a few hours sorting out the 2nd bedroom so that everything was accessible and the desk was clear ready for the ten feet of shelves for the study. To relieve the boredom I talked to Sue next door. We had a walk on Sunday as far as Solihull railway station and called in at the Colebrook pub. It was packed with about 100 men and 5 women - talk about equality over cooking the Sunday lunch! At work in the lunch hour I mooched around town and bought the Habitat catalogue to see what our house could be like if we had the money. After work we went to the 'Pretenders fancy dress' shop to hire spanish outfits for a party on Saturday. More bomb scares in the city so I think I'll stay in at lunch times for now."

15th November 1981: I think we invited the neighbours.
"The crime prevention officer came to see us about house security and to advise on locks. A visit to 'Protectitall' was next and we had to spend £41 on making our house burglar proof. Margot wants a joint housewarming party at her house (our old house) so we are organising it and even Alain and Christiane from Paris want to come. It is giving me a headache as I feel responsible for everyone having a good time by inviting them. Also I'm worried that my friend Barbara would bring along her husband's marijuana smoking friends. I needn't have worried, the party went well and Alain filmed it all on video. Everyone had left by 4 a.m. apart from our solicitor John who was last to go. Today we had to have a sleep in and our French friends went back to Paris, Jane back to Peterborough by which time we had to rush round to Margot's to help clear up, but she had done it."

29th November, 1981: My father-in-law becomes Worshipful Master and it's Grandma's 85th birthday.
"We called in to see my cousin Shonagh in her flat over the Cresset Centre in Bretton - a new part of the ever expanding city of Peterborough. There was a Christmas Fair which we looked around. I need some ideas for the office 'Christmas Dip'. We all wrap a present to be put in a large festively decorated bin and everyone takes a present out to put under the tree at home. Apart from that, people at work have bought all their Christmas presents and I haven't even bought one yet. I did buy flat shoes for walking round the shops as my high heels are doing me no good, so that is a start. As my father-in-law is now the Worshipful Master at his Masonic Lodge, Steve was helping him with the table plan for Ladies Night. This event has clashed with my Grandma's 85th birthday party and Mum was not pleased. I can't seem to keep everyone happy."

River Welland   Deeping St. James   Me, brother Ian & Gem.

13th December, 1981: My new dentist is a ray of sunshine in a freezing cold office.
"The buses were on strike, the traffic was atrocious and I was 20 minutes late for work. In the afternoon my new dentist Julian Perry walked into School Office, who everyone fancies, even Glenda's mood softens when he is around. It has been so cold in the office this week starting at 55°F and only rising to 68°F if we are lucky. Instead of Christmas shopping at lunch time I've been looking for thermal vests. By Friday it was snowing continually and it took an hour, that is twice as long, to get to work. The office temperature only reached 61°F all day. This weekend I sat in the sun in our bay window writing Christmas cards and the lads across the road were making a very impressive igloo. The lights have been flickering and we have been warned of power cuts, due to the unrelenting snow. In the evening Steve braved it as he needed to see a man about a bungalow. I am glad we are not in Scotland as the temperature in Glasgow has been -13°F."

20th December, 1981: Remote control - no more getting off the settee to change channels.
"Our new portable t.v. arrived - with remote control! It was still snowing with blizzards and despite bleeding all the air out of the radiators at home, it was still cold. The interviewees for the Dentistry courses failed to turn up because most were snowbound. We were sitting working in our coats at one point as

we were so cold. The Christmas Incidentals still took place and when Terry White popped in to ask if I was going, the whole office was convinced I would be dragged on to the stage! I worried about this until I heard that I would be sitting with Jean and Jim on the balcony. The freeze continues and the water pipes in the garage are frozen so I can't use the washing machine. Stayed in - too cold to go out and watched 'Hi-de-hi' on t.v."

26th December, 1981: Coldest winter since 1890 and snowiest since 1878.

"These past few days the shops have been full to bursting and a lot of plastic is being used to pay for everything. We had our staff Christmas lunch at the Centre Hotel and I wore my new blouse which looked as if I'd slept in it. At 4 p.m. my boss came round with the sherry bottle and glasses. Steve collected me at 5 p.m. and we went to the Aston Council House party and as that finished just got the tail end of the Baskerville House party. My eyes were stinging from all the smoke. Christmas Eve and I was cooking for Steve's family - prawns in whisky, burgundy lamb and a pudding called Christmas snowballs. Christmas Day and opened our presents - Human League L.P. and Chanel No. 19 (the right number this time). Church with Steve's parents, Christmas lunch at their house and travelled to my parents for Christmas dinner in the evening. Freezing fog but we found our way. Today was Boxing Day and the River Welland was frozen solid. We took the dog for a walk on it. Malcolm came over to meet my cousin Sally-Ann and he brought his skates for the river!"

1982

12th January, 1982: In the deep midwinter frosty wind made moan.

"The river is still frozen over so we had one last walk on it for the novelty. We will remember the Winter of 81/82! Back to work after celebrating the new year in at the Old Boys Club. Everywhere is crowded with 'sale' shoppers. You wouldn't think there was a recession! We made up another 5 gallon vessel of wine and I read my book on 'classic slums'. The heating had been fixed at work thankfully but the big freeze is still on. There is ice on the inside of the windows at home even though the central heating is on. My 29th birthday today and the girls in the office

Begum Madhui   Soondi.

bought me letter writing paper with tissue lined envelopes (luxury), Badedas Bath Foam and After Eight mints. We had a lunchtime drink at the Gunmakers Arms and Steve took me for a slap up meal to the Tile House in the evening (now the Ristorante Dal Forno, Tilehouse Lane, Shirley). We were the only ones in there who had braved the weather on a Monday night. A fan heater was brought in to bring the dining room up to a decent temperature."

31st January, 1982: Belfast, Dublin and Guinness cake.
"The office temperature has gone from one extreme to the other - we are sweltering at 80°F. Lots of work and we now have a lovely temp lady called Shelagh from Belfast and the best thing is that she is 'unflappable'. Glenda brought in some Guinness cake as it was her birthday on Wednesday. Although she is not Irish, we serenaded her with 'In Dublin's Fair City, where the girls are so pretty, I first set my eyes on sweet Molly Malone '. I hoped she was amused and touched by our feeble efforts, although the singing was dire! There was a rail strike so more chaos on the roads. We went to a fancy dress party in Peterborough - I was a saloon girl, Steve a jungle explorer and Jane and Chris were cave men. It caused a stir in the Gordon Arms where we all met before the party at Scoops (SueCooper's)."

28th February, 1982: The ghost could have been my ancestor with important information!
"At work I discovered a new way into the city centre shops

through the General Hospital Gardens. I was also on the look out for the 'Lady in Grey' - the ghost of a Matron who used to work there, although more hospital staff have encountered a figure of `a kindly old man with a clay pipe in his mouth`, and this, on one occasion was confirmed by the night sister. She saw the phantom vanish, on reaching a recently-constructed wall. `He is just such a friendly old chap we don't want to bother him`. This weekend we have noticed that the car does not like being washed. Water seems to seep into the engine which causes it to keep stalling. It did this after being cleaned with the hosepipe on Sunday at Deeping St. James level crossing! I was driving my Mum to collect eggs from a farmhouse. The engine stalled on the railway lines, and Mum got out and ran, leaving me to try and get the thing to start. Eventually the engine came back to life. I am hoping perhaps that the trains do not run on a Sunday in which case we were not in danger."

20th March, 1982: The garden is a 'blank canvas' so Steve is now interested in gardening.

"The t.v. and video have been fixed on to a 'pivotelli' which is an arm attached to the Wall - no need for a shelf or table which suits a husband who is a minimalist. Steve has become interested in the garden now that we have a 'blank canvas' - just lawn and he is enjoying drawing up a design plan. I was reading the Solihull News when a man from the local nursery came round to give advice on the types of shrubs and trees for a north facing garden. I noticed that Sam the cat and a squirrel were watching the proceedings nearby. I relaxed in the evening watching a four part serial called 'Alexa' from a book by Andrea Newman. Although I don't like the character Alexa, as she runs off with her best friend's husband, I do like the name and we have lots of Alexander McDonalds on the family tree, so it is an abbreviation of an old family name. On my mother's side I don't know how we would make a modern name out of Jabez or even worse on Steve's side - Ferdinand! We were having an amusing discussion about this whilst driving out to the Cherry Tree Motel. Steve is designing a factory for Keith who took us out to Sunday lunch and we met his new lady friend Vicky." Reader: We named our daughter Alexa Rani. The name Rani, meaning Indian princess as there are two Indian Great Grandmothers on the George family tree - Madhui related to a Nawab (similar to a British peerage) and Soondi the servant girl!

23rd April, 1982: A new shopping centre and I remember the quirkiness of the old one.
"Bought a surrealist poster. Enjoyed a goblet of wine at Beaumonts with Julie at lunch time. I was fed up at work to rang up the BBC for a job application form. Avoncroft Open Air Museum and lunch at a pub by the canal was a good choice for an outing. Also the Botanical Gardens was a wonderful jungle type venue for the Architects' Dinner Dance although a bit cramped at the meal where we were packed on to long tables touching shoulders. At Easter we saw the new Queensgate shopping centre in Peterborough. Very ultra modern with a glass lift in the middle, steel tubing, marble floor and lush green plants. An old department store called Farrows was demolished to make way for this. I think it sold fabrics and as a child with my Mum, we sometimes called in after shopping at the Co-op across the road (I still know the 'divi' number). I remember the unusual payment system in Farrows. Money was put in a capsule and in a pipe where it shot off to the cash office and your change and receipt came back quite quickly through all the pipes overhead in the shop, the same way! Back in Solihull and I started an evening class - disco dancing. It is based on Pans People, Legs and Co and Hot Gossip!. The women there were all housewife types so I don't know how this is going to work but our teacher Rita is hopeful."

30th May, 1982: An ideal 'Situation Vacant' in a place called Hull.
"Started ballroom dance classes with Steve and we began with a quick step and waltz. The hospital was having a day of industrial action so we could leave at 3.30pm as the caretaker was locking up. As I had some unexpected free time I decided to look through the Architects' Journal when I got home and noticed in the 'Situations Vacant' section a Principal Architect's job at Hull City Council '. I put a ring around it and left it on the coffee table. We took Steve's brothers and their canoes with us to Mum and Dad's. They found it great fun on the river, just as much as skating on it in the winter. After we had extracted a poor sparrow from the cat's mouth, we took the dog for a walk across the fields and ended up at the Rose in Frognall and their beer garden. We were the only ones there and the landlady had the ironing board out behind the bar - multitasking."

19th June, 1982: The Paddle Steamer Lincoln Castle moored in the shadow of its replacement.
"I had a phone call from Steve in Hull to say he had got the job! Went out and bought OS maps and any books and information on Hull and the surrounding area. We went to see Steve's parents and told them the news - they were pleased but taken aback and my mother-in-law said she would be spending all of her 2 week annual holiday with us. I hope she was joking. This weekend we drove to Hull on the A38 leaving at 6.50 a.m. and arriving first in Beverley at 9.30 a.m. to do some house hunting. Looked around Hull too and the old dock areas. Stayed in a cheap and cheerful B & B in Ryde Street off the Beverley Road in a small terraced house, a bit like Coronation Street. The highlight of our day was a meal on the now redundant PS (paddle steamer) Lincoln Castle moored on the Hessle Foreshore with a superb view of the engineering achievement that took this boat out of action - the Humber Bridge."

29th June, 1982: Whistlestop Tour and more for our money in the north.
"Breakfast at 9.30 a.m. and we set off for the docks and coast. Paid £1 and went down to Spurn Head - a nature reserve, had a drink at Withernsea and dinner at Hornsea. More house hunting in Beverley. Travelled home on the motorway. Heard that the Princess of Wales had given birth to a son - William. I had to hand in my notice at work - Glenda thinks I am pregnant - the rest of the office were quite shocked that I'm going in 2 weeks. The Estate Agent came round to put the house on the market - we have only been in it 8 months. The good thing is that, as far as houses go, we can get more for our money in the north!"

11th July, 1982: Goodbye to being a Brummie - I am off to 'God's own county'.
"Sold the house in a week for £31,750 - that must be a record time. The office staff came to Beaumonts Wine Bar for a 'leaving drink' and I took a photo of the girls outside afterwards. At my presentation lots of nice things were said about me and I was presented with a book 'The History of Birmingham.' My last day and such a hot and heavy atmosphere. I was clearing out my desk and drawers. At lunch time I sat in the churchyard to cool off in the breeze and I would come to realise that there would be things I missed about the West Midlands. At 5.30 p.m. I skipped out of

the building rather too happily! This weekend we packed a few things as we are camping out in a flat until we find a house. Hull City Council have kindly given us temporary accommodation in Orchard Park - sounds like an idyllic garden village!"

The girls from the Dental School office, the end of an era.

blurb